150073
US HISTORY

*Theodore Roosevelt, Culture,
Diplomacy, and Expansion*

Theodore Roosevelt, Culture, Diplomacy, and Expansion

 A New View of American Imperialism

RICHARD H. COLLIN

LOUISIANA STATE UNIVERSITY PRESS
BATON ROUGE AND LONDON

Designer: Albert Crochet
Typeface: Linotron Galliard
Typesetter: G&S Typesetters, Inc.

Library of Congress Cataloging in Publication Data

Collin, Richard H.
    Theodore Roosevelt, culture, diplomacy, and expansion.
    Bibliography: p.
    Includes index.
    1. Roosevelt, Theodore, 1858–1919.   2. United States—
Foreign relations—1897–1901.   3. United States—Foreign
relations—1901–1909.   4. United States—Territorial
expansion.   I. Title.
E757.C65   1985   973.91′1   84-25094
ISBN 0-8071-1214-3

The author gratefully acknowledges permission to quote from the following: Brigadier
General Frank McCoy, untitled manuscript, May 19, 1919, in Theodore Roosevelt Collection, Harvard University, the Houghton Library, Cambridge, Mass., reprinted by permission of the Houghton Library. Elting E. Morison, John Blum, and Albert Chandler,
eds., *The Letters of Theodore Roosevelt*, 8 vols., Harvard University Press, Cambridge,
Mass., 1950–54, reprinted by permission of Harvard University Press. The Papers of
Henry Cabot Lodge, the Papers of John D. Long, and the Papers of Agnes Storer, Massachusetts Historical Society, Boston, Mass., reprinted by permission of the Massachusetts Historical Society. Various documents in RU 45, Box 108, Smithsonian Institution
Archives, Washington, D.C., reprinted by premission of the Smithsonian Institution
Archives.

For my parents, Esther and Barney,
and for my wife, Rima

Contents

Preface and Acknowledgments

My historical relationship with Theodore Roosevelt began almost twenty years ago. I am not at all sure that a personal meeting, even if it were possible, would be as rewarding. Theodore Roosevelt would undoubtedly charm and impress me, but the gulf between an academic historian and a successful president is one not easily bridged. Besides, we have other differences. Roosevelt was an aristocrat; I am a first-generation son of emigrant working-class parents from England, and a member of a family that rarely even considers voting Republican. As a child of the depression I grew up thinking that *Franklin D. Roosevelt* and *president* were synonymous; FDR's death was my first inkling of the possibility of monumental change in the world.

The Theodore Roosevelt I have written about is not the Theodore Roosevelt that most people admire. Once in a frivolous moment, I thought of titling the book "His Name Wasn't Teddy," but reconsidered, lest I be remembered as the historian who tried to end the Teddy legend. Nothing can (or should) change the enduring affection for the aristocratic president known universally by his nickname. That affection reflects the unique relationship of Americans and their presidents and the magic of charisma. This book is not about the legendary Theodore Roosevelt but about the Theodore Roosevelt I have been working with, a historical figure of substance as well as charm.

I am grateful for the advances in technology that changed my working habits as this book progressed. The book began as a longhand draft on legal pads; it was transcribed by typists, edited, retyped and reedited many times. In its final stages, the manuscript was copied onto computer disks. Perhaps the most comforting blessing of the computer as a writing instrument is its elimination of the mountain of paper that inexorably grows as a book progresses. The computer did not exorcise my mistakes, but at least it effectively hid the physical evidence.

Many persons helped in the research and writing of this book. Grants by the University of New Orleans College of Liberal Arts Organized Research Fund were timely and helpful. The staffs at the Library of Congress, the National Archives, the Smithsonian Institution Archives, the Freer Gallery of Art Archives, and the Massachusetts Historical Society were consistently helpful and kind. Wallace Finley Dailey, the curator of the Theodore Roosevelt Collection at Harvard College, was especially attentive to my many inquiries.

A number of librarians at the Earl K. Long Library of the University of New Orleans have been especially helpful over a long period of time. To Evelyn Chandler, Sybil Boudreaux, Greg Spano, Anthony Tassin, and Donald Hendricks my deep gratitude for their invaluable assistance and their patience. I am also grateful to Margaret Fisher Dalrymple and Catherine F. Barton of Louisiana State University Press for their support.

Professor Willard B. Gatewood, Jr., of the University of Arkansas and Professor William H. Harbaugh of the University of Virginia read earlier versions of the manuscript; their suggestions improved the final version, and I am grateful for their careful readings, and their useful critical comments. Although the final book is a collaboration between the writer and the editor, it is the writer's name that appears on the title page. For the record, let me thank Shannon Sandifer for her meticulous editing of the final manuscript. My wife, Rima Drell Reck, by her example, her presence, and her intellect, offered essential support through all the stages of the book.

The book's inevitable errors I hereby blame on the computer, though we all know who is responsible for computer errors.

Abbreviations

AHR	*American Historical Review*
FRUS	*Papers Relating to the Foreign Relations of the United States, 1861 –* (Washington, D.C., 1861–)
JAH	*Journal of American History*
JSH	*Journal of Southern History*
LC	Library of Congress
MRL	Elting E. Morison, John Blum, and Alfred E. Chandler, Jr. (eds.), *The Letters of Theodore Roosevelt* (8 vols.; Cambridge, Mass., 1950–1954)
MVHR	*Mississippi Valley Historical Review*
NA	National Archives
ONI	Office of Naval Intelligence
PHR	*Pacific Historical Review*
RG	Record Group
RU	Record Unit
SIA	Smithsonian Institution Archives
Works, Nat. Ed.	*The Works of Theodore Roosevelt*, National Edition (20 vols.; New York, 1926)

Theodore Roosevelt, Culture, Diplomacy, and Expansion

Introduction

Theodore Roosevelt was already a master at creating political legends when he became president in 1901. With the help of journalists, historians, and Roosevelt's own ability to steal the spotlight, the legends— especially of the sickly Teddy who became a virile cowboy and of the big stick—have become folktales. Roosevelt hated the nickname Teddy with its terrible childhood associations: "No man who knows me well calls me by the nickname. . . . No one of my family, for instance, has ever used it, and if it is used by anyone it is a sure sign he does not know me."[1] Nevertheless, Roosevelt allowed the nickname to project for him the aura of an ordinary man of the people, which was more politically attractive than the image of an intellectual, an aristocrat, or an urban dandy.

Theodore Roosevelt was hardly the first president to foster an image that differed from reality; successful American presidents are gifted at building images. William McKinley went out of his way to appear powerless and even simpleminded, a presidential tactic Abraham Lincoln raised to a classic level. Andrew Jackson, hardly a plain man of the people, led a political revolution by pretending to be democracy incarnate in his battle with the intellectual and aristocratic John Quincy Adams. George Washington, a soldier, aristocrat, and gentleman, used both the pomp of power and the simplicity of the new America's republican mores as symbols of the new presidency.

Most political myths are not as seriously at odds with reality as

1. TR to John Moulder Wilson, December 9, 1902, in MRL, III, 392.

Theodore Roosevelt's. The idea that modern America's first almost-intellectual president was at heart merely a power-hungry adolescent is as misleading as the idea that Roosevelt created the imperial presidency single-handedly. Roosevelt's image as an intrepid big-game hunter and fearless soldier helped Americans to accept a president who befriended poets and artists, and made it possible for Roosevelt, the gentleman and aristocrat, not to appear effete. The bigger problem of his image lies with Roosevelt's diplomatic ideal of "speak softly and carry a big stick."

Roosevelt first used the big stick phrase to attack the Republican machine while he was governor of New York. Cartoonists picked up the phrase, and the image, and often drew caricatures of Roosevelt carrying a huge club studded with spikes. Roosevelt understood the irony of a popularity that came from a distorted image: "It is very curious. Ever since I have been in the presidency I have been pictured as a huge creature with enormous clenched teeth, a big spiked club, and a belt full of pistols, . . . and yet all the time I have been growing in popularity." Before the phrase became politically identified with him, Roosevelt was aware of its dangers: "If a man continually blusters, if he lacks civility, a big stick will not save him from trouble; and neither will speaking softly avail, if back of the softness there does not lie strength, power." By the end of his presidency, the popularity of the phrase had triumphed over Roosevelt's own skepticism; he not only accepted but embraced the distorted image.[2]

But the image of big-stick diplomacy was rarely realized. Roosevelt, as his critics have frequently observed, did not always speak softly—he often bellowed. And the United States did not have the diplomatic luxury of a big stick. As president, Roosevelt frequently complained of an inadequate navy and an almost nonexistent army. America's best strategic advantage lay in its geographic situation—for three centuries effective isolation from the world's most powerful European navies and a prodigious land mass that made amphibious invasion almost inconceivable.

2. Henry Pringle, *Theodore Roosevelt: A Biography* (New York, 1931), 279; Joseph B. Bishop, *Theodore Roosevelt and His Times* (2 vols.; New York, 1920), I, 240; Address at Minnesota State Fair, September 2, 1901, in *Works, Nat. Ed.*, XIII, 474–75. See also TR to Whitelaw Reid, December 4, 1908, in MRL, VI, 1410, and TR, *Autobiography* (New York, 1913), rpr. *Works, Nat. Ed.*, XX, 524.

However, physical isolation was no longer a sufficient safeguard in Theodore Roosevelt's time. The United States had become a modern industrial nation dependent on free world trade. Africa had been totally colonized, China was in danger of a similar partition, and Latin America was a tempting undefended area for strong and ambitious European navies. Technological innovations had diminished the protection offered by the huge oceans and had made modern navies swifter, more efficient, and capable of intervening anywhere in the world. The end of America's natural geographic isolation as an effective defensive buffer called for a more active naval policy. Strategic necessity demanded the prevention of tactical footholds in key places by foreign powers. Americans had long resisted European efforts to control a Central American canal, or to divide Latin America as Africa had been divided. But by 1900 with Germany and Japan as new and threatening ambitious powers, America had to change its defensive posture—not to become imperialistic as historians have argued, but to better defend its newly vulnerable prosperity.[3]

Strategic necessity, not imperialism nor the big stick, caused American intervention in the Philippines and Panama. Americans were reluctant to appear to imitate even vaguely anything European. The United States Senate disliked Spaniards being in Cuba and wanted them out, but the Americans wanted no part of the Cubans themselves, as the Platt Amendment clearly shows. Because much of America was racist in 1900, the idea of making Cubans and Filipinos citizens was abhorrent. The Americans managed to get the Spaniards out of Cuba and the Philippines, and in Cuba were successful in getting themselves out as well. In the Philippines, however, the getaway was interrupted by an unforeseen Philippine war for independence. When Panama's volatile situation was added to the Philippine episode, the big stick legend became almost a permanent part of American history. Who is not familiar with the swashbuckling Teddy Roosevelt and his big stick making war on the Spaniards in 1898 (both in the Philippines and Cuba), on the Colombians in 1903, and with the cruise of the Great White Fleet, on the Japanese in 1907?

3. The strategic necessity argument is summarized best in John A. S. Grenville and George Berkeley Young, *Politics, Strategy, and American Diplomacy: Studies in Foreign Policy, 1873–1917* (New Haven, 1967), 267–96.

The big-stick legend was aided by European imperialism, which had been a part of European history for all of the nineteenth century. However, by 1900 classic imperialism was fading, a victim of the same modernism that made American geographic isolation no longer feasible. Colonies, which had been seen as assets in times of population surplus, were no longer practical. Colonists resisted political and economic domination and became a liability to the mother country; even as wealthy a nation as Great Britain could ill afford to establish new colonies. Imperialism was dying a natural death. It was rescued not as a historical reality, but as part of a literary and journalistic myth, and in its new meaning European imperialism and Theodore Roosevelt's big stick became inextricably united in legend, journalism, and history.

The best case against the old imperialists was Britain's messy war with the Boers of South Africa. Although Britain eventually won the war, the cost was monumental. The Boers in resisting won the sympathy of the world and made forced colonization permanently unfashionable. The Filipinos, who resisted first Spain and then America, were as important as the Boers in making imperialism unattractive. The Americans were as surprised in the Philippines as the British had been in South Africa. Had there been any instinct for further imperial adventures, the Boer and Filipino episodes convinced Western governments of the foolishness of the undertaking. Pleas such as Kipling's inspirational writing actually confirm the death of the old imperialism. A living institution does not need slogans such as the "White Man's Burden" in order to flourish. Kipling's efforts were rhetorical exercises on behalf of a burdensome anachronism.

Literature, however, proved to be the dramatic turnaround that saved the concept and symbol of imperialism, if not the reality. The Manchester *Guardian* sent one of the shrewdest of English writers, economist John A. Hobson, to write about imperialism by connecting it to the Filipinos and Boers. What had been a descriptive word for centuries now became one of the most striking of modern pejoratives: Hobson, a gifted writer, made the fiascos that were the death throes of a movement—and irrelevant to classic nineteenth-century imperialism—the symbols of a new imperialism. At the same time that Hobson was presenting the image of modern imperialism to the world, journalists

William Randolph Hearst and Joseph Pulitzer were putting a big stick in Theodore Roosevelt's hand. Ironically neither imperialism nor the big stick had much to do with what was happening in the world in the early twentieth century, but the images have stuck and have clouded historical reality ever since.[4]

This book is an attempt to replace the myths with historical perspective. Because the expansion in early twentieth-century America was cultural rather than diplomatic, it cannot be adequately described as imperialistic. Renaming the Executive Mansion and restoring its original function as the president's residence was a significant symbol of the old, and new, American commitment to aesthetics. Architects Charles McKim and Daniel Burnham, veterans of Chicago's White City in 1893, worked closely with the new president to create a symbol of distinction and leadership for the new America. The establishment of a European-type salon in the White House set the stage for fuller American participation in world matters with nations that considered themselves civilized and advanced. The Roosevelt salon was a dramatic change from the diplomatic parties that had previously made Washington a provincial backwater. President and Mrs. Rutherford B. Hayes liked serving grape juice instead of champagne; they impressed some Ohioans but left Europeans convinced that the United States was neither a nation nor a people to be taken seriously.

Nations that find themselves in a state of permanent disrespect generally have to fight for anything they can get, including what is rightfully theirs. Japan's wars with China in 1894–1895 and with Russia in 1904–1905 are gory examples of war substituting for respect. For the Japanese the world's disrespect came both from cultural ignorance and racial intolerance. A nation with a strong culture (and a common one) will be able to win more battles by diplomatic bargaining than by force of arms, which is why the White House and the new salon were important stepping stones often overlooked in the Roosevelt presidency. To know a people one must understand both their politics and their poetry,

4. For the change in the concept and usage of the word *imperialism*, see Richard Koebner and H. D. Schmidt, *Imperialism: The Story and Significance of a Political Word, 1840–1960* (Cambridge, England, 1964). A good summary of Hobson's assignment and its effect is in Oron J. Hale, *The Great Illusion, 1900–1914* (New York, 1971), 4–6.

and the Roosevelt administration made the first modern attempt to remind the world that Americans had a poetry. In the same era and independently of the cultural stirrings in Washington, Americans were reminding themselves and the world of their history, with two celebratory world's fairs, and of their uniqueness, with Frederick Jackson Turner's frontier thesis of American history, which posited the settlement of the West as more decisive in American society than its European heritage.

The new White House, the European-type salon, the fancy state dinners, the wines, were not simply window dressing to impress European diplomats. Theodore Roosevelt was too much of an aristocrat even to try to impress European royalty. John Dewey, the philosopher, in his perceptive obituary for Roosevelt in 1919, explained the president's success by his uncanny ability to be both in step with the people and to lead them where they wanted to go.[5] Americans wanted to go everywhere, and do everything in the age of Roosevelt. One American, Charles Lang Freer, a classic gilded-age businessman in the late nineteenth century who turned not only to art but to Oriental art, symbolizes an entire generation of American millionaires turned art collectors. Freer's vision is more important in American history than the shrill arguments of the anti-imperialists or the exhortations of active imperialists such as Albert Beveridge. But we have become so accustomed to the irrelevant arguments that we ignore the story of how one railroad man from Kingston, New York, and Detroit, Michigan, taught himself about art and became one of the world's leading connoisseurs. Eventually, Freer battled along with Theodore Roosevelt to establish the first American national art museum. Freer and Roosevelt are both a part of the new American expansiveness that extended far beyond simpler ideas of empire and strategy.

In an attempt to dispel the myths, the diplomacy of Theodore Roosevelt's era deserves to be reexamined. The legend that Roosevelt's famous cable to Commodore George Dewey precipitated the war with Spain still persists, though specialists have discarded the notion for some time. The Philippine-American war was a tragedy of cultural ignorance on both sides, rather than an example of ideological imperialism or even

5. *Dial*, XLVI, February 8, 1919, pp. 115–17.

practical expansion. The United States took the Philippines to prevent Germany from taking them, and to prevent a disruption in the European balance of power. Theodore Roosevelt's indifference to the continued American occupation of the Philippines is at odds with the image of Roosevelt as a champion of expansion.

Under presidents McKinley and Roosevelt a century-long cultural and diplomatic antagonism with Great Britain was set aside, leading to the detente that has characterized twentieth-century relations between the two English-speaking peoples. The Alaskan boundary dispute with Canada, which threatened the new spirit of cooperation with Britain and is generally cited as a classic case of the Roosevelt big stick, is instead an example of tough diplomacy and a good compromise. Unfortunately any firm diplomacy by the Americans has generally been dismissed as another example of either the big stick or imperialism.

Cultural and diplomatic changes worked together to enable the new American nation to assume a leadership role in a world already teetering on the brink of the chaos, war, and revolution that characterizes twentieth-century history. Theodore Roosevelt thought he made the difference between peace and war in the first decade of the century, and that claim is a valid answer to the charges that Roosevelt was a bellicose warmonger who led an aggressive America on its path to world domination. More important than world economic domination is the emerging American cultural leadership, a phenomenon that has little to do with political imperialism.

The cultural efflorescence that began the twentieth century started in cities like Chicago, New York, Detroit, Boston, and Washington, D.C., where museums, new art collections, and symphony orchestras flourished and eventually grew. In the decade after World War I, Ernest Hemingway and E. E. Cummings became recognized major writers; by the end of World War II American art and culture were dominating a war-weary world. Abstract expressionism, action painting, pop art, and American western films became the dominant forms of international art. American popular culture overwhelmed the world. But Theodore Roosevelt was no more responsible for Franz Kline's paintings than he was for Pearl Harbor or Panamanian unrest in the sixties. To view Roosevelt's presidency, and in turn all American history, in terms of diplomacy or economics, ignoring the equally important cultural developments, produces inaccurate history. The big stick is the straw man of the Roosevelt era. The Freer Museum and even the Nobel Peace Prize Roosevelt received for settling the Russo-Japanese war are also valid as symbols of his era.

The Roosevelt symbols were part of the heritage of the age. He encouraged the idea of the big stick, and journalists were quick to use it. Roosevelt also helped corrupt his own historical image when in 1911 he told an audience in Berkeley, California, "I took the Canal Zone and let Congress debate and while the debate goes on the Canal does too."[6] It was a statement both arrogant and inaccurate. Part of the excitement of the age of Roosevelt came from the rise of modern journalism. The new Merganthaler Linotyper developed in 1886 and the discovery of photoengraving as an efficient printing process led to the first mass market for newspapers in America. Hearst and Pulitzer competed wildly for the cheap mass market with pictures, sensationalism, and even lies, if necessary, to increase circulation.

Overdramatization of diplomatic matters (especially those concerning Spaniards in Cuba), speculations that passed for fact, and overwhelming political partisanship were the journalist's way of testing the new waters. Theodore Roosevelt was a benefactor as well as a victim of the new journalism. Both the Democratic newspapers and the party misjudged the public response to the Panama controversy. The staunchly Democratic New York *Times* was convinced that the Panama controversy opened the way for Democratic judge Alton B. Parker to easily defeat shaky incumbent Roosevelt. The *Times* was wrong. Panama was Roosevelt's strongest issue in his startling landslide victory in 1904. Unfortunately most of the semitruths, innuendos, and outright lies that were part of partisan political journalism of the time were picked up first by Latin American papers, and later by historians, and have kept Panama a murky historical issue.

6. There are two versions of the Canal Zone speech. The cited passage comes from the standard account in the New York *Times*, March 24, 1911, p. 1; a less harsh version was reprinted in the *University of California Chronicle*, April 1911, p. 139, rpr. in part in Albert Bushnell Hart and Herbert Ronald Ferleger, *Theodore Roosevelt Cyclopedia* (New York, 1941), 407. For the argument that Roosevelt may never have intended even the milder of the two versions, see James F. Vivian, "The Taking of the Panama Canal Zone: Myth and Reality," *Diplomatic History*, IV (1980), 95–100.

Roosevelt, however, used the papers well. He attacked muckrakers in 1905, though the reform journalists were mostly sympathetic to Roosevelt programs. Roosevelt's biggest battle with the press came in 1884 when as a Mugwump (gentleman reformer) he opposed James G. Blaine's nomination as president. When Blaine was nominated by acclamation, the Mugwump journals expected reformer Roosevelt to leave the Republican party in protest as gentlemen before had done. Roosevelt astounded everyone by choosing to remain in professional politics even at the cost of publicly recanting and paying lip service to Blaine's candidacy. Roosevelt felt he had made the right choice and never forgave the insensitive intellectuals and journalists who put principle before politics. In battling the newspapers from 1884 through the postpresidential war intervention campaigns in 1915 to 1917, Roosevelt and the newspapers remained constant adversaries.

The papers responded with gestures of love and hate. There are more unkind caricatures of Theodore Roosevelt than of any other president. There are also more sources critical of the president for the historian who wishes to use them. The battles between Theodore Roosevelt and the press came to a climax at the end of his presidency. Incensed at a New York *World* election-day editorial indicating that he, his brother-in-law Douglas Robinson, and presidential candidate Taft had been corrupted by payoffs from Panama (palpably untrue and known to be by the Pulitzer paper involved), Roosevelt sued the *World* for libel. The actual libel suit pitting the federal government against a newspaper was a fiasco. Roosevelt was bitter, vindictive, self-indulgent, and as angry as he had ever been. The *World*, forced to defend itself in a landmark legal action, collected an astonishing amount of information on the Panamanian Revolution, later reprinted in a government document as *The Story of Panama* following an exhaustive congressional investigation. Roosevelt, Douglas Robinson, and Taft were all cleared of any wrongdoing, the government's libel suit against the *World* was dismissed, and the inside story of the entire Panamanian episode was made a part of the public record.[7]

7. *The Roosevelt Panama Libel Case Against the World and Indianapolis News* (New York, 1910); Clyde Pierce, *The Roosevelt Panama Libel Cases* (New York, 1959); *The Story of Panama: Hearings on the Rainey Resolution Before the Committee on Foreign Affairs of the House of Representatives* (Washington, D.C., 1914).

9

In spite of the silliness of a president's suing a newspaper for libel and the petty opportunism displayed by Pulitzer's papers in using a fabrication just before an election, *The Story of Panama* is so valuable that it probably balances the indiscretions of both Pulitzer and Roosevelt. But in spite of all the public information available, the big-stick legends and the innuendos about Panama and the Panamanian Revolution still persist. In the controversy over returning the Panama Canal to Panama, history was the chief American victim. The original acquisition of the Canal Zone in 1904 and its return in 1980 to Panama were both reasonable actions in the context of their times, even though in the 1980 debate President Carter felt it necessary to condemn the taking of the Canal Zone in order to justify its return to the original inhabitants. When Roosevelt defended his assertive Panamanian diplomacy in 1903 with the idea that the Panama Canal advanced world civilization, American historians and journalists dismissed the arguments, often with ridicule.

Yet Roosevelt was on familiar ground with a cultural argument for a Panama Canal. The French regarded canals as a positive contribution to world peace and civilization through improved communication and transportation. French philosopher Henri Saint-Simon had urged improved transportation as a national movement in the 1820s. When Ferdinand de Lesseps built the Suez Canal in 1869, its completion was celebrated by an event symbolizing the international cultural achievement, a specially commissioned opera by an Italian composer to celebrate a French canal. Giuseppe Verdi's *Aïda* was first performed at Cairo in 1869 to commemorate the finishing of the Suez Canal, which was generally regarded at the time as a monumental advance in world civilization. Panama's canal began with the same impulse. When the French were badly defeated by the Germans in the Franco-Prussian War of 1870–1871, French patriots and nationalists looked back to Suez as a more suitable national endeavor for Frenchmen than war. National poet Victor Hugo publicly pleaded with de Lesseps to create another miracle for France. De Lesseps took up the challenge and looked to Panama, not realizing that enormous physical difficulties made a private company's plans to build a canal a monumental impossibility in Central America. But de Lesseps, Hugo, and the French shopkeepers who subscribed the money for both Suez and Panama, saw the Panama Canal as a work of art and of peace. So did the president of the United States and most of Latin America's newspapers and governments, until the partisan diatribes in the American newspapers obscured the grand achievement that the Panama Canal represented and made it another squalid episode in big stick and imperial imagery.

The real history of the age of Roosevelt is not the diplomatic battles over the Panama Canal nor the party battles over control. It is the story of enormous and monumental cultural change, in all of the world and especially in America.

One cannot overestimate the amount of change and the effect of it upon nineteenth-century Americans. As sensitive a person as Henry Adams felt he had to make a choice between the dynamo culture represented by the Centennial Exposition at Philadelphia in 1876 and the virgin culture of gothic cathedrals in the more familiar medieval France that Adams revered. Theodore Roosevelt loved both worlds. But he welcomed the changes that he had not caused. Henry Adams' friends in the East (mainly) brooded and opposed all change, especially cultural: Dickens and Scott were Boston's favorite authors in 1900, Herman Melville was hardly mentioned in Barrett Wendell's definitive *Literary History of America*, and that Brahmin view of literature mentioned poet Walt Whitman only to note that the French seemed to like him. The anti-imperialists were anti everything, tired anachronisms losing power and influence in a nation whose main energies were clearly in the West. In a previous age Henry Adams would have been called upon to preside over his country as had his ancestors, John and John Quincy. In 1880 Adams was reduced to writing an anonymous novel (*Democracy*) parodying the Grant and Hayes administrations with a heavy hand. No one was asking Henry Adams for leadership or advice. No one was listening to the tired Brahmins of Boston culture.

No wonder, however, that sensible sensitive men would be overwhelmed by the vast changes in America. In the forty years between 1860 and 1900 the changes were boggling. Population had more than doubled from 31 million to over 75 million. Exports of manufactured goods had increased from 38 to 189 million dollars. Corn production increased from 838 million bushels to over 2.5 billion bushels; railroad tracks jumped from 30,000 miles to 193,000 miles, and the labor force went from just over 10 million to just under 30 million workers. Industrial capital had increased from 1 billion to 10 billion dollars. Cities were growing at an amazing rate; the wave of immigration had become a torrent; California and the East were united by no less than four transcontinental railroads. The business cycle, always volatile, reached new heights (or depths) in the 1893–1897 depression; the corporation, the trust, the new techniques of big business, seemed to be running out of control.[8]

Change was everywhere. The new national ambition of Germany was frightening. China, in its Boxer Rebellion, showed signs of ancient pride and modern discontent. Britain was no longer the unchallenged king of the sea; America was no longer an isolated provincial backwater; Japan was certainly a new power to be reckoned with. No one ever dreamed that the Japanese would be ready so soon to successfully challenge Russia, the oldest monarchy in the world. Japan's victory in the Russo-Japanese War was a triumph of the new East over the old West, and a wrench for those who believed passionately in Oriental racial inferiority.

Theodore Roosevelt had challenged tradition in 1881 by becoming a professional politician and not a corporate lawyer, like many of his fellow gentlemen and Harvard graduates. In 1901 Roosevelt was willing and able to lead a new America through the changes that engulfed the world. It was Theodore Roosevelt, an American aristocrat with a passion for duty as strong as the old idea of noblesse oblige, who led the nation, not the imperialist and warmonger of popular legend.

The image of Theodore Roosevelt was closely tied to the misfortunes of his major political rival, Democratic president Woodrow Wilson. Wilson's years culminated an era of hope and optimism and a belief in progress and evolution that died when the United States Senate failed to ratify Wilson's dream of world order through the League of Nations. World War I, devoid of the saving grace of Wilsonian idealism, ap-

8. Harry J. Carman and Harold C. Syrett, *A History of the American People* (2 vols.; New York, 1952), Statistical Tables, I, 712–31; Harold U. Faulkner, *The Decline of Laissez Faire, 1897–1917* (New York, 1951), 8–9; George Mowry, *The Era of Theodore Roosevelt and the Birth of Modern America, 1900–1912* (New York, 1958), 1–15; Harold U. Faulkner, *The Quest for Social Justice* (New York, 1931), 1–51.

peared a stunning reversal of progress and civilization. For many writers the war was an incredible joke played upon history. In the disillusionment that followed, all words became suspect as did history, culture, art, and tradition. Writers turned to brief prose styles—the Hemingway sentence was a formal reaction to the inflated rhetoric of patriotism and reform. In poetry imagery replaced regular rhyme; poet E. E. Cummings eliminated punctuation; artists went beyond abstraction to surrealism, which denied even the appearance of reality; and in music serial form replaced the centuries-old harmonic scale.

In history and biography the 1920s became the age of debunking. Helped by the popularization of Freudian psychology, writers attacked revered heroes and institutions. In America the Puritans and George Washington were their victims. Poor Theodore Roosevelt would have had a tough time with just the literary fashions of the decade following his death. But he fared even worse. His biographer, Henry Pringle, a journalist who hated almost all politicians, having spent a lifetime covering them, and who was fascinated with the new fashions in biography, made his portrayal of Roosevelt a classic case of Freudian debunking. Pringle ignored the aristocratic background, Roosevelt's sense of duty, any glimpse of intellect, and created the image of the semiadolescent big-stick bully either hungry for political power or obsessed with psychological feelings of frailty. Pringle, a poor man's Henry Adams, wrote well, was thoroughly plausible, won a Pulitzer Prize, and wrote so dominating a biography that it has remained the definitive portrait of the first Roosevelt.[9]

Revisionist historians following America's recent history can easily make the twentieth century an unhappy mélange of new American imperialism. How easy it is to connect the Philippine war of 1899 to 1902 with the Korean or Vietnam conflicts. Even easier is taking Latin American complaints at face value and making Panama the symbol of all American imperialism and the beginning of an era. Diplomatic historians critical of American dominance in the latter twentieth century have no trouble accepting Pringle's insensitive legend of a Napoleonic Roosevelt

9. See Pringle's prior political studies, especially *Big Frogs* (New York, 1928), a collection of essays on well-known political figures whose flaws are scathingly examined, and *Alfred E. Smith: A Critical Study* (New York, 1927).

and connecting it with an American imperial tradition and presidency.

The New Left historical emphasis on economic and intellectual motives, on American shrewdness rather than innocence, is a useful corrective to the old notions of America as an innocent victim of European corruption and scheming. But the revisionists tell only a part of the story. Economics and empire were not the only American motives; they may not even have been the decisive ones. Theodore Roosevelt as an aristocrat disliked businessmen as a class. For most of his life and presidency he distrusted them and regarded them as materialistic and soft. He found repellent the catechism of the modern American businessmen—corporation law. He refused to become a lawyer in 1881 and attacked courts and the law as a radical in 1912. To make a man who disliked lawyers and businessmen and who knew little and cared less about foreign markets the leader of the new imperialism is logically absurd. The twin legends of a new American imperialism led by the father of the big stick make colorful images and weak history.

For Theodore Roosevelt the business interest was dangerous to democratic government. He spent his entire presidency trying to control business hegemony and to assert some kind of control over a society that had not yet accommodated its institutions to the corporate age.

America and Americans in the age of Roosevelt adjusted to the new growth and change and to new European and Asian perceptions of American change. The worldwide revolution of modernism is infinitely more useful in explaining the changes in the twentieth century than the repetition of inaccurate and anachronistic slogans of imperialism and the big stick. The changes, the new circumstances, the dilemmas and their solutions are the subjects of this work. I hope, in the end, that we will have a clearer and a different notion of both Theodore Roosevelt and the nature of American society in one of its most creative and exciting decades.

Part I

The New President

The news of President William McKinley's assassination, said Theodore Roosevelt, "seemed literally incredible." Roosevelt and the country were stunned when Leon Czoglosz shot President William McKinley at 4:07 P.M. on September 6, 1901. The shot, fired at point blank range while McKinley was on a receiving line at the Pan American Exposition in Buffalo, was fatal, though the president seemed to rally after the first shock. McKinley was immediately moved to the residence of the world's fair president, John G. Milburn, located on the exposition grounds. Roosevelt, on a speaking tour in Vermont, joined the entourage at the fallen president's bedside the next day. The violence of the deed shocked Roosevelt. But even more puzzling to him was why anyone would want to harm a man as plain as McKinley, a man who made few enemies, who represented "in every instinct and feeling . . . the men who make up the immense bulk of our nation." McKinley, Roosevelt observed, "is a man hardly even of moderate means." The assassination of such a simple man went beyond "ordinary wickedness."[1]

For a week the stricken president remained at the Milburn house while overly optimistic doctors predicted a full recovery. The presidential advisers left Buffalo and the week seemed to promise a welcome return to routine. Roosevelt rejoined his wife Edith and the children, and after his arduous speaking trip of the week before, he looked forward to the relaxation of climbing Mount Marcy, the Adirondack's highest peak. Theodore Roosevelt was already bored with the vice-

1. TR to Henry Cabot Lodge, September 9, 1901, MRL, III, 141–43.

presidency. He made extra speaking trips to keep alive his flickering political hopes for 1904, fretted about his inactivity, and even planned to take a law degree to help pass the time. The impatient vice-president had reached the fog-shrouded peak of Mount Marcy on Friday, September 13, and was descending the mountain with his old friend Noah LaCasse when the party was met by guides bringing grim news. President McKinley was dying. Vice-president Theodore Roosevelt had been summoned once again to Buffalo.

For the nation the change from William McKinley to Theodore Roosevelt was physically and spiritually tumultuous. The gentle, self-effacing Ohioan, who sang "Nearer My God to Thee" as he lay dying, was a genuine bedrock nineteenth-century American elder statesman. The young president, who was eventually to become the symbol of the new century, began his term in dramatic and exhausting fashion. Racing down the treacherous Adirondack slopes without pausing to sleep, Roosevelt covered the twelve-mile descent to the Tahawis clubhouse in a little over three hours, barely pausing to remove the mud that covered him. A team of three relay drivers, equipped with horses and buckboards, carried the new president the additional and still treacherous thirty-five miles to the railroad station at Balliston Spa.[2] A special train carried Roosevelt through the state's most populous cities—Albany, Utica, Rome, and Syracuse—en route to the grim rendezvous in Buffalo. Roosevelt remained alone throughout the trip, avoiding both the press and the company of friends. He arrived in Buffalo at 5:30 A.M. on Saturday, September 14, and went directly to William McKinley's bedside to pay his last respects to a man he had genuinely loved and admired. McKinley had died three hours earlier.

At 2:00 P.M. on the same day, in the house of his old friend Ansley Wilcox, the official mourning site for the dead president, Theodore Roosevelt took the oath of office from Judge John R. Hazel. On hand in the Wilcox library was a small group headed by the senior McKinley cabinet official, Secretary of War Elihu Root. Roosevelt's ascension to the presidency was a somber moment in American history.

2. Dorothy Taylor, "Noah Lacasse, Presidential Hiking Mate," *Adirondack Life*, II (Spring, 1972), 9–11.

Theodore Roosevelt was one of the least likely members of his generation to become the twenty-sixth president of the United States. Born on October 27, 1858, Theodore was the second child and first son of Martha and Theodore Roosevelt, Sr.; his birth marked the beginning of the seventh generation of male Roosevelts to be born on Manhattan Island. The family had begun its American life when Klaes van Roosevelt had emigrated to New Amsterdam in 1642. An aristocrat by social status if not overwhelming wealth, young Theodore had the classic gentleman's schooling: private tutoring and trips to Europe rather than formal learning in school. Although Theodore was a sickly child prone to frequent and disabling attacks of asthma, his health was not especially unusual in an age that lacked the benefit of antibiotic medication or even the knowledge that germs cause disease. Roosevelt's colleague Elihu Root was even frailer as a child and considerably sicklier as an adult, yet he hunted and hiked as vigorously as Roosevelt. Root lived, complaining of poor health, into his nineties.

The comfortable world of New York City society and politics was the most significant factor in Roosevelt's early life. Even though the Civil War was a discordant note in the Roosevelt family household—Martha was a southerner by birth—Theodore's young years were relatively serene. Roosevelt, Sr., a stern but understanding father, recognized early that his son was more independent than most members of his class, and advised young Theodore to choose either a profession that produced enough wealth to maintain the standard of living he was accustomed to, or to consciously sacrifice wealth for the pleasure of doing whatever he wanted to do. Theodore Roosevelt came to be best known as one of America's most gifted politicians, but his political skills at their best never matched the genius he displayed in natural science, his earliest and most consistent passion. It was a profession he returned to throughout his crowded political career.

Roosevelt's share of his father's estate, $125,000, was large enough to give him an independent start, but not sufficient to maintain his simple but expensive standard of living. Educated by travel in Europe, private tutoring, and a gentleman's bachelor's degree from Harvard in 1880, Roosevelt married his college sweetheart Alice Lee. Seeking a career after graduation, he published his first book, *The Naval War of 1812*, which offered some hope of a career in history. He tried law in an attempt to earn a substantial living, but he hated both the study and the practice of law, a dislike that set him apart from most of his peers, the most successful of whom became powerful and wealthy corporation lawyers before coming to politics.

In 1881 Roosevelt turned suddenly and unexpectedly to politics as a career. For a gentleman of the time, politics was not an accepted pursuit. Ever since Andrew Jackson had initiated the myth of political humility in his battle in 1824 with the gentlemanly John Quincy Adams, the last of the Massachusetts-Virginia dynasty of aristocratic presidents, it had become impossible for anyone with the taint of a gentleman to succeed in American political contests. Bright presidents like Lincoln affected humble log-cabin origins; most aristocrats took Henry Adams' road and rebelled against a society that rejected their leadership. Roosevelt, however, hated law, had no taste for banking, and no talent for business. He wanted no part of teaching or writing history as a full-time profession. Historians, Roosevelt wrote, have the time to research and write properly not because their profession demands it, but because they are ignored by the general public. Once a historian achieves popular recognition the necessary leisure is lost. "Requests to do second rate work" come from publishers, and the historian is besieged by other time-wasting requests. On the other hand, the bad historian—a "day laborer" who collects facts—is "absurd and mischievous," two of the most derogatory terms in the Roosevelt lexicon. Unfortunately, "these small men do most of the historic teaching in the colleges." Roosevelt was elected president of the American Historical Association in 1912, an irony, since it was not quite the presidency he had been seeking.[3]

Roosevelt, unhappy with the prospect of law, history, or teaching, took destiny in his own hands by forcing himself upon the working class politicians in a silk-stocking New York Republican club in 1881. From the beginning young Roosevelt's chief stock in his new political trade was the noblesse oblige of the earliest aristocrats. Because of his uniqueness—virtually the only gentleman in American politics—Roo-

3. TR to William Peterfield Trent, February 23, 1898, in MRL, I, 782–83; TR to George Treveleyan, January 25, 1904, in MRL, III, 708.

sevelt rose quickly. He emphasized his uniqueness, wearing three-piece suits and conspicuous glasses, and exaggerating his already distinct diction. As a state legislator in a particularly corrupt assembly, Roosevelt won national attention both as a reformer and as an outspoken critic.

The real turning point came in 1884, a tragic year for Roosevelt. In February his young wife, Alice, died in childbirth; on the same night his beloved mother, Mittie, also died unexpectedly. In 1884 Roosevelt suffered a number of severe political setbacks as well. Prevented by custom from serving another term as an Albany legislator, he joined with Henry Cabot Lodge of Massachusetts to campaign against James G. Blaine in the Republican presidential nominating convention. Despite Roosevelt's active opposition, Blaine was nominated. The political defeat and especially his deep personal loss prompted Theodore Roosevelt to escape to the West. He had recently invested much of his patrimony in livestock and rangeland in the still wild Dakota territory, giving him a rare national breadth doubly unique for an eastern gentleman. He became a self-taught cowboy in much the same way he had become a self-proclaimed politician.

Roosevelt's personal life took an upward turn in 1886 when he was reunited with his childhood friend, Edith Kermit Carow; they were married in November. Had he wished, Roosevelt could have remained in the West to become one of the first senators from the new Dakota states in 1889. Instead he set his roots squarely back in his native New York. His political prospects, however, plummeted with an ill-advised attempt to become mayor of New York City, justified on the dubious grounds of duty to party. Roosevelt finished an ignominious third to Democratic elder statesman Abram Hewitt and Chicago radical Henry George. That political mistake notwithstanding, Theodore Roosevelt was in control of his destiny.

Edith and Theodore were passionately in love, in spite of their Victorian embarrassment at the idea of second love and second marriage. The mansion at Oyster Bay, originally designed and named Leeholm for his wife Alice, was finished and renamed Sagamore Hill. The disastrous winter of 1887–1888 wiped out most of Roosevelt's western investments and consequently most of his patrimony. In spite of apparent social standing and a reputation for inherited wealth, the Roosevelt family

21

endured a life of genteel poverty in the service of a government that paid its public officials little. On a civil service commissioner's annual salary of $3,500, Roosevelt maintained residences in both Washington and Oyster Bay, entertained with cautious abandon, and began a family that eventually numbered six children.

As civil service commissioner under two presidents, Roosevelt enhanced his reputation as an honest reformer and bellicose do-gooder. Republican Benjamin Harrison originally appointed Roosevelt; Democrat Grover Cleveland reappointed him. In 1895 when he became a New York City police commissioner, he helped reorganize one of the nation's most corrupt forces into one of the first honest urban police departments. His role as police commissioner was well publicized, and his exploits became legendary, though New Yorkers soon grew tired of the truculent and shrill moral lecturing that accompanied the reforms.

When Republican William McKinley was elected president in 1896, Roosevelt as a loyal Republican had earned a position in national government. After much political cajoling by his friend Senator Lodge and others, Roosevelt was named President McKinley's assistant secretary of the navy. Roosevelt was an adept administrator and a useful spokesman for the younger generation of Americans who favored Pacific expansion as well as war with Spain. When the war he advocated came, Roosevelt went against the political advice of his friends, who felt that Roosevelt's work in organizing the Navy for the war had made him a major political figure. He cited duty rather than personal gain as the reason for leaving Washington and organizing the Rough Riders, a volunteer cavalry group that achieved unexpected fame in the War of 1898 in the Battle of San Juan Hill.

After the war the Republican party in New York State found itself hopelessly embarrassed by a series of canal scandals and looked to returned war hero Theodore Roosevelt as the only chance—albeit a slim one—to maintain their hold on the New York governorship. Roosevelt's return to elective politics was not especially notable. He won by the barest of margins, defeating the overconfident Democrats, who lost a sure election through arrogance and bad timing.

Theodore Roosevelt's margin of victory, though precarious, was enough to assure his future presidential candidacy and serious consideration as a national leader. His term as governor was important. He was an able administrator who could match wits and determination with one of the oldest political machines in the country. Roosevelt's independence, and his challenges of Boss Thomas Platt's previously unquestioned authority, frightened Senator Platt seriously enough to cause him to plan Roosevelt's political demise. Platt ingeniously maneuvered Roosevelt into the Republican vice-presidency, a role that turned from political quicksand into an unexpected springboard to the presidency.

On hearing that Theodore Roosevelt was McKinley's choice for vice-president in 1900, Mark Hanna, McKinley's chief political adviser, demurred, warning that "that damned cowboy is only a breath away from the presidency." Hanna was both right and wrong. Roosevelt would be president. But Roosevelt was no damned cowboy. Indeed, he was just the opposite—an urban aristocrat, unique for both America and the Republican party. Theodore Roosevelt's genius consisted not only of being in the right place at the right time, but in having the intellectual ability to take the presidency and his country into the uncharted times of a new century in which change would become the new tradition, and revolution and war the most striking historical characteristics of the age. Roosevelt was able to unite in his political image the idea of the American cowboy that pleased the nineteenth-century American, while at the same time returning in substance to the aristocratic style that had merged so effectively with revolutionary democracy in the first years of the nation.

Theodore Roosevelt was well aware of the differences between himself and William McKinley. McKinley, Roosevelt grieved, was a simple man, representative of a simple America and the triumph of American political democracy. He was one of the people. Theodore Roosevelt, though he worked hard at being accepted, was not one of them. For Roosevelt his own assassination would be comprehensible. McKinley's was not. McKinley was a good man for his time. He resisted the inevitable conflicts with the world but eventually he was compelled to bring a reluctant America into a new and modern age. Theodore Roosevelt did not create the world in which Boxers rebelled in China and the Boers in South Africa, nor did he wish to fight Filipinos in Asia. But unlike McKinley, Roosevelt was not surprised at the changes, and he was determined that America would have something to do with them rather than blindly reacting to Europe's mistakes. The old order was giving way. The third world, unbeknown to anyone, was already making its first demands, while most of the world's leaders were still arguing about a second world of colonialism and imperialism already on its way to political obsolescence.

Automatic colonization ended at the same time as the automatic American frontier. The world was changing, America with it, and the new president did not understand all of the changes. Unlike his predecessors, however, he was sympathetic to change and intellectually willing and able to deal with it. Also unlike his predecessors, Theodore Roosevelt would be a leader with a perspective grounded in intellect and literature rather than corporate law. By not only leading and adapting to change but by becoming the very symbol of change in the twentieth century, he was able to make peace with the new economics of the twentieth century, the new powers of the presidency, and the peculiar politics of American democracy. With the new presidency of Theodore Roosevelt, style, intellect, and leadership once again had taken up residence in the White House after an absence dating from the defeat of John Quincy Adams in 1828.

1 / Setting the Stage
American Cultural Expansion and Charles McKim's Restoration of the White House

"It's like living over the store," complained Edith Kermit Roosevelt shortly after the new first family moved into the Executive Mansion. The original president's house had been designed with two purposes: to provide living quarters for the first family and to present an august symbol of the dignity of America's new democracy. A century of disrepair and a hodgepodge of presidential styles had reduced the once imposing structure to the shambles the Roosevelts found in September, 1901. Even at its best, the Executive Mansion would have been sorely tested by the unusually active Theodore and Edith, their six growing children, and their menagerie of pets, including frogs and horses. Theodore Roosevelt half-jokingly complained: "I can run the country or be Alice's father. I cannot do both."[1]

Americans were deeply touched and frightened by William McKinley's assassination, and the scars remained visible for several months. Even when the immediate horror of the McKinley assassination abated, official memorials remained as constant reminders: flags stayed at half-mast; government stationery was overwhelmed by a stark black border. In the wake of McKinley's death, Theodore Roosevelt was expected to be a caretaker rather than a dynamic leader. The difficulties of living in uncomfortable quarters were part of the many unpleasantries of the Roosevelt family's new duties.

The White House was still officially called the Executive Mansion.

1. Sylvia Jukes Morris, *Edith Kermit Roosevelt: Portrait of a First Lady* (New York, 1980), 222. There are many variations of TR's remark about Alice; see Owen Wister, *Roosevelt: The Story of a Friendship, 1880–1919* (New York, 1930), 87, for one version.

And it was a mess. Its deterioration and poor physical condition reflected a century in which America's energies and vision were directed westward. The idea of an urban capital, a strong central government, or the style of an elegant eastern seaboard family were as foreign to the spirit of middle nineteenth-century America as was the idea of electing an aristocrat to the presidency. The symbolism of James Hoban's original designs suited the Virginia-Massachusetts dynasty of founding fathers; it ill suited the majority of presidents who served after the demise of aristocracy in American politics and after the triumph, with Andrew Jackson and William Harrison, of the politics of the plain man. In 1901 Theodore Roosevelt became the first urban aristocrat to sit in the Executive Mansion since John Quincy Adams was swept away by the tide of Jacksonian democracy in 1828.

Both damage from the War of 1812 and changing national priorities assured the continued deterioration of the president's home. In 1814, when the triumphant British stormed through Washington, the Executive Mansion was singled out as an appropriate symbol for destruction. Unfortunately for American aesthetics, the British were as unsuccessful in completely destroying the original building as they were in reestablishing British rule in North America. The old Hoban building was ruined, but its shell remained intact, and it was upon the rotten shell that the penurious political architects of the nineteenth century practiced their worst art. The art involved was hardly architecture. To mix politics and architecture in a country unconcerned with the symbols and trappings of leadership is to abdicate any pretense of art. Politics took over and the president's house gradually reflected the country's indifference. The national symbolism that had mattered so much in Washington's and Jefferson's ambitious plans mattered not at all, and the seat of government became a hodgepodge of styles and utilitarian compromises that made it just another eastern house.

Ulysses S. Grant and Rutherford B. Hayes added greenhouses to the sweeping vista, transforming Jefferson's dream of ancient Rome into a suburban plant nursery. Chester Arthur, one of the few American leaders to be aware of, or practice, the good life, with the help of Louis Tiffany and the installation of new wine cellars, transformed the Executive Mansion interior into the style of a late nineteenth-century urban bordello. The Tiffany glass was beautiful, if inappropriate, and in one decade the mansion passed from barbarism to decadence without a pause for civilization. Centennial America in 1876 and into the 1880s still had little sense of its own destiny or what, if anything, it demanded from its leaders. When Hayes was president, diplomats drank grape juice from champagne flute glasses while his teetotal first lady tittered at the crowd. When Chester Arthur took over, the parties were lavish, there was less tittering and more drinking, but the nation's heart and soul were firmly in the West. In the 1880s Washington was hardly a real city, and it remained one of the world's most provincial capitals. The arrangement suited everyone. American leaders were as provincial as their capital city.

Less obvious and more serious than the changing architectural styles of the Executive Mansion, or the social styles of its occupants, was the continued physical deterioration of the buildings. Prevented by the marginal political aesthetics of official architecture from considering any real changes, structural or historical, Congress let the buildings limp from year to year with makeshift cosmetic repairs. No one tried to rehabilitate the buildings because no one knew how badly dilapidated they were. When Theodore Roosevelt took over, the buildings were no longer fit as offices or residence. And in the tragic circumstances of his ascension to the presidency, even Theodore and Edith Roosevelt failed to realize just how bad living over the store was going to be.

Under the Harrison and Cleveland administrations further attempts to clear up the more obvious mess at the Executive Mansion had been stymied by congressional and party politics. The more ambitious the plan, the more difficult it was to get past the political architects who influenced congressional decisions. Simpler plans had a better chance for success. In 1899 Colonel Theodore Bingham, President McKinley's superintendent of public buildings, developed his own plans for restoring the mansion. Bingham's plan, a shrewd composite of acceptable politics and makeshift architecture, would have easily passed Congress a decade or even a year before. But in 1900 Bingham and Congress ran afoul of the American Institute of Architects, meeting in Washington to celebrate the centennial of the nation's capital.

The AIA immediately and publicly condemned Bingham's improvement plan, leaving the buildings untouched by architectural or political hands. The AIA action, however, was startling evidence that an era of aesthetic indifference had come to an end. Just the very fact that the city of Washington was celebrating its centennial marked a change in a culture starved of tradition and history, and dependent for its strongest legends on an untrammeled wilderness. But the American Institute of Architects' denunciation was more than a historical accident. After almost a century of aesthetic indifference, America had changed. A remarkable new interest in architecture and an overwhelming passion for European art had overtaken those Americans with money to spend, and they were making up for centuries of absent traditions by rampaging through Europe, buying priceless medieval, renaissance, and modern art treasures.

Chicago led the way. Mrs. Potter Palmer, like many Chicagoans, had graduated from Renoir, newly fashionable in New York, to the marvels of Spanish painting, and with the Martin Ryersons in the 1890s, was adding Spanish and Italian treasures to the permanent collection of the Art Institute of Chicago. Chicago led the way not because it had the wealthiest collectors; New York and probably even Detroit could outspend Chicago. But Chicago was one of the rare American places where two levels of art could exist side by side. Old art or culture was taken care of by the wealthy collectors. New art, best expressed in the soaring skyscraper architecture of Louis Sullivan, was springing up throughout the living city itself. Chicago was the hub of the new American aesthetics.

In 1893 at the meeting of the American Historical Association in Chicago, Frederick Jackson Turner announced that Americans had been looking in the wrong place for the origins of the unique American spirit. Turner pointed West. The American West, Turner told the small scholarly audience, was the key to all that was great, living, and significant in American history. For Turner the real America had its roots in the West, not the East, and certainly not Europe. With Turner's thesis Americans found a unique indigenous culture in their own westward movement. But the Americans of the 1890s were not the same hardy frontier pioneers who had settled the West. They were products of a new America with enough wealth to purchase a commodity so precious that previous generations hardly knew it existed.

They could afford leisure, leisure to travel, to read, to look—whether at paintings, churches, cities, or society—and to see. The process of American cosmopolitanism had begun before the 1890s. Henry James's novel *The American*, published in 1877, portrays the classic American, Christopher Newman, learning about Paris, art, Europe, and eventually life. In the Louvre Museum at the beginning of the novel, Newman was unable to tell the difference between a fair copy and the museum original. He learned fast. So did the Americans. Museums sprang up everywhere, especially in the more prosperous industrial cities. Paintings became a socially acceptable way for entrepreneurs to gain entry into the previously closed social circles of the older cities. Henry James's American could partake of two worlds by the end of James's cautionary tale. Newman never really lost his innocence. And he never stopped longing for the artifacts of real civilization, which for Americans meant not their own West, but the priceless and timeless culture of old Europe, or the even more ancient art of Asia.

In 1893 Chicago was a city breathtaking enough to inspire Henry Adams, a determined eastern Brahmin in culture, to acknowledge its primacy. And Chicago in 1893 fulfilled Norman Mailer's later characterization as "the great American city."[2] Chicagoans had little history, but they liked the idea of history and had decided to stage the Columbian Exposition of 1893, an extravagant affirmation and demonstration of four hundred years of America's existence.

However, they celebrated not with wild west exhibits, nor with parades of Indians, mountain men, horses, or pioneers. Chicago would celebrate America's anniversary with a great White City of its own, an instant old city built in the best tradition of French beaux-arts architecture, dazzling in its perfection and awesome in its conceit: an ancient city as an additional entity beside what was already one of the world's most engaging communities. No wonder the White City dazzled Henry Adams. Who could fail to be dazzled by the effrontery of an American city trumpeting to the world its huge advantages of space and wealth? Where else could an established city afford to build another city? Equally important, as suggested by the largesse of the lakefront site, was Chi-

2. Norman Mailer, *Miami and the Siege of Chicago* (New York, 1968), 85.

cago's breathtaking demonstration that architectural traditions, which had taken Western civilization centuries to accumulate, could be reproduced in a flash (What is two years in European history?) as temporary buildings in an American historical celebration.

The White City was a historical tour de force as well as an architectural miracle. That it was a reactionary piece of architecture unnaturally plunked down in the middle of an open prairie is not beside the point; it is the point. Chicago and America could show the world (and itself) that not any of the traditions of Europe, or later of Asia, were beyond the enterprising American. The White City showed that America could have its land and skyscrapers as well as the worst or best of Europe's architecture. Paintings were easy to move if one had the money and the taste. But Chicago's White City was an act of artistic creation. The Americans did not buy the buildings. They built them, just as they built their own skyscrapers. And in building the White City, Chicago clearly announced to the world that the new America was no longer the backward, provincial, prairie utopia Europeans had for a century taken for granted.

The new age of America, or cosmopolitan America, arrived not in 1898 in the Philippines or Cuba, not in 1901 with Theodore Roosevelt's presidency, but in 1893 and 1894 in the great White City of Chicago. Everything else, including the restoration of Theodore Roosevelt's White House, springs from this catalytic event. Ironically, Chicago's historical White City was more influential in its time than its unique and indigenous skyscraper architecture. The White City, reactionary though it might have been in its architecture, was a perfect source of inspiration for Americans who viewed cities and urban life as sources of class strife and ugliness and as symbols of a distasteful and crowded European civilization. Architect Daniel Burnham's White City made a beautiful city appear possible. Indeed, the City Beautiful Movement, which sprang from the influence of the Chicago world's fair, began a grass roots movement in urban America to redesign existing cities to make them more attractive. Not until the White City showed the way were many Americans willing to accept the permanent existence of urban life in America. Turner's historic pronouncement in 1893 gave Americans their frontier legend. Burnham's White City softened the blow of the closed frontier and made the future of the American city an aesthetic and social challenge rather than an unadulterated nightmare. The twentieth-century American city would continue to lack the charm and tradition of most European cities, but at least now there were influential Americans willing to make the effort to transform America's urbanity into something more than ghetto chaos.

Throughout America the spirit of the White City dominated the new urban architecture. Beaux-arts state capitols, banks, and huge boulevards sprang up. For the first time civic associations were devoted to aesthetic matters and urban planning: parks, museums, and attractive new buildings were all part of the new consciousness of America's suddenly discovered urban destiny. Eventually the new aesthetic awareness reached the nation's capital and helped break the almost century-long decline of Washington, D.C., the only American city originally planned on a European model.

Although Chicago supplied the initial aesthetic impetus, Detroit was the major connection between the new city and national political power. In the late nineteenth century, Chicago and Detroit had both become the leading cities in the American railroad industry. Chicago was the hub of the huge national rail system, Detroit the manufacturing city that built many of the railroad cars. The railroad was as central to nineteenth-century American society as the automobile to twentieth-century America. Many of the great American fortunes were made by the railroad car builders of Detroit.

So much money was made that American entrepreneurs, following the fictional odyssey of Henry James's *American*, turned to Europe and its art with as much passion, initiative, and enterprise as they had used to build their business empires. The men who had made their fortunes in Detroit's railroads turned, almost as a group, to collecting serious art. Detroit, along with Chicago, became one of the aesthetic entrepôts of Western civilization. Culture was the means by which the newly wealthy could gain social acceptance. James Scripps, newspaper publisher and Detroit outsider, helped establish the Detroit Museum of Art in 1888 mainly as a personal entrée into a theretofore closed society.

Scripps's zeal for social acceptance through aesthetic glory became the classic American way. New museums sprang up in most major Amer-

31

ican cities, and even in the east, where large museums were well established, lavish new gifts multiplied their holdings. The American urban museum movement in the last decade of the nineteenth century was closely related to the City Beautiful Movement; both drew their major public inspiration from the example of Chicago's White City. While museums were an ideal way for outsiders to acquire social acceptance, the new American desire for art, tradition, and culture was as much aesthetic as social. In every city, insiders as well as outsiders bought art for themselves and eventually for their urban museum.

James McMillan was one of the Detroit insiders. He led the consolidation of the railroad car business in Detroit, when he established the American Car foundry, a giant corporation that virtually smothered the competition. McMillan, although interested in art, turned in a different direction than aesthetic urban philanthropy, choosing national politics instead. In 1889 when McMillan became Michigan's new senator, he brought to Congress for the first time an active American aesthetic presence.

American culture was represented not by an accidental aesthete, but by one of the foremost industrialists the nation had produced. McMillan was as adept in national politics as he was at building industrial empires; by the time Theodore Roosevelt became president in 1901, a time when senators rarely shared power with anyone, be it other congressmen or presidents, the Michigan senator was widely regarded as one of the most influential men in Congress. McMillan's power base was the Senate Committee on the District of Columbia, a previously insignificant Senate committee, which in McMillan's hands took over the nationalization of the City Beautiful Movement and made the reestablishment of Washington as a model European city its main goal. McMillan chose Detroit newspaperman and aesthete Charles Moore as his chief aide in 1891.

Moore, already on intimate terms with many of Detroit's artists, collectors, and industrialists, quickly mastered the art of national politics, and by the turn of the century had become an expert behind-the-scenes political manipulator. Like McMillan, Moore was knowledgeable about art and architecture, and a passionate advocate of the new American aesthetic consciousness. Although in later years Charles Moore emerged from behind the scenes to write substantial biographies of architects Daniel Burnham and Charles McKim, papers on Washington's urban history, and scholarly articles on art and aesthetics, his most influential role remains as the behind-the-scenes man during America's transition from provincial developing country to a cosmopolitan urban nation. Theodore Roosevelt's presidency began at about the same time that this startling American efflorescence in art, architecture, creativity, and urban development was becoming apparent.

By the time Theodore Roosevelt had assumed the American presidency in 1901, James McMillan had consolidated his power in the Senate and had made the District of Columbia Committee an important aesthetic and political tool. McMillan was convinced that the time had come to restore Washington to Charles L'Enfant's original plan—a city of broad vistas, monuments, and boulevards—and to make the capital the symbolic leader of the now burgeoning American City Beautiful Movement. Daniel Burnham, who had become the president of the American Institute of Architects for 1894 and 1895, had just returned from his first grand architectural tour of Europe. McMillan convinced Burnham to direct a new government agency, an autonomous Park Commission attached to McMillan's District of Columbia committee and funded by the Senate. The Park Commission was to study plans for the new Washington and to advise the government on ways to revitalize and beautify the nation's capital. McMillan convinced Frederick Law Olmsted, Jr., the urban and park planner, Charles McKim, the distinguished New York architect, and Augustus Saint-Gaudens, the American sculptor, to join Burnham on the Park Commission and draw up a comprehensive plan for Washington.

The Washington plan was neither political nor provincial in its vision. In an unprecedented move, McMillan arranged for the four members of the Park Commission to tour the major European cities for ideas on how to deal with Washington's specific architectural difficulties. Washington's most immediate problem involved the Pennsylvania Railroad's Union Station. The terminal's tracks marred the previously unbroken vista of L'Enfant's impressive Mall. The McMillan master plan endeavored to maintain the Mall and its majestic effect, to prevent the bureaucracy from encroaching upon Washington's still ample undeveloped land, to preserve the magnificent Rock Creek Park, and to educate Congress and the people about the aesthetics of grand cities.

The four members took their charge seriously and diligently recorded the ideas culled from their trip to Europe on behalf of the United States government. That trip symbolized the beginning of a new American attitude and a new aesthetic political power, and goaded Speaker of the House Joseph Cannon, who resented the power of Senator McMillan that made it possible for him to circumvent Cannon's traditional control of the congressional purse. Charles Moore acted not only as clerk of McMillan's committee, but as secretary of the new Park Commission, keeping its records, acting as an adviser, and even participating in many of the informal architectural discussions. Moore also further developed his newsman's instinct for significant developments and his new political ability to cut through Washington's red tape. The stage was set for the District of Columbia committee to launch its new plan for the nation's capital, not only with a complete blueprint for maintaining the idea of the original French city, but for a complete restoration of the symbolic seat of government, the buildings and grounds that have since been called the White House.

Theodore Roosevelt had the knack, at the most successful stages of his life, of being in the right place at the right time, a phenomenon writers call Rooseveltian luck. There can be disagreement about whether the president was really lucky. Roosevelt did not regard his assumption of the presidency by assassination a stroke of good fortune, but for most people Roosevelt's accidental presidency seemed like his good luck and McKinley's bad luck. But Roosevelt's knack would have little historical significance if, at the same time, Theodore Roosevelt did not have the gift of seizing available opportunities. From the start, Roosevelt could take the smallest opening, and by dint of determination, self-dramatization, or electrifying leadership transform the molehill of opportunity into a veritable mountain. Consigned by political fate to a minor job as civil service commissioner, Theodore Roosevelt made that small role the beginning of a flourishing national political career, establishing his reputation as a reformer. In equally minor positions from state assemblyman to police commissioner, Theodore Roosevelt made small jobs appear large and glamorous. There is hardly a more famous assistant secretary of the navy or a better known volunteer cavalry colonel.

When Theodore Roosevelt moved into the Executive Mansion he had things to think about other than restoring the residence, making it a symbol of a new America, or even attempting to convince Congress of the need for renovations. But the machinery for a major restoration of the president's house was already in place. Senator McMillan's District of Columbia committee had hired the Park Commission to redesign Washington. The AIA had already made standard political architecture unacceptable when it had condemned the Bingham plan. Charles Moore thought that there might be a chance to include the Executive Mansion in the Park Commission's Washington work, and when the chance came both Moore and Roosevelt seized the opportunity.

Theodore Roosevelt took the first and most symbolic step. Although the press and the public referred to the president's home as the White House, its official title remained the Executive Mansion. In one of his first executive orders as president, Theodore Roosevelt officially banished the turgid *Executive Mansion* from official documents and presidential stationery. Almost from the start of the Roosevelt presidency the White House became both the colloquial and the official name. But except for renaming the building, Roosevelt had no further plans. Nor did Congress when it made its customary appropriation of $16,000 for annual maintenance and upkeep.

Edith Roosevelt innocently (we must assume) asked Colonel Theodore Bingham to ask the noted architect Charles McKim, in his capacity as a member of Senator McMillan's Park Commission, to discuss with her how best to spend the $16,000. When Bingham passed on the request to McKim, the drama began. At first Charles McKim refused to have anything to do with such a paltry sum. For McKim, the White House was a disgrace, and $16,000 was an insult. He complained bitterly to Charles Moore, citing specific and obvious White House defects and what was needed to set them right.[3]

Few successful newspapermen are bashful by temperament. Even fewer politicians are timid. Charles Moore quickly took advantage of a golden opportunity. He arranged for a meeting between Charles McKim

---

3. Charles McKim to Charles Moore, April 9, 1902, in Charles Moore Papers, LC; the first glimmer of planned changes in the White House before Roosevelt became president can be found in Charles McKim to Charles Moore, August 26, 1901, in James McMillan Papers, Box 2 of Moore Papers.

and Edith Roosevelt, knowing full well that McKim would not cooperate in any way with a miserly $16,000 upkeep appropriation. Edith did not know that, although she may have been somewhat puzzled by the thoroughness of McKim's two-day examination. The actual state of disrepair at the White House exceeded even McKim's worst expectations. He shocked Edith, but not Charles Moore, at the end of the inspection: "I am sorry to tell you that sixteen thousand dollars isn't enough to clean the White House let alone repairs."[4]

Moore took the depressed McKim back to the Senate office building, where he repeated the long tale of woe to Senator McMillan. McMillan listened with interest and interrupted only to ask the thoroughly dispirited architect for a rough estimate for full repairs. McKim, on the spot, figured $100,000. Unknown to McKim, Senator McMillan went to the Appropriations Committee, in session at that very moment, and added $130,000 to the government's budget, demonstrating his own power in Congress and also his shrewdness in interpreting the architect's estimates. (Even McMillan's additional $30,000 would prove insufficient in the end.) McMillan enjoyed telling Moore that afternoon of the new appropriation of $100,000 for the White House and an additional $30,000 for offices.[5]

McKim had not only obtained the money, but also the first approval of his new plan to separate the president's living quarters from the government offices, a historic return to the first design of the White House as the president's residence and symbolic seat of government. McKim was ecstatic. "In this day of miracles," he wrote, "I thought of the improbability of the whole thing, and am writing now in the frame of mind of a man more likely to go off on a spree than home to dinner!"[6]

The architect and the president were in agreement about the major new idea in McKim's plans for the White House. Roosevelt had publicly complained that the mixture of living and working quarters was inefficient and inconvenient. The issue had never before been as obvious, since no previous president had ever tried to use the Executive Mansion as a home for six young and lively children. Even after the sepa-

4. Charles Moore, "Makers of Washington," Chap. XIX, p. 135, in Moore Papers.
5. *Ibid.*
6. Charles McKim to Charles Moore, April 17, 1902, in Moore Papers.

ration of living and working areas had taken place, the Roosevelt children delighted in mixing their games with presidential duties. Guests at the White House could count on mischief that varied from the evening pillow fights between president and children to the pranks with young Archie's horse, transported to the second floor by way of the official White House elevator. On one occasion Speaker of the House Joe Cannon was introduced to the Roosevelt children's collection of snakes while trying to discuss a tricky matter of politics with the president. The large Roosevelt family dramatized the need to separate as much as possible matters of home and state.

When Theodore Roosevelt asked to meet Charles McKim on April 19, 1902, both men had determined independently to push for a substantial refurbishing of the Executive Mansion, but neither at the time realized how extensive the project would ultimately prove to be. The architect had already scheduled a meeting with his most trusted contractor, Norcross and Company, "to go over the White House from cellar to garret, with a view to determining what should be done to renew its interior walls and partitions, and at the same time to determine upon a site, dimensions, and general treatment of the new temporary office building."[7]

Norcross' findings shocked everyone. Some of the original Hoban building still existed, never having been replaced, since cosmetic changes had always taken precedence over structural and maintenance matters. The original wooden plumbing pipes were still in use, though they no longer functioned as originally designed but instead served as misplaced rainspouts. Some of the still standing structural beams bore evidence of the fire that destroyed the main building in 1814; they were charred and should have been replaced at the time. The Executive Mansion's heating plant was exhausted. Sharing a crowded basement were a welter of heating and electrical pipes, all in poor condition and obviously unsafe. The main elevator, a physical shambles, worked intermittently. Not only had the buildings been poorly maintained, the additions made during the century were ill designed for modern needs. Servants lived in crowded attic quarters that were substandard even in primitive urban America. And at the other end of the social cycle, guests at White House recep-

7. *Ibid.*

tions had to retrieve their coats and wraps from a hall floor, since the President's house had no cloak or dressing rooms.[8]

McKim was shocked at the Norcross findings and consulted fellow commission member Daniel Burnham, who confirmed the results of the inspection. Burnham went further than either Roosevelt or McKim in calling for a separation of the living quarters from the official offices. By suggesting a permanent placement of the living quarters in Lafayette Square across from the original White House, Burnham hoped to avoid placing an additional temporary office building on the White House grounds, fearing it would become permanent, like all the other temporary additions.[9] To add to the architect's dilemma, Theodore Roosevelt insisted that whatever work was to be done had to be finished within four months. Roosevelt knew that at least part of the time the government would be run from Sagamore Hill, and he feared the disruption that longer delays might cause. But the biggest problem was the amount of money required to undo the damage and neglect of almost a century.

The case seemed hopeless when fate and Charles Moore intervened once again. With Senator McMillan on business in Detroit, it was left to Moore to deal with Charles McKim's disappointment over the insufficiency of the original architectural estimate. McMillan's cavalier approach to appropriations had finally caught up with him. In the past he had kept the aesthetic appropriations involving the Park Commission exclusively in the Senate, a routine maneuver on small appropriations, but both illegal and irregular on anything large. The White House was looming as a large and growing expense after the Norcross inspection. Moore knew he could add whatever amount he needed with Senator Allison's Appropriations Committee still in session, but there was a point where the concurrence of the House of Representatives could no longer be taken for granted. Moore knew that point had been reached when, in gently probing Joe Cannon's attitude, he was told, "Those damned architects are fooling Senator McMillan again." Cannon was still rankled by the idea that the Senate had sent the four members of the Park Commission on a European tour without House approval.[10]

8. Moore, "Makers of Washington," Chap. XX, pp. 185–86, in Moore Papers.
9. Daniel Burnham to Charles Moore, April 14, 1902, in Moore Papers.
10. Philip Jessup, *Elihu Root* (2 vols.; New York, 1938), I, 279–81; Moore, "Makers of Washington," Chap. XIX, p. 136, in Moore Papers.

To Moore's surprise, however, House Speaker Cannon objected not to the idea of restoring the Executive Mansion, but to the piecemeal process of additional appropriations. Cannon indicated that if he were given the total at one time he might be willing to support the program. "I must know the total amount needed, the color of the baby's hair before the baby is born." Moore's encouragement lasted barely a moment. Cheered by Cannon's receptivity, Moore asked McKim to prepare a revised estimate of the cost. When he received it, the usually imperturbable Moore was boggled. McKim's figure of $440,641 seemed astronomical. Rather than even try Joe Cannon's generosity again, Moore immediately called the White House and requested to see the president on a matter of extreme urgency. Theodore Roosevelt was in his barber's chair when Charles Moore told him of the new estimate. Roosevelt responded in the manner of any prospective homeowner—with surprise and horror. "That is four times what you told me before." [11]

Moore, however, pointed out that for the first time Speaker Cannon indicated his possible support. Roosevelt agreed. "Tell Uncle Joe I approve." Moore, seeing all manner of political obstacles, declined to take the initiative. "No, Mr. President, you are the one to tell Mr. Cannon." [12] Roosevelt met with Cannon, and to practically everyone's surprise and relief, the Speaker of the House not only agreed to the new estimate but volunteered an additional sum for replacing the worn out furniture. The Sundry Civil Act appropriated $475,445 for repairs and furnishings for the White House and $65,196 for an additional office building capable of future enlargement.

Even indifferent congressmen were impressed by the detailed architectural report of the White House condition. McKim and Norcross had found "the President's office in an unsafe condition," and reported especially severe problems in the electrical system: "the electric wiring was not only old, defective, and obsolete, but actually dangerous." So bad was the condition of the buildings that the $165,000 originally intended to cover the entire restoration was to be used "merely putting the house in order and making it safe." The architects had made a major

11. Moore, "Makers of Washington," Chap. XIX, p. 136, in Moore Papers.
12. *Ibid.*

discovery while looking through architectural records in the Library of Congress. "Old prints and plans of the house showed that by a return to the original design the White House can be put into such a condition that it will serve every use intended for many years to come, and that the increased demands for room in the house can be met in a dignified and a satisfactory manner at a cost which is small when compared with the plans for either a new residence or additions to the present building, both of which are objectionable from many points of view."[13] With McKim's professional arguments, McMillan's powerful support, and Speaker Cannon's cooperation, the bill easily passed Congress. The only matter for debate was the name of the buildings. Charles Moore had used the original name, the President's House, the Senate substituted Executive Mansion, and Theodore Roosevelt overruled both names and made the colloquial White House the official designation. The president signed the act on June 20, 1902.

Although McKim and Moore had won a monumental appropriations victory, the architect and his builder faced an enormous task. Not only had they undertaken a major restoration, but they had promised, at the president's insistence, to have it completed by December 1, 1902, in one hundred working days. While the work progressed, the Roosevelt family took up residence in a nearby house at 22 Jackson Place. McKim sympathized with Roosevelt's urgency in having the renovations completed quickly. At the heart of the McKim plan, and its architectural inspiration, was the return to the original idea "that the White House was planned and constructed as a residence." McKim firmly believed "that it is useless to expect to secure a harmonious structure by doing over any one portion of the house. If the work is to be done at all the entire house should be treated as a single problem." Roosevelt fully agreed. He already lived in a house designed for both work and living at Sagamore Hill, and he knew that McKim's idea was practical. McKim further satisfied the president with an unequivocal timetable: "Provided work begins on June 12, the living portions of the house and the office building

13. "Repairs to the White House," Report of McKim and Norcross, April, 1902. Also see McKim's handwritten notes and sketches, "For President Roosevelt," April, 1902; Memorandum, McKim, Mead, and White, May 24, 1902 (typed with handwritten corrections), all in Moore Papers.

can be ready for occupancy October 1; and the remaining portions of the house by December 1; this can be guaranteed."[14]

The work went smoothly. Both of the Roosevelts consulted with architect McKim, but the changes they asked were relatively minor. Charles Moore volunteered to be the intermediary between the architect and his presidential clients. Moore assured McKim that Mrs. Roosevelt was "very heartily in favor of the changes you propose," while at the same time he submitted to the architect a three-page list of additional matters. Moore reported spending an "hour and a half with Mrs. Roosevelt," during which time the president came in three or four times "to impress upon me certain ideas that he [wished] brought *forcibly* to your attention."[15]

Legend has it that the president hated the Hayes greenhouses so much that he told McKim to "smash the greenhouses." No one liked them, and probably Charles McKim hated them even more than the Roosevelts. But the greenhouses did serve the important function of supplying the huge amount of plants and flowers used for official White House functions. McKim ingeniously arranged for the largest greenhouse to be moved and reassembled at the Botanic Garden, where it continued to produce White House plants. Thus the greenhouse was preserved and the White House grounds freed of an eyesore that had upstaged the elegant East Room—the site of the grandest diplomatic receptions—since the Hayes administration. It was Charles McKim, not Theodore Roosevelt, who reveled in the destruction of the other greenhouses: "It is too good to believe that those excrescences, the greenhouses, are to be abolished or rather 'smashed,'" McKim told Moore when the plans had finally been worked out.[16]

McKim was happy to delegate the details to Moore. "I am very glad to learn that Mrs. Roosevelt had roped you into her horizon," he told

14. "Repairs to the White House," Report of McKim and Norcross, April, 1902; Memorandum in Regard to the White House, June 5, 1902 (printed for the use of the Senate Committee on the District of Columbia); see also Daniel Burnham to Charles Moore, April 14, 1902, all in Moore Papers.

15. Charles Moore to Charles McKim, May 17, 1902, in Moore Papers.

16. TR to Colonel Theodore Bingham, June 28, 1902, Theodore Roosevelt Papers, LC; Edith Kermit Roosevelt to Charles Moore, July 2, 1902, Charles McKim to Charles Moore, July 11, 1902, both in Moore Papers; William Ryan and Desmond Guinness, *The White House: An Architectural History* (New York, 1980), 154.

Moore. Edith Roosevelt was specific in her demands. "I have marked the chintz that we prefer, and have returned the others to you by express today. I do not like my writing desk at all. I think it ought to be made to match the furniture, which is rosewood, carved with big birds, I should say about fifty years old." Edith discussed the Blue Room samples that she and Alice liked, "but the President still thinks it would make an ugly evening room, so to satisfy him I would like to know exactly how you propose it should look completed." McKim listened carefully and used most of the Roosevelt family suggestions.[17]

Politics was not completely absent from the White House work. Colonel Bingham, superintendent of the White House grounds, was not happy with the way things had gone. His own plans had been demolished by the American Institute of Architects, he had to suffer the growing influence of the aristocratic McKim, and he fretted as his bureaucratic power gradually eroded. Bingham did not give up easily. McKim saw the danger in June when he complained to Moore that Bingham's interference would be intolerable. "I understand that all payments are to be made by him. It should be distinctly understood in my agreement, with the President, that he is to have nothing to do with the work in any way, either as to passing on its character, or authority to question the amounts which from time to time will be certified by us." On June 18 McKim, noting that his builder was ready for immediate clearing of the White House, worried over possible delaying tactics by the bureaucratic keeper of the grounds. Such tactics finally led to McKim's ultimatum of July 11, 1902, in which he again declared Bingham's interference "intolerable" and insisted Bingham's role "be restricted to that of Inspector and Disbursing officer." McKim complained that "with all we have undertaken to do in the short time at our command, it is a little too much to have to contend with Col. Bingham's methods."[18]

McKim's victory over Bingham was total. The president, writing to Bingham on July 14, 1902, carefully instructed him not to interfere with McKim, and informed him that the penalty clause Bingham had

17. Charles Moore to Charles McKim, May 17, 1902, in Moore Papers; Edith Kermit Roosevelt to Charles McKim, Box 8, in Charles McKim Papers, LC.
18. Charles McKim to Charles Moore, June 12, 1902, and July 11, 1902, in Moore Papers.

decided to invoke on the architects was not a part of Bingham's domain. Roosevelt's highly detailed letter places strict limits upon Bingham's responsibility and deals with the complicated overlapping of the restoration funds and the normal White House building appropriations. The letter is firm but conciliatory. Roosevelt had to use all his diplomacy and charm to keep his building superintendent and architect from damaging the restoration. For McKim, however, the resolution was total. To Charles Moore he wired on July 15, 1902, "Successful visit Oyster Bay. Greatest relief." McKim was impressed with the nature of his victory. He met the president and "presented the matter fully to him, in the presence of Mrs. Roosevelt and the Secretary of War." As they sat on the piazza, "the President sent for Secretary Cortelyou and dictated a letter to Colonel Bingham." [19]

McKim was also pleased with the progress of the work, "although the house still suggests the recent evacuation of an enemy." With a labor force of six hundred men, the work progressed with little serious friction or delay. The press remained critical during the renovations, displaying a skepticism that only the finished work would eventually allay. On details of furniture and decoration, the architect worked with the Roosevelts. McKim even relented on the president's desire for stuffed heads to replace McKim's beautifully proportioned lion heads as a decoration. Moore wired McKim: "The President desires me to thank you heartily for your generous offer. Unfortunately he already has two mooses heads." A $2,000 appropriation had been included in the original legislation for the "purchase of large decorative game heads for the dining room under special instruction of the President." On October 30, McKim wired Moore, who was in Detroit attending to the details of Senator McMillan's funeral: "All quiet on the Potomac. President moves in tonight." The architect had finished the White House itself on schedule. The remaining details concerning the grounds and the office building were finished by the end of the year. [20]

19. TR to Colonel Theodore Bingham, in MRL, III, 293–94; Charles McKim to Charles Moore (cable), July 15, 1902, and July 17, 1902. See also Bingham to McKim, July 5, 1902, and McKim to Bingham, July 10, 1902, all in Moore Papers.

20. Charles McKim to Charles Moore, July 17, 1902; "Two Elk Heads at Present," McKim to Moore, October 30, 1902, both in Moore Papers; War Department, Sundry Civil Act, June 28, 1902; Moore to McKim (cable), November 5, 1902; McKim to Moore, October 30, 1902, both in Moore Papers.

While the rush to complete the restoration was at its height, the press, largely neglected, began to write unfavorable articles on the new White House. Charles Moore was chosen to set the record straight. His vehicle was a commissioned article in the prestigious *Century Magazine*, which used the same material to be presented to Congress in the final report of the architects. Moore's article is carefully and fully illustrated and offers a comprehensive history of White House architecture before McKim. Moore's commentary on the actual restoration is more of a panegyric to McKim than a critical commentary, but it serves well as the best defense, apologia, or argument in favor of his impressive work. More important in Moore's article is the revelation of what the architect, the president, and even the Congress had in mind in redoing and renaming the presidential house.[21]

Of the East Rooms, where the new administration would conduct its social diplomacy, Moore wrote, "The scene of so many social triumphs and brilliant spectacles had undergone transformation." Moore told his readers that the walls were now white, the distracting paintings were on display elsewhere and the floor rivaled "the floors of Versailles and Fountainbleu." Moore's main emphasis was on the social changes the renovation had brought about. The dining room was rebuilt without Chester Arthur's Tiffany screen, the Blue Room where the president received guests was redone, and the Red Room now served as either a smoking room or as an additional apartment for overnight guests. The architects had set out to make the White House a grand showplace. Gone were the symbols of an age more concerned with commerce than with prestige. Perhaps the old greenhouses are the best symbol of what the change meant. Moore eloquently defends their removal.

> On the west the beautiful terrace of Latrobe had been perverted by constructing upon it a series of greenhouses that smashed into the fine features of the main building with all the results of an end-on railway collision; on the east the garden sloped toward the house instead of away from it; and a great fountain and terrace were placed on the axis of the Treasury Department, ignoring the White House itself in most cavalier fashion. On the south the Latrobe colonnade, with its fine stone columns, like some old cloister, had

21. Charles Moore, "The Restoration of the White House," *Century Magazine*, LXV (1903), 807–31.

been closed by building against it a heterogeneous collection of cheap glass houses—one for a President fond of grapes, another for a Chief Magistrate who fancied big cucumbers! The rooms in this terrace, designed for house offices, had become the accessories of the greenhouses, as if the President of the United States were a commercial florist.

The new spirit demanded a new vista:

Now, on the occasions of large receptions, the guests drive into the grounds by a new entrance, opposite the west front of the Treasury. Alighting at a spacious portecochere, they enter a corridor formed by the east terrace.[22]

McKim and Roosevelt's relationship continued after the White House restoration. McKim actively continued his work with the Park Commission and its struggle to keep ugly government buildings from overwhelming the capital. McKim could play politics as well. He later advised the president "that Mr. Cannon and the Park Commission are now friends." Cannon agreed to a new commission to advise on the location of capital buildings and, McKim added, "the Speaker has further promised to see and consult you."[23]

The McKim restoration was not universally acclaimed. The most embarrassing immediate failure occurred at the first State dinner when the still incomplete electrical system failed at the worst possible moment. And a recent architectural history, while praising McKim's inspired transformation of the original basement into reception rooms, finds the entrance hall closer in appearance to a 1900 bank than to Hoban's original plan. Roosevelt, McKim, and Moore, in all their official and semi-official articles and messages, emphasized the modesty of the plan, its expression of stately simplicity, and its reflection of the original building plans, conceived for a simpler time. Moore made it clear that the original premise of the White House as a residence and not a government office was the great triumph of the McKim restoration.[24]

The Roosevelts personally approved the changes. Writing to his son Kermit, a month after moving back in, Roosevelt thought "the changes have improved [the White House] more than you can imagine." The

22. *Ibid.*, 830, 825.
23. Charles McKim to TR, March 13, 1905, in Charles McKim Papers, LC.
24. Ryan and Guinness, *The White House*, 156; Senate Documents, 57th Cong., 2nd Sess., No. 197, Serial 4439, p. 15; Moore, "Restoration," 830–31.

president understood the change in style as well: "The changes in the White House have transformed it from a shabby likeness to the ground floor of the Astor House [the Times Square Hotel] into a simple and dignified dwelling for the head of a great Republic."[25] The new consciousness, the new century, and the new president now had a setting in keeping with the ambitions of a people who moved as eagerly as their president from the provincial life of the frontier to the more worldly outlook of a fully developed industrial nation.

25. TR to Kermit Roosevelt, December 4, 1902, in MRL, III, 389; TR to Maria Storer, December 8, 1902, in MRL, III, 392.

2 / Theodore Roosevelt's Salon
Style in the American Presidency

"Distinguished civilized men and charming civilized women came as a habit to the White House while Roosevelt was there. For once in our history we had an American *salon*."[1] Owen Wister's description of the Roosevelt White House is apt. Theodore and Edith Roosevelt added the dimension of style to American government. Novelists, painters, poets, artists, and journalists came to the Roosevelt White House, stayed for an evening or a week, mingled with the political regulars, and discussed everything from the day's events to ancient history, or any one of hundreds of subjects on which the president of the United States was able and eager to talk. Roosevelt's letters to political allies and to writers frequently closed with a serious and well-considered invitation to spend some time at the White House. The Roosevelt dinner table could be expanded almost at will. Not all of the six Roosevelt children were always at home, or at every dinner, but enough of them were to make any meal at the White House a family affair—with famous guests.

John Hay and Henry Adams were frequent visitors, as were members of the cabinet and old Harvard friends. When a visiting politician was in town whom Roosevelt wished to talk with, he became one of the diners along with the week's resident writer or hunter. The talk was lively and usually dominated by the president. How much Roosevelt talked was determined by the mixture of guests. Wister distinguished familiars and unfamiliars. When an unfamiliar took to the customary quick and informal repartee, the newcomer could easily dominate the evening's conver-

1. Owen Wister, *Roosevelt: The Story of a Friendship, 1880–1919* (New York, 1930), 124.

sation. More frequently the president discoursed on a new or favorite old topic with his guests. Edith was a relaxed hostess who enjoyed her evenings as first lady; the children, experienced in adult dinner parties, rarely became a problem.

Theodore Roosevelt is best known and most admired as the classic man of action. His acerbic friend Henry Adams remarked that Roosevelt "showed the singular primitive quality that belongs to ultimate matter—the quality that medieval theology assigned to God—he was pure act." Adams' description is witty and inaccurate. Roosevelt combined an excess of personal charm and magnetism with a unique eclectic intellect. He read in three languages—English, French, and German—and managed to get by in others, including the archaic Old Norse. He read voraciously, and he remembered virtually everything he read. Roosevelt's range bordered on the miraculous. When one White House guest, apparently showing off, cited a book on Icelandic literature, Roosevelt eagerly discussed a dozen other books on the exotic subject. He read and loved the ancient literature of Norway, and wrote a learned article on the Irish sagas that casually referred to German and Norse equivalents. His honors as president of the American Historical Association in 1912 and honorary president of the Gaelic Literature Association were earned, not by-products of his presidency.[2]

In the letters written during his presidency to distinguished English historian George Otto Trevelyan, Roosevelt revealed a working knowledge of recent historical literature and a professional grasp of history that was remarkable. He used difficult historical analogy with a sense of the complexity of historical comparisons. Roosevelt's history was carefully thought out; his frequently anguished letters to Trevelyan revealed a sympathy for world dilemmas that included Turkish treatment of Armenians and Russian treatment of Jews. Roosevelt's historical thinking is far from the big stick image. He was aware of presidential and national limitations and of questions that went beyond the normal scope of an American president. In his letters his intellect dominates; in person Roosevelt's charm could be overwhelming.

2. Henry Adams, *The Education of Henry Adams* (Boston, 1918), 389; Edward Wagenknecht, *The Seven Worlds of Theodore Roosevelt* (New York, 1958), 70; "Ancient Irish Sagas," *Outlook*, December 16, 1911, rpr. in *Works, Nat. Ed.*, XII, 131–46; "Dante and the Bowery," *Outlook*, August 26, 1911, rpr. *Works, Nat. Ed.*, XII, 98–105.

Roosevelt possessed the rare gift of absolute concentration. He read continuously and quickly. Anecdotes abound about Roosevelt's voracious reading appetite. He read Tolstoy's *Anna Karenina* in a rainstorm in the Dakotas, Shakespeare's plays while on a safari in Africa, Lecky's *History of Rationalism in Europe* in the men's room (for the light) on a swaying train to Cairo in 1910. He kept a book by the White House door for the odd moments of waiting for other members of his party. When he read a magazine he would read a page quickly, tear it out, and continue until the magazine had been literally consumed. He could go from absolute concentration on a difficult book to an equally complex conversation without losing the thread of either. Roosevelt possessed a photographic memory for the printed word and could reproduce from memory virtually anything he had read. In addition, he probably knew and could identify more birds by their songs than any other man of his time. One of the most touching moments in modern history is the meeting of Roosevelt and Viscount Gray, London's Foreign Minister during World War I, when the two statesmen paused in 1915, and compared their knowledge of birds singing, before talking about more momentous diplomatic matters.[3]

Yet the Roosevelt gifts that appear so abundantly in letters and in spoken conversations rarely appear in Roosevelt's many books. Except for an occasional piece of luminous prose in the natural history works, most of Roosevelt's published books are seriously flawed and, when compared to the letters, intellectually disappointing. In his historical work Roosevelt would often bog down in irrelevant detail. *The Naval War of 1812* mixes extraneous fact with some useful history; the four-volume *Winning of the West* does not. It is a morass of random information. Some of the Roosevelt potboilers—biographies written for series—are seriously hindered by scholarly impatience. While working on one less than memorable biography, Roosevelt urgently wired Henry Cabot Lodge asking for the date of his subject's death so that he could finish the book. "I hesitate to give him a wholly fictitious date of death." Of all his books, the most difficult for Roosevelt was *Thomas Hart Benton*, which he was trying to research and write while in the Dakota Ter-

3. Viscount Gray of Fallodon, *Fallodon Papers* (Boston, 1926), 64–69; see also TR, President Roosevelt's List of Birds Seen in District of Columbia, March 27, 1908, printed, in Theodore Roosevelt Papers, Series 16, LC.

ritory—an impossibility. "The Bad Lands have much fewer books than Boston has," he wrote Lodge. Roosevelt was aware of his shortcomings and yearned to be able to write with the right word and the right rhythm. "I do not like a certain lack of sequitur that I do not seem to be able to get rid of." Roosevelt reserved his most lavish praise for writers who produced polished finished prose. Roosevelt edited everything he wrote, but few versions of his prose began well or are memorable in their final form, except for the letters, which are not as carefully edited.[4]

Roosevelt displayed a well-developed taste for writing, art, literature, and history even as an adolescent. His earliest aesthetic sensibilities were recorded on his first European trip at the age of twelve. In Sorrento, he observed "well preserved frescoes on the wall and mosaics." The fifteen-year-old Roosevelt wrote that the temple at Karnak by moonlight "gave rise to thoughts of the ineffable." By graduation from Harvard and marriage in 1880, young Roosevelt was an old hand in museums, at ease with art and exhibiting a well-developed critical facility. He wrote his sister Corrine of his admiration for the Louvre Museum but not for French painters "except Greuze"; after visiting the Netherlands Roosevelt reported fully on the state of European painting. "Rembrandt is by all odds my favourite." Rubens continually offended Roosevelt's Victorian sensibility.[5]

The awareness, taste, respect, and affection for works of imagination gave President Theodore Roosevelt influence as a taste maker. Because the president liked art and literature, art and literature became more fashionable within the country, in much the same way as in later years James Bond novels became popular when John F. Kennedy was president, and golf when Eisenhower was in the White House. Although Roosevelt lived in a time before culture had begun to dominate American leisure, the president's social life and cultural preferences received enormous coverage in the daily newspapers and had a wide influence.

4. TR to Henry Cabot Lodge, June 7, 1886, in MRL, I, 102, TR to Lodge, March 27, 1886, in MRL, I, 95. For a persuasive defense of Roosevelt as a stylist and professional writer, see Edmund Morris, "Theodore Roosevelt as Writer," Colloquium, May 17, 1983, at Woodrow Wilson International Center for Scholars.

5. TR to Anna Bullock Gracie, January 2, 1870, in MRL, I, 5; TR to Anna Gracie, January 16, 1873, in MRL, I, 6; TR to Corrine Roosevelt, June 6, 1881, in MRL, I, 48–49. For his full critique of Dutch painting, see TR to Corrine Roosevelt, August 14, 1881, in MRL, I, 51.

Much of the reporting was frivolous, and like historical writing on Theodore Roosevelt, it emphasized the colorful and dramatic, exaggerating Roosevelt's physical activities at the expense of the intellectual. Nonetheless, the variety of White House visitors was well publicized. The president's eclectic taste, his passion for intellect and imagination, as well as for horseback riding and hunting, was well known and respected. Probably the virile presidential image made his less active interests both acceptable and familiar to the public.

Roosevelt's strong critical preferences, however, were not always helpful. His close personal friendship with Owen Wister involved many critical discussions between president and novelist on Wister's writing. Although in most instances Wister remained single-minded, it is possible that the prepublication changes in the *Virginian* inspired by Roosevelt's objections weakened the final version of the novel. Roosevelt objected to the realistic natural scenes. When Wister toned them down, he made his book more popular with the public but less distinguished as literature.

Roosevelt's taste varied. He quickly picked up his son's fondness for the unknown poetry of Edwin Arlington Robinson. Roosevelt's review of Robinson's poetry reveals the president's genuine critical ability as well as his broad cultural background. Impressed by the unique quality of "gray" in Robinson, Roosevelt compared the poet's metaphorical use of cold with the paintings of J. M. Turner. Roosevelt was sensitive to the problems of writers trying to earn a living in a society that was just beginning to support its art and culture. He was concerned, too, about the effect of expatriation upon writers in general, and Robinson in particular. Roosevelt finally convinced Robinson to take a two-thousand-dollar-a-year position as special treasury agent with presidential assurances that the job's minimal duties would not interfere with Robinson's writing.[6]

Neither respectability nor fashionability is relevant in assessing the importance of presidential taste. Roosevelt did not collect art because

6. TR to James Canfield, August 16, 1905, in MRL, IV, 1303; TR to Edwin Arlington Robinson, March 27, 1905, in MRL, IV, 1145; TR, "The Children of the Night," *Outlook*, August 12, 1905, rpr. in *Works, Nat. Ed.*, XII, 296–299; TR to Richard Watson Gilder, March 31, 1905, in MRL, IV, 1155, 1145n.

he felt he should. He liked and disliked individual artists, and he was genuinely affected by art and literature. It really does not matter that Longfellow's poetry, a Roosevelt favorite, is simple, or that Robert Grant's *Unleavened Bread*, another presidential favorite, is a dreary moralistic novel of the time. Simply by reacting to art and literature personally, Theodore Roosevelt made them part of the new American consciousness, which in the early twentieth century was already undergoing a transformation from provinciality to cosmopolitanism. The influence of the White House did not cause the new culture. Cultural activity grew rapidly in the large urban areas of Chicago, New York, and Philadelphia. For one of the few times in the American presidency, the White House was not a fortress of philistinism or indifference to the arts.

Roosevelt was active in encouraging the arts. When Charles Freer tendered an important collection to a government not yet ready to consider a national art museum, the president himself intervened in favor of acceptance. Even on small matters the president was helpful. In 1908 when the Boston Museum wished to convey its gratitude for help on a project to a Japanese artist who was in political trouble at home, Roosevelt gave the museum's message directly to the Japanese government.[7]

Roosevelt's comprehension of culture was unique among Western leaders of the early twentieth century. When the Russo-Japanese war of 1904–1905 became imminent, nearly every European leader regarded the conflict as one between the civilized West and the backward East. Roosevelt was the exception. Fascinated with Japanese history, he began a study of ancient Japanese culture. Roosevelt studied Bushido, learned the ancient samurai traditions, and became aware of a centuries-old Japanese culture, which he felt was equal to that of the West, even if markedly different. Theodore Roosevelt became one of Japan's few allies in the war with Russia, and eventually he was able to make peace between the two rivals. The Nobel Peace Prize that Roosevelt received for settling the Russo-Japanese War was as much a recognition of his cultural perception as of his diplomatic achievement. Of the Western world's leaders, Roosevelt alone understood the Japanese and treated them as equals with the West.

7. U.S. Department of State, Decimal File 13,968, June 4, 1908, RG 59, NA.

With the growth of cities, new wealth, and leisure, more Americans than ever before were ready for the urbanity of culture at the start of the twentieth century. Theodore Roosevelt's own curiosity and delight for art and literature were obviously real; the authenticity made the Rooseveltian presence enormously and continuously influential. During the presidency and after, when sharing Norwegian mythology with King Olaf of Norway (in 1910 while belatedly accepting his Nobel Peace Prize), talking about birds with Viscount Gray of Fallodon outside London in 1915, or reviewing books on art, literature, history, and natural history, Roosevelt brought to the country and to the White House a sense of style absent in American life since the earliest days of the Republic.

Seeing Theodore Roosevelt's presidency from a cultural perspective should change the common stereotype of the bellicose expansionist associated mainly with imperialism and jingoism. Roosevelt's taste for civilization became America's taste and helped ease the clash between American cultural ignorance and European pretension. One of the most difficult diplomatic problems Theodore Roosevelt faced in the early days of his presidency was the ingrained European statesman's habit of denigrating America as a cultural backwater. Americans judged other peoples by their political sophistication, efficiency, and their devotion to democratic principles. Europeans and Latin Americans looked for far different values, frequently cultural. America's prestige automatically rose during Theodore Roosevelt's presidency when the American president, his cabinet, and many of his diplomats, such as the cultured back-bay Bostonian George von Lengerke Meyer, no longer looked and acted like uneducated yahoos. The new American cosmopolitanism, radiating from the White House as well as from America's established cities, had as much to do with America's new place in the world as Roosevelt's dramatic diplomatic initiatives.

Diplomacy and culture were related and worked hand in hand. Wealthy Americans were making their peace with the older and newer art in both Europe and Asia. America, during Theodore Roosevelt's presidency, was expanding its cultural horizons; it was not expanding its colonial holdings. The influence of the White House was continuously on the side of the cultural expansionists. Although the support was mostly indirect and symbolic, the effect of the Roosevelt presidency was to bring America closer to the world. The new mutual understanding of a shared cultural heritage with Europe softened, but did not entirely eliminate, the American claim of uniqueness.

Led by a president who liked and responded to art, and who entertained artists and writers at the White House, Americans backed off from older assumptions that art and artists were too effete for a virile democracy. With the expansion of American cultural understanding, it became possible for the United States to become an equal partner with other advanced world peoples, in culture and imagination as well as in diplomatic influence. Without this new cultural equality, the Americans, already committed to messianic democracy, would have had little recourse but to depend on force to compel even minimal European toleration of American diplomatic equality. As it was, the detente between the English and the Americans, promoted by cultured statesmen such as John Hay and indirectly by gifted American expatriate artists like Henry James and James Whistler, began before formal diplomacy confirmed the new American status.

A political leader like Theodore Roosevelt, who could understand Norse epics as well as Oriental traditions of ancient Bushido, made the cultural changes even more dramatic and emphasized the positive influence of the new America to the world. Roosevelt as president introduced what Henry James's fictional character Christopher Newman searched for: a new relationship with the old world that did not relinquish the American virtue of uniqueness. Presidential style is not simply a succession of well-planned dinner parties, sophisticated vintages of imported wines, or carefully balanced invitation lists, even though these are the routine elements of an efficient diplomatic court. Style is a continuous quality, and in the Roosevelt White House it never stopped, since style was already an integral part of the man and family who were to lead America in the first decade of the twentieth century.

Wister was right. Theodore Roosevelt's American salon was unique, indispensable, and a significant part of the diplomatic maturity (expansion) brought about by the new conditions of wealth, leisure, and prosperity in the world's newest middle-class industrial nation. Theodore Roosevelt's style is much more important than his so-called big stick in explaining America's sudden emergence as one of the leading world powers under his presidency in the early twentieth century. The Roosevelt salon comprised both the usual formal entertainments that have become a tradition in the American presidency and the informal everyday dinners at the White House.

George Washington, who established the custom of lavish entertainment and the pomp of the presidency (which is often at odds with the democratic image of the new Republic), managed to satisfy the demands of both pomp and democracy by staging elegant open houses and bowing to his resplendently dressed guests. Thomas Jefferson regaled his guests with elaborate wines and international cuisine, and he did it frequently—sometimes several times a week. Except for the aberration of the teetotal Hayes administration, the formal White House dinners and receptions were standard events in the American presidency from the beginning. Superficially there was little difference between the McKinley and the Roosevelt formal dinner parties.

There were, however, subtle differences. Edith Kermit Roosevelt made the formal entertainments both a sacred trust and a personal joy. Edith had always loved to entertain and had done so successfully on a small scale, but until Theodore became president, Edith's resources were limited. The Roosevelt income had never been large enough to cover the social ambitions and traditions of the large family and at the same time allow enough money to raise six children and keep two residences. For Edith Roosevelt large-scale entertaining had been neither affordable nor appropriate. For a first lady, entertaining was not only appropriate, but a requirement of the office.

Although the president personally paid the direct costs of the dinners and receptions, the indirect expenses were paid from White House or State Department budgets. Theodore Roosevelt's salary as president was much larger than his previous wages as a government employee, and the indirect allowances were substantial enough that the Roosevelt family could look upon the presidency as an undreamed of luxury. Edith Roosevelt loved the idea of entertaining on a grand scale and made the onerous responsibilities of feeding enormous groups of people a happy challenge. Faced with the prospect of entertaining over fourteen thousand guests at the five major White House receptions of 1902 and

1903, Edith Roosevelt planned her details with the dedication and ingenuity of a general preparing for battle with a prodigious opposing army.

Before Edith Roosevelt became first lady, catering for the White House was divided between several firms in the Washington area and dominated by Jules Demont's catering company. Edith Roosevelt, however, was more attracted by Charles Rauscher's impressive credentials. Rauscher had begun his career in food at Delmonico's in New York, and he was not bashful in advertising his background on his letterhead. Edith's reasons for choosing Rauscher as the sole White House caterer are not entirely clear. She may simply have wanted to make a dramatic change from the past, or perhaps she was impressed with the Delmonico heritage, or liked the constant arguments that dominated the new partnership. The White House continued to use Jules Demont to supply its elaborate desserts, but when Demont tried to regain some of his lost business he was curtly told, "Your letter has been received and you are informed that arrangements have already been made." Probably as a sop to Demont, he was permitted to cater one last official event, a supper dance on January 3, 1902.[8]

The partnership between Charles Rauscher and Edith Roosevelt was a distinguished one. Together the two made the receptions, entertainments, and formal dinners at the Roosevelt White House memorable at the time and impressive in historical retrospect. Taken by themselves, neither the dinners nor the arrangements are particularly interesting or significant. But in examining the effort made by the first lady and her caterer, it is obvious that the Roosevelts took the social side of the presidency seriously. Edith worked hard at making the events notable, and in the process provided a glimpse of the image the president of the United States wished to present to the world.

Beyond the bickering and the haggling over prices and services, which made the Rauscher-Roosevelt relationship an exercise in frugal domesticity, there was an attempt to bring knowledge, cosmopolitanism, and

8. Jules Demont to Colonel T. W. Symons, October 27, 1903; Symons to Demont, October 28, 1903; Colonel Mead Bingham to Demont, December 10, 1901, all in "Official Functions of the President, 1902–1916," 24 vols., in RG 42, NA.

sophistication to the White House functions. Some of the effort reflects Edith's own social pretensions, but both of the Roosevelts were dedicated to making the American image impressive, to demonstrate that the Republic could entertain as knowledgeably and as impressively as Europe. In short, the Roosevelt White House was dedicated to the idea that America in the twentieth century was more than equal to the worldliest of powers, even in matters a republic traditionally cares little about. In the grandness of the style, Edith Roosevelt returned to a tradition that George Washington and Thomas Jefferson had begun.

The details of the planning are nearly as intriguing as the actual events. Colonel Mead Bingham handled the thankless task of mediating between the first lady and the chief caterer. The association between Rauscher and the White House began on October 29, 1901, when Charles Rauscher told Colonel Bingham that "the price I am stating for the Buffet Supper is a special price as I am very anxious to have the honor to serve Mrs. Roosevelt. Anything that Mrs. Roosevelt would like to change on either menus, I am only glad to do so and make new suggestions." Rauscher's proposal showed an inclination to haggle within reason, and it was a rare Rauscher proposal that did not produce some change in menu, wine, or price. The battleground varied. Edith Roosevelt, in accepting Rauscher's proposal for one of the first large dinners, spelled out the details of the agreement (always through Colonel Bingham, never directly). Rauscher was told that "the price is for ninety persons more or less and includes everything which goes with furnishing the dinner, including any extra linen, china, chairs, etc., that may be needed in addition to the White House equipment. The price includes all wines, liqueurs and everything mentioned on your submitted menu." [9]

The requirement that Rauscher's waiters "be colored" is not an indication that Mrs. Roosevelt was one of the century's first equal opportunity employers, but a casual reminder of standard matters of caste, race, and class in the America of the time. Since the White House staff was colored, the additional serving staff must also be colored. Bingham

9. Colonel Mead Bingham to Charles Rauscher, December 14, 1901, in RG 42, NA.

was not at all bashful in spelling out the requirement and the reasons for it.[10] The famous Booker T. Washington dinner at the White House had already occurred in October, and though the Roosevelts had taken social racial questions casually then, the outcry from the southern press about entertaining a Negro for dinner was never forgotten by anyone at the White House.

By December 18, 1902, Rauscher and Edith were working well together, and the cabinet dinner of December 18, 1902, one of the smaller formal dinners, is representative of how official Washington dined during the Roosevelt years. Appetites and menus were equally prodigious. The meal began with raw oysters on the half shell (fresh bluepoints) and turtle soup. Fresh Kennebec salmon, sweetbreads, saddle of mutton, and terrapin a la Baltimore made up the next (but not the main) course. The pièce de résistance was "cancaback" ducks. Many vegetables and side dishes accompanied the main dishes. All Roosevelt dinners included champagne (a frequent matter for discussion between Edith and Rauscher), and in addition sherry, sauternes, and red Bordeaux were served. A much later cabinet dinner for seventy-two persons is similar. Oysters and terrapin were again on the menu, and the early course included "Potomac bass and filet of venison with roasted quails as the main course." Specific wines were listed for each course to guide the diners (or perhaps the caterer).[11]

Politicians ate well in early twentieth-century America. One of the first of Edith Roosevelt's changes was putting "the pièce de résistance after the secondary entrees." The menus were composites of French with American translations, some of which were left to poor Colonel Bingham's imagination. In one early plaintive letter to Rausher, Bingham asks, "What is the United States for Tartelettes a la Moelle?" Ruinart champagne was the usual Roosevelt favorite but Edith loved to debate about champagne with Rauscher. On November 3, 1903, in response to a continuing discussion, Rauscher submitted his entire list of champagnes, including "my own direct importation." Edith ignored Rauscher's choice completely and designated three champagnes for White House use: the usual Ruinart Brut, a Duc de Montabello Brut,

10. *Ibid.*
11. Menus are in RG 42, NA.

and the 1893 vintage of Casanove Vin Monargue. She then instructed Rauscher not to list any of the wines by shipper or vineyard on the official menus. It is not clear why, since some future menus do cite specific wines. Edith also added another condition to the arrangement; the caterer would be henceforth responsible for both dishwashing and any breakage that resulted from his new responsibility. As always the eager caterer accepted the new terms.[12]

Perhaps because of the constant changes either suggested by Rauscher or initiated by Edith Roosevelt, the Roosevelts' formal entertaining became grander and more elegant than the previous presidential celebrations. The newly restored White House, particularly designed with large-scale entertaining in mind, would probably have made even ordinary dinners more resplendent than before. But although food and drink were the most entertaining of the arrangements, they were far from the most demanding. Throughout the presidency, Edith and her social aides were concerned with the planning of seating arrangements that would not disrupt the delicate social rules and protocol of official Washington. Every function had its own seating list, which was in effect a pecking order of power and prestige. The president was always number one. Number two could vary. In normal circumstances it was the vice-president unless the chief executive of another nation was in attendance. At state functions the cabinet took precedence over foreign ministers, but at cabinet members' homes the order was reversed. Army and Navy officers were fifteenth in the pecking order as a class and were seated by grade and within the grade "according to the date of commission." The details for each function were immense, and seating arrangements were usually specified by a list accompanied by a chart.[13]

One of the secrets of the Roosevelt success was the meticulous planning Edith insisted upon for every event. Nothing was left to chance if it could be planned in advance. For the Diplomatic Dinner of 1903, 3,487 persons were invited and 2,139 attended. Each finger bowl con-

12. Colonel Mead Bingham to Charles Rauscher, December 4, 1901; wine list is in Rauscher to Charles McCauley, November 3, 1903; wine instructions are in McCauley to Rauscher, November 5, 1903, in RG 42, NA.
13. Colonel Theodore A. Bingham, "Order of Precedence," February 12, 1900; see also the table of guests invited and attending at the different receptions, "Seasons of 1902–03 and 1903–04," both in RG 42, NA.

tained a small lily of the valley. Palms, crotons, and other plants between the tables were to be five feet tall and the flower requisition called for "2000 spikes of Roman hyacinths (white)." For larger parties such as the New Year's reception different rules were required. The memorandum instructed the staff of "an important change." The line would pass through the two south doors rather than the north as before. A boggling 6,821 persons attended to see the president, the first lady, and the "behind the line guests" comprising the cabinet and the Supreme Court.[14]

By the beginning of the third White House social season Edith's memoranda to the staff were intricately detailed instructions specifying who would face the first family, when the Marine band would play, who would escort single ladies to the tables, and who the senior guest of the evening was—an important detail, for the senior guest was the only person to be informed that the president was ready to have dinner. Nothing was left to chance socially. The two White House aides Major Charles L. McCauley and Colonel Thomas W. Symons would "seek to introduce partners to each other and to assure themselves that each guest knows his seat and function." Music was always supplied by the Marine Band (which had been banished during the presidency of Thomas Jefferson). The music was meticulously scheduled but without any discernible pattern. For the Diplomatic Reception of January 8, 1903, the band, presumably playing a broad assortment of seminationalistic music, began with a Sousa march, proceeded to a German opera overture (Weber's *Oberon*), and wandered from there into the semi-popular music of the time.[15]

The White House music was consistently less grand than Rauscher's food or champagne but had the advantage of being considerably less expensive. Indeed, the music was furnished at the government's expense; the food and drink were paid for by the president out of personal funds. The division reflects the relative low cost of even grandiose food

14. Table of guests invited and attending, "Seasons of 1902–03 and 1903–04;" "State Dinners," two-page memorandum "approved by Mrs. Roosevelt," November 15, 1903; George H. Brown, "Description of the floral decorations of the table at the 'Diplomatic Dinner' held in the State Dining Room of the White House—January 15th, 1903;" Memorandum for New Year's Reception, 1903, all in RG 42.
15. "State Dinners," November 15, 1903, in RG 42, NA.

at the time and the Roosevelts' feeling that the presidential salary was sufficient for such a high standard of living.

The less elaborate meals at the White House—luncheons with the presidential family and a mixture of political and social friends—were also memorable. Oscar Straus, the secretary of commerce, described the informality: "The President throws off his official harness, which he does very readily, and expresses himself with that freedom which is so natural to him. He was as buoyant and full of spirits as a young college graduate. He has a wonderful fund of humor."[16] At the smaller luncheons and informal dinners, the Roosevelts entertained in grand family style with the president generally acting as chief entertainer.

Oscar Straus, before he became a member of the Roosevelt cabinet, was invited to a White House dinner in 1904 when both Edith and Alice were away and Theodore was host. "Dinner was announced, and we walked into the dining room without any idea of precedence, just as informally as at one's own house. The President took the head of the table and assigned the seats." With the ladies off, the president announced that "we have come together to do some business," and from a slip of paper he indicated several subjects he wished to discuss. The guests included Dr. Lyman Abbott, editor of *Outlook*, future attorney general William H. Moody, Attorney General Philander C. Knox, Bureau of Corporations Chief James A. Garfield, and businessman-politician Oscar Straus. The mixture of public and private persons was characteristic of the Roosevelt presidency. The subjects were not easy ones: southern response to Roosevelt's Negro policy and the election of 1904. Abbott and Straus, the overnight guests, had additional words with the president before retiring. Breakfast at 8:15 A.M. with four of the children at home—Archie, Kermit, Ethel, and Ted, Jr.—became a continuation of dinner topics, with the president serving coffee. A short walk after breakfast concluded at 9:30 A.M., and the president was ready for his office duties.[17]

In many ways the informal meals were extensions of the Roosevelt cabinet meetings. Tuesday and Friday were cabinet days beginning at 11:00 A.M. Seating arrangement (by chronological order of the crea-

16. Oscar Straus, Notebooks and Diaries, Box 22, in Oscar Straus Papers, LC.
17. Box 4, in Straus Papers.

61

tion of the cabinet position) was the only formal part of the Roosevelt cabinet. Meetings were informal, beginning with general conversation. Except for occasions in which a particular issue was uppermost, the president asked each member for matters of interest. On general matters the entire cabinet discussed the question.[18] Roosevelt consulted an enormous number of people on every conceivable issue at every opportunity—during official office hours, in cabinet meetings, and at meals, which were mixtures of social and business matters.

Sometimes visiting celebrities with unfamiliar intellectual specialties would fascinate the president, who loved to hear discourse on subjects he did not know, one way in which he assembled the enormous fund of trivia (or scholarship) he delighted in displaying. Roosevelt "would talk first as if a decimal and then as if a tunnel was the only thing in the world he had ever loved: he would refer to the Thames and Severn tunnels . . . to the monetary system in China, or the currency experiments of Frederick the II of Hohenstaufen."[19] Some of the regulars would bait an overly serious celebrity and be laughingly brought to task afterwards by the amused president.

Although "sometimes an unfamiliar would prove a delightful surprise," it was when none but familiars assembled "that Roosevelt let himself go, that the whole company let itself go, that it became sheer luxury to listen to those distinguished and brilliant men turning their minds loose to play." The topics varied from government shoptalk to Henry Irving's acting, the Wright brothers' airplane, the president's luck with jujitsu, or the writings of Walter Scott or Mark Twain. Nor were the evenings simply stag affairs. The women, though they seldom led a conversation, were as "civilized" and as "cultivated" as their men. Mrs. Oliver Wendell Holmes, Mrs. John La Farge, Nannie Lodge, and Emily Tuckerman added to the exchange of wit and repartee.[20]

Not every dinner was as spectacular as the gathering of January 12, 1905, with Henry James, the novelist whose expatriation had riled the president, Henry Adams, who loved to bait Roosevelt, and artist-friends John La Farge and Augustus Saint-Gaudens. James liked Roosevelt as

18. Oscar Straus, Diary entry, Box 22, in Straus Papers.
19. Wister, *Roosevelt*, 125–27.
20. *Ibid.*, 128.

little as the president admired him, though in 1914 they made an ideological if not personal peace when both became leading champions of immediate American intervention in World War I. James disapproved of Roosevelt's attempt to make a court; Edith thought Henry James charming; and Theodore was at his best in warding off the nastiest barbs from Henry Adams.[21]

Roosevelt took his salon into the outdoors as well. He rode frequently with Elihu Root, General Leonard Wood, Gifford Pinchot, or James Garfield, his favorite riding companions. An aide to Wood and one of the original Rough Riders describes the route:

> They were not the usual park rides, but on wood roads through Rock Creek Park and over the fields and rail fences nearby. He made the vogue for the riding habits of official Washington, and instigated the system of chaining bridge paths throughout the parks of Washington.
>
> On one of these rides, when I was mounted on a hired crock, much to my disgust he bolted and dashed by the President and Mr. Root. Instead of annoying the leader, he let out his own horse with a wild Indian yell, and everybody let go to a full run and joined in a wild helter-skelter horse-race. There was never any thought on his part of formality or place when out for sport.[22]

Roosevelt fenced, boxed, wrestled, played tennis, while frequently complaining in letters of remaining out of shape because of his White House duties. Hiking through Rock Creek Park was a favorite Roosevelt exercise, but none more celebrated than the jaunt with the French Ambassador Jules Jusserand, a member of the Tennis Cabinet. Frank McCoy's description of the afternoon is one of the best:

> One spring afternoon the Colonel [TR] was leading a party of five or six down the riverside from the chain bridge to Georgetown. It was a favorite walk of his, not only on account of the beauty of the river gorge and rush of the waters, but there was an old quarry just below the chain bridge, up the wall of which he loved to clamber from the rocky riverside of a gentle woodland path skirting the cliff. It gave a little touch of mountain climbing, which had early been one of his favorite sports. I think he was one of the early American members of the Alpine Club of London.

21. Sylvia Jukes Morris, *Edith Kermit Roosevelt: Portrait of a First Lady* (New York, 1980), 288; Leon Edel, *Henry James, the Master, 1901–1916* (Philadelphia, 1972), 266.

22. Brigadier General Frank McCoy, May 19, 1919, untitled transcript, in Roosevelt House Papers, Theodore Roosevelt Collection, Harvard College Library.

After reaching the top he swung down the path, which soon dropped into a ravine full of flowers and a babbling brook, and followed it down to the river again.

Just below there was much smooth reach of water, and Jim Garfield casually remarked that he wished it were a little warmer and we could have a swim. The Colonel remarked "I am warm enough for a swim, and we will have it." So everybody stripped, and gulped as they dived into the cold waters of the Potomac in April. I said all stripped, but on second thought the French Ambassador looked somewhat ludicrous still wearing his kid gloves. No doubt everybody noticed it, but of course nothing was said until, returning from a swim across the river the Colonel could hold in no longer. As he stood up near the shore ready to come out he remarked "Pardon my curiosity, Mr. Ambassador, but why do you wear your gloves?" The Ambassador came back without a moment's hesitation and said "But we are near Washington and might meet some ladies," upon which we all laughed with the joy that comes from a spring afternoon and the joke on the Colonel. Nobody enjoyed it more than the Colonel. He could get no further or any better explanation for the kid gloves.[23]

Roosevelt's style dominated the nation's press even when he traveled from the White House. In Oyster Bay or on hunting trips in Mississippi or Colorado, and after the presidency on the trip to Africa and Europe in 1909 and 1910, the Roosevelt personality remained colorful and striking enough to ensure that the papers would always be filled with humorous and charming anecdotes of one of history's most electric personalities. But the colorful and anecdotal incidents may have blurred the real significance of the Roosevelt years. The charm, the humor, and all of the engaging antics of the man and his family set precedents for the charismatic presidents who followed and are still tangible reminders of the Roosevelt style. But the significance is not in the colorfulness of the man or his exuberant personality, but in the nature of the style Roosevelt brought to the presidency and to the nation.

The nation was in the process of a transformation from a rural and agricultural to an urban, industrial, and financial society. No longer a frontier civilization secure in the isolation of a huge undeveloped continent, the United States, without conscious planning, had passed from one historical phase to another. Such a change is never easy; the bitter

23. *Ibid.*

struggles of the 1920s between the city and the country testify to the difficulty of coming to grips with the realities of modern city life and the new American urbanity. Equally dramatic was America's change from cultural and diplomatic outsider to mature world leader.

Theodore Roosevelt was the first urban president, the first aristocrat, and the first cosmopolitan since the founding fathers. He brought style to the White House after years of plainness and provinciality. Part of the excitement that Roosevelt produced was that of his own unique ebullient personality, but the other part of the change was the bringing of civilization itself to the American government. For the first time, America had a leader who read and revered books, greatly admired art, liked and respected artists, and appreciated the uniqueness of his own country's culture without remaining ignorant or fearing the heritage of the oldest of Western or Eastern culture. With the Roosevelt salon, the country moved from a provincial and essentially ignorant nineteenth-century self-image to a cosmopolitan and knowledgeable twentieth-century sense of itself.

Theodore Roosevelt has come to personify the change in America from nineteenth to twentieth century. He changed the presidency, its power, its scope, and its possibilities. Perhaps the least tangible of the changes lies in the style Roosevelt brought to the presidency. But in the early twentieth century, cultural changes in Europe and America preceded the political, diplomatic, and economic upheavals that coincided with the trauma of the Great War that began in 1914. Roosevelt's style and the White House salon played a substantial role in accommodating America to the change that engulfed the entire world in the early twentieth century.[24]

24. Jan Romein, *Watershed of Two Eras: Europe in 1900* (Middletown, Conn., 1978); Edward Tannenbaum, *1900: The Generation Before the Great War* (New York, 1976).

3 / Cultural Expansionism
Theodore Roosevelt and Charles Freer's
New National Art Museum

Even the old Horatio Alger myth, which took the legendary American hero from rags to riches but no further, changed in the new America. Novelist Henry James refined the myth by sending his wealthy American heroes to Europe searching for a taste of history or culture. At the end of the nineteenth century, real-life American millionaires began to resemble and even surpass Henry James's fictional characters. Charles Lang Freer, a successful Detroit millionaire, became the prototypical Jamesian hero and refined the Horatio Alger myth almost beyond recognition. Freer made his millions building railroad cars in Detroit. He then amassed one of the world's great collections of Oriental art. Charles Freer, a self-made millionaire and self-taught art collector, became in 1906 the donor of America's first national art museum.

Freer's impulse to donate his art to the public was not an unusual one, nor was his initial urge to collect art. For the self-made man in the late nineteenth century, collecting art had become as important as amassing a fortune had been in past decades. The same acquisitive process dominated both pursuits, and it became more an obsession than a vocation or hobby for most of the collectors. Freer was different. From the beginning his tastes were more specific, his interest more intense, and his final national vision almost completely unique.

Other millionaires created museums or donated their collections. James E. Scripps, in 1888, gave the Detroit Museum of Art his Renaissance collection. In Chicago Mrs. Potter Palmer and Martin Ryerson brought Europe's treasures to the burgeoning Art Institute of Chicago. In Boston Isabella Gardner opened her own small museum, as did

Henry Clay Frick in New York. But until Charles Freer no one had thought of donating art or a museum to the national government. Indeed, the struggle of Freer to make his vision a reality is one of the best demonstrations of the enormous changes taking place within America. When Theodore Roosevelt became president in 1901, Freer was still a provincial collector working from his home in Detroit. By 1905, the beginning of Roosevelt's second term, Freer's vision and his collection had assumed a national focus, and the idea of a national museum of foreign art located in the nation's capital became both a political and an aesthetic issue. The culmination of the battle to establish the Freer Gallery of Art in Washington, D.C., was a triumph for nationalism over provincialism in the new America. Eventually the Freer Gallery, founded in 1906, paved the way for a national museum of monumental proportions in the nation's capital. Freer's triumph also assured that the Smithsonian Institution, the caretaker of America's material culture, would assume responsibility for America's first national art collections.

Charles Freer could not have picked a better time to make his own collection a national rather than a local gift. Theodore Roosevelt, after assuming the presidency in 1901, had begun an ambitious domestic political program that eventually gave the federal government responsibility for the economy, displacing the state and municipal governments that had dominated regulations before. In diplomacy Roosevelt was in the vanguard of the younger group of American expansionists who saw America more as a world power in her own right, rather than a provincial nation protected by geography from the ambitions of other world powers. In culture the new president was already a distinguished world citizen. He had known European art and literature well enough to be able to criticize artists and writers since youth. For Theodore Roosevelt, French painting, Oriental culture, and even rare and archaic forms of literature or art were familiar matters. What most Americans might consider foreign art was for Theodore Roosevelt, as for Charles Freer, the commonplace of everyday living. Freer's vision of giving his unusual art to all the American people was consistent with Theodore Roosevelt's vision of a world community in which America played a central role.

Neither Charles Freer nor Theodore Roosevelt worked in a cultural vacuum. Art and culture had come to America with a vengeance. Mu-

67

seums were flourishing in virtually every urban area; the City Beautiful Movement did not halt the spread of American urban ghettos, but it did increase the number of parks and attractive urban buildings, as well as stimulate an awareness of the aesthetics of architecture. American expatriate artists were becoming more and more influential. Henry James and James Whistler were famous already; Mary Cassatt and Maurice Prendergast were waiting in the wings.

By 1906 Gertrude and Leo Stein from San Francisco were among the most influential collectors of new European art and were directly influencing even the most radical new European painters. The European influence was strong in America, especially prominent in the new museum collections and in the popularity of beaux-arts architecture inspired by the Chicago world's fair in 1893. But increasingly America influenced Europe. American collectors were the most active art buyers in the world, buying both European and American art; increasingly, American artists were creating work that stood on its own merit. The changes in the cultural world, produced by the new America, were at least as striking as those caused in the diplomatic world by the Spanish-American War.

One major result of America's war with Spain in 1898 was the acquisition of the Philippines and a new awareness of the place of Asia in world diplomacy, especially in matters affecting America. American art collectors were already making their own way into the older cultures and art of China, Korea, and Japan. Charles Freer's passion for Oriental art began with his initial interest in the paintings of James Whistler, who, like the French impressionists, had become fascinated with Oriental art and symbolism. Whistler introduced Freer to Japanese art, and the artist's and the collector's mutual interest in old Oriental symbolism cemented their friendship and allowed the intimacy to survive both Whistler's legendary irascibility and Freer's aloof coolness.

Charles Freer was born into genteel middle-class poverty in Kingston, New York, in 1856. His first series of jobs were matters of chance. He began as an accountant for a cement manufacturer with offices in the same building as the local railroad. The introduction to the railroad industry opened the way for Freer's successful career. He formed a partnership with Frank G. Hecker, and together they went to Logansport,

Indiana, to run the small Eel River Railroad. Eventually the partners made their way to Detroit and the safe corporate harbor afforded by James McMillan's American Car and Foundry Company. Many businessmen who could afford to collected art in the early 1880s. Most of the collectors were motivated by fashionability or social prestige. A decent art collection marked a man as more a gentleman than a robber baron and made it possible for a newly transformed industrialist to gain access to the exclusive social circles of the older cities.

Charles Freer was unique from the start. For Freer, art was never a means to something else, but an end in itself. He studied it, became more enamored of the world of art than of transportation, and for a while managed to balance the two vocations acceptably. James Whistler upset the precarious balance. Freer first encountered Whistler's art in 1886, made his first purchase in 1887, and personally met the artist on a trip to London in 1890. Already a passionate collector and traveler, Freer went one step further on his European trip in 1894 and became a unique patron of art. Because of their wealth, American collectors were already effectively acting as patrons, though their primary interest was to collect paintings, not to support artists. From his earliest time as a collector, Freer tended toward a close relationship with artists, which suggested a collaboration resembling the older practice of patronage. Freer admired the Medicis' encouragement of Renaissance artists and gave credit to the patrons for helping to make possible the great art the Renaissance produced.

Freer began to limit his collections and allegiances. He did not support his favored artists with grants or subsidies; instead he visited with them, wrote letters of encouragement, and befriended them. Increasingly he purchased works from the artists themselves rather than the dealer middleman. Whenever he could, Freer would promote museum exhibitions of artists he liked, advise artists of opportunities, and share his knowledge with other collectors. Charles Lang Freer was already preparing for his role as a democratic American counterpart of the Italian Medicis.

By 1899 Charles Freer had retired from the railroad business to devote all his time to art, now his overwhelming passion. He was well read, universally admired, well traveled, and already an expert on Whistler as well as Oriental art. Freer's expertise was reflected in the collections overflowing his Detroit house, which had been specifically designed to show off the connoisseur's collections. By 1902 Freer had further defined his taste and his philosophy. "I am confining my collection of American painters to the work of five men—Whistler, Tryon, Dewing, Thayer, and Church which is a very narrow group, I know, but it sympathizes with my highest ideals of American art." Freer had become a professional. He knew there were better painters than the ones he liked, but he preferred to specialize. "I don't consider him [Church] as great an artist as either George Inness, A. H. Wyant, or Winslow Homer, and neither of these three men is included in my group."[1]

Freer had gone beyond collecting and being an art connoisseur. He played the informal patron to artists he particularly liked, a role that eventually evolved into his unique idea of being patron to the nation and giving the United States its first national art museum. Thomas Dewing, whom Freer continually advised to raise his prices and to whom he frequently lent money, was the first artist he befriended, Whistler the most important. Freer's concern over Whistler's failure to achieve proper recognition in his native America led to Freer's initial impulse to create an American national art museum. Freer confidently assured an anxious collector concerned about one of Whistler's paintings "that eventually it will go to the American National Museum," well before there were any serious plans for creating such a museum.[2]

The group of professional art collectors to graduate from the fierce world of American industrial competition remembered well the competitive days of railroad finance and merger. Their new world easily impinged upon the old; the competition that had been so keen in the railroad business remained as vigorous in art. Freer knew that "thoroughly fine paintings by first class men are advancing rapidly in price, and the number of buyers are rapidly increasing. When Morgan, Wagner, Whitney, Yerkes, Clark and other giants get their fighting blood up, and it

1. Charles Freer to William K. Bixby, February 7, 1902, in Freer Papers, Freer Gallery of Art.
2. Charles Freer to William Burrel, August 20, 1902, in Freer Papers.

seems to be nearing the boiling point, we little fellows will have to go to bed and stay there." Freer had no desire to compete with the big boys. He disdained the parochial world of the local art museum and the social side of art collecting.[3]

By 1900 Charles Freer had already chosen a different path. His friendship and respect for Whistler increased even as the ill-tempered artist began his final physical decline. At the time Whistler died in 1903, Charles Freer remained disturbed by Whistler's lack of recognition. Freer never doubted the democratic possibilities of art education. He was keenly aware that everything he knew about art he had learned himself. He became more acutely aware of the enormous cultural ignorance of fellow collectors, the general populace, and Americans who had never had the chance to develop their cultural tastes or inclinations. His own collection had begun to reflect a sensibility akin to that of creative artists. Freer began to see the collector-patron in a close relationship with the artist himself and as an integral part of the aesthetic process.[4]

Charles Freer and Theodore Roosevelt were two of the outstanding nationalists and internationalists of their time. It is fitting that the two men worked so closely together in the political struggle to establish a national American art museum. Roosevelt and Freer met and spoke together briefly in 1902 at a party given in Detroit by Senator Russell A. Alger. Meeting Theodore Roosevelt in Detroit may have rekindled Freer's plan for a national art collection. Freer probably mentioned the idea that evening, perhaps to Roosevelt, who would have thought it perfectly natural. Charles Moore, Senator James McMillan's aide, who was equally knowledgeable about art and politics, also talked to Freer and began the wheels turning. Moore sent Freer a detailed letter about the Smithsonian Institution, material about its collections, and an analysis of its leaders. With its founding in 1847, the Smithsonian had been appointed the nation's official museum. Although there were some

3. See Helen Nebeker Tomlinson, "Charles Lang Freer; Pioneer Collector of American Art" (2 vols.; Ph.D. dissertation, Case-Western Reserve University, 1979), I, 114–46; Freer to William Bixby, February 7, 1902, in Freer Papers.

4. For Freer's unique modern form of patronage, see Nicholas Clark, "Charles Lang Freer: An American Aesthete in the Gilded Era," *American Art Journal*, XI (October, 1979), 58–60.

minor collections of art in the Smithsonian vaults, the museum's main function had been to house technical artifacts and instruments of material culture.[5]

The Smithsonian liked *things* and reflected the predominant nineteenth-century American ignorance of and disinclination toward serious art. For the Smithsonian, art was strange, mostly foreign, and costly to acquire and to maintain. Charles Moore knew that it was the only existent national collection; he also knew first hand of congressional reluctance and ignorance in cultural matters. The Smithsonian was far from ideal, but it was the obvious starting point. Freer carefully considered Moore's suggestion of the Smithsonian as a possible home for his art, and although Freer moved cautiously, he agreed to meet with Moore and the Smithsonian directors to discuss the gift.[6]

Charles Moore was excited by Freer's idea of contributing his entire collection to the government. He knew, however, that the political obstacles were monumental. But Charles Freer was not an impatient man. He was content in his new life and cautious in his expectations. He had long since ceased to haggle with art dealers or artists over prices. He resisted bargaining as he resisted the blandishments of dealers or friends urging a particular work of art upon him. Even if it meant giving up the acquisition of a cherished painting, Freer would not bargain or compromise. His firmness was frequently effective in winning a battle in which compromise would not have worked.

In spite of a strong sense of inner confidence, Freer paused before committing himself to what he knew would be a difficult struggle. After Whistler's death in 1903 Freer was still not sure. "I have not reached a final conclusion," he told Moore on his return from Whistler's funeral. But Freer was moving toward the decision. Although he had reservations, he told Moore, "Before I decide their permanent home, I had

5. "Roosevelt Chronology," in MRL, IV, 1353; Tomlinson, "Freer," 423–24. For the most detailed analysis of the Smithsonian Institution's organization, as well as a critical evaluation of its function as a national scientific museum, see the 1903 Smithsonian Institution report by the Committee on Organization of Government Scientific Work, File 2.1.2.1.33, Box 602, in Gifford Pinchot Papers, LC; Charles Freer to Samuel P. Langley, December 3, 1902, Freer to Charles Moore, December 3, 1902, both in Freer Papers.
6. Charles Freer to Charles Moore, August 19, 1903, in Freer Papers.

better add as much as possible to the quality and importance [of] this collection." In the same letter he added, "I am constantly adding important articles to my collection and I hope to make the group eventually worthy of the custody of the Smithsonian Institution."[7]

Freer's house had become overcrowded, looking more like a gallery than a home, and he became increasingly concerned that his art was not sufficiently protected or suitably displayed. Two events helped Freer make his decision. When Whistler's death threatened a further distribution of the artist's work to other museum and private collections, Freer was tempted by the possibility of keeping as many of the paintings in one place as possible. Freer could not help noticing the publicity accompanying the opening of Isabella Stewart Gardner's Boston Museum House on New Year's Day, 1903. He knew the time was near for donating his own collection; the pressures from Detroit and other art centers would increase with the opening of each new museum.[8]

Charles Moore was playing his accustomed role as diplomatic intermediary. For some reason Moore and Freer regarded the tentative Smithsonian decision as a matter of top secrecy, perhaps to avoid too early an emotional commitment, or to make the Smithsonian feel less pressure. Charles Moore wrote in positive terms to the Smithsonian on Freer's behalf August 1, 1903, even before Freer had made a final decision. He enclosed Freer's own letter from Madrid and told Dr. Cyrus Adler, the assistant director, that "Mr. Freer has the finest examples of Whistler's work." Moore knew that the death of an artist brought extra publicity and a respectability often missing in the artist's lifetime. A new interest in Whistler's work had begun throughout the world; Charles Moore hoped to pique the Smithsonian's interest. Moore cautioned Adler that "the matter [of a Smithsonian donation] has not been dropped but is still looking after. Of course, this is confidential between Mr. Langley [the Smithsonian director] and you and me." In his best conspiratorial manner, Freer, as soon as he returned from Europe, told Moore to come and visit to discuss "as fully as possible the matter we have under consideration." When Freer confided "some progess is being made," he

7. Charles Moore to Dr. Cyrus Adler, August 1, 1903, in RU 45, Box 108, SIA.
8. Charles Freer to Wilson Eyre, December 4, 1902, in Freer Papers.

had already decided to donate his collection to the Smithsonian. Obviously the only progress that had occurred was wholly in Freer's mind, since the negotiations with the Smithsonian had not really begun.[9]

Freer's main preoccupation was reserved for Whistler. The Copley Association of Boston was holding a Whistler retrospective in March, 1904, and Freer told the exhibitors that the best way to get French permission for the loan of Whistler's *Mother* was through John Hay, the secretary of state. Freer blithely advised the planners to use Charles Moore as an entrée to Hay. Moore took that opportunity to arrange the first formal meeting between Freer and the Smithsonian's director and secretary Samuel P. Langley.[10]

Throughout the negotiations between Charles Freer and the Smithsonian Institution, Samuel P. Langley, the Smithsonian director, appears to be the benchmark American philistine, ignorant of art, unwilling to take chances, and a curious obstacle to a natural opportunity for the Smithsonian to enlarge its cultural influence. But Langley was not a boor or a villain. He was not even a typical bureaucrat. He had not only accepted gifts of art before, he had fought bitter battles with the rival Corcoran Gallery of Art for the privilege. One gift to the government by the estate of artist Joseph Henry remained in solitary exile from 1874 until 1896, when Sam Langley decided it rightfully belonged in the Smithsonian. The Smithsonian's secretary was indeed a character and an adventurer. He had participated in a bizarre Tahitian fire-walk ceremony in 1901, but his most striking adventure occurred before the bitter battle with Freer began. On October 7, 1903, Sam Langley took off in his own flying machine to prove that flight was possible. Langley's trip was wholly unsuccessful. His plane lost a wing on takeoff from his Potomac River houseboat and never reached land, crashing nearby. Another attempt, just nine days before the Wright brothers' successful flight at Kitty Hawk in December, was equally unsuccessful. With a little luck and a better launching strategy, Langley's plane might well have flown. S. P. Langley, in spite of the failures, is still remembered as a

9. Charles Moore to Dr. Cyrus Adler, August 1, 1903, in Freer Papers.
10. Charles Freer to Richard Rice, December 1, 1903; Freer to Hooker Abbott, December 1, 1903, both in Freer Papers.

pioneer in aviation history and not as the bureaucrat who resisted the formation of a national museum of art.[11]

Moore, Freer, and Langley met together for the first time in March, 1904, to discuss the donation. Langley was clearly reluctant to encourage either Moore or Freer. Moore was able to demonstrate his political prowess by following up the meeting with a reception that evening for Freer at Senator Alger's Washington residence. Freer appeared eccentric to those who did not know him. He exuded a clear confidence, a sense of quiet mission, and a disinclination for negotiating. He had made it clear that his offer was unique and not negotiable, especially rebuffing attempts to dilute the personal nature of the collection. Langley liked art but had never before faced a bequest in which control remained with the donor and not the museum.[12]

He felt that Freer was asking too much. The idea of the collector as educator, or even as a kind of artist, was entirely new at the time. Indeed, it is not familiar now, though museums are willing to segregate substantial gifts of individual donors, rather than integrating the paintings into other museum holdings. In 1904 collectors were not recognized as patrons of art, as modern counterparts of the old Medicis, but were regarded instead as crude industrialists who had suddenly discovered culture. But Freer remained patient even in the face of discouragement. He never wavered in his conviction that men like Langley would eventually be convinced.

Nine months elapsed before Samuel Langley was willing to entertain a formal written offer from Charles Freer outlining the proposed gift to the government and Freer's nonnegotiable terms for its acceptance. Freer's formal offer of January 3, 1905, included 100 framed paintings by Whistler, 60 drawings, 150 lithographs, 575 etchings, the Peacock Room decorations, 60 framed paintings of Tyron, Dewing, and Thayer, 510 Japanese Kahemono screens and panels, and 950 pieces of Oriental pottery. "My great desire has been to unite modern work with masterpieces of certain periods of high civilization harmonious in spiritual and

11. Geoffrey Hellman, *The Smithsonian: Octopus on the Mall* (Philadelphia, 1967), 132–58, 160.
12. Charles Moore to Samuel P. Langley, February 19, 1904, in RU 45, Box 108, SIA.

physical suggestion, having the power to broaden aesthetic culture and the grace to elevate the human mind." Freer noted that his "censorship, aided by the best expert advice" was necessary to maintain "harmonious standard quality." [13]

Freer's terms called for the construction of a building to house the collection. The $500,000 expenditure was to be paid by Freer's estate, with future maintenance to be paid by the United States government; no additions or changes were to be permitted even after Freer's death. Freer made it clear that the final legal details remained to be worked out. He also suggested the appraisal by a committee of experts at Detroit. "It will be a source of satisfaction to me to exhibit the collections to such a committee." [14]

From the start Freer's insistence on the integrity of the collection was the main sticking point. Had the Smithsonian been free to make the collection a temporary exhibit, or to store it in an out-of-the-way place with an occasional painting drawn from storage for display, Langley might have been willing to talk about details. But bureaucrats were not accustomed to following someone else's rules. From the beginning, it seemed that Freer's gift and his accompanying conditions might overwhelm the museum's other functions and its personality. Freer would not even permit "other" art to be exhibited with his own collection. Senator John B. Henderson, a member of the Smithsonian board of regents, had seen other wars in his long life. Henderson, at various times in his political career an active Democrat and a staunch Republican, served as the Union party senator from Missouri in the Civil War Congress. Henderson was outraged by Freer's exclusivity. "I presume that his collections will not fill a house of such proportions as can be built with half a million dollars; and if we can neither add to nor deduct from the collection, then the building with all its treasures simply becomes a monumental mausoleum to preserve the memory of one of the world's

13. "Memorandum in Regard to the Freer Proposition," no date, Freer Folder, Box 20, in Charles Moore Papers, LC; Charles Moore to Samuel P. Langley, January 29, 1904, February 19, 1904, Langley to Freer, December 16, 1904, all in RU45, Box 108, SIA; Tomlinson, "Freer," 426.

14. Langley's and the Executive Committee's response to Freer's verbal offer is included in Samuel P. Langley to Freer, December 16, 1904; Freer to Langley, December 27, 1904, both in RU45, Box 108, SIA.

rich men, of whom we have far too many already." Senator Henderson was wrong. Freer could fill any size building, or even an entire city, as he added to his already large collection. Freer's response was classic: "I regard my collection as constituting a harmonious whole, and of benefit as a unit to students [and] the public not subject to the whims of a transient museum director." To follow the suggested modification of relinquishing artistic control is "so serious as to defeat the main purpose that induces me to make my offer to the Institution." [15]

In 1919 Freer relented and just before his death waived the exclusivity condition. In 1905 he exhibited no flexibility at all. Freer felt that he had carefully thought out the best disposition of his collection and he remained adamant. His characteristic unwillingness to bargain, his extreme patience, and the apparent reasonableness of his position made Freer confident of eventual victory. Freer's confidence, however, was based on a false assumption. He knew the worth of his collection. He assumed that the regents of the Smithsonian or any protoprofessional body would immediately perceive the obvious value of his art. He had not counted on the abysmal cultural ignorance of bureaucratic Washington. The world that Charles Freer lived in was far different from that of his countrymen. Art was not a universal language, even in America's elite classes, as Freer was soon to painfully discover.

Bureaucrats, even in 1905, had perfected the technique of the stall. They delayed as long as possible, but pressed by Freer, the Smithsonian finally named its committee to visit the collection in Detroit. Freer loved to display his art. Charles Moore, in his role as officer of Detroit's Union Trust Company, wrote to Samuel Langley praising Freer's collection, welcoming the Smithsonian committee to Detroit, and at the same time warning Langley that the presentation Freer always insisted upon was elaborate. [16]

The committee—inventor Dr. Alexander Graham Bell; Bell's daughter, Marian; Senator John B. Henderson; Dr. James B. Angell, the president of the University of Michigan; and Smithsonian secretary Langley—were not nonentities, but they were hardly specialists in Ori-

15. John B. Henderson to Samuel P. Langley, January 6, 1905, Freer to Samuel P. Langley, January 18, 1905, both in RU45, Box 108, SIA.
16. Charles Moore to Samuel P. Langley, January 29, 1905, in RU45, Box 108, SIA.

ental art nor even moderately discerning connoisseurs. They certainly did not relish the prospect of seeing Freer's two thousand objects one at a time. Freer, once having made up his mind, remained convinced of the value of his proposal. To sculptor Augustus Saint-Gaudens early in February, 1905, just before the expected visit, Freer wrote: "I feel a possibility of accomplishing . . . something worthwhile. On the other hand, if I were to scatter my means while I might do some good, I do not feel that it could possibly equal what I hope to do in a single direction." [17]

Two members of the committee became ill and the trip had to be postponed. The committee would have preferred an indefinite postponement. But Freer was not that easily discouraged. He asked Langley to reschedule the viewing before April, since "I have agreed to contribute very largely from my collection of paintings by Mr. Whistler for the Memorial Exhibition to be given in Paris under the auspices of the French government." [18]

The regents were fighting a losing battle in hoping that Freer would become discouraged or that the trip to Detroit could be indefinitely postponed. Newspapers had picked up the Freer story and were in complete support, and Charles Moore kept the Washington press well supplied with the latest news. Freer remained optimistic because of the impressive newspaper support, though he was aware that the Smithsonian was still reluctant. In writing to his old business partner Frank Hecker on February 25, Freer felt "there is little probability of the gift being refused. The leading newspapers of the country have treated the matter with unexpected liberality and breadth of vision and while of course the committee are entirely incompetent to judge the value of the collections, the Board of Regents itself will be favorably influenced by the attitude of the leading papers of the country." [19]

Freer overestimated the power of the press to overcome cultural ignorance or bureaucratic timidity. The committee's visit to the Freer house

17. Charles Freer to Augustus Saint-Gaudens, February 13, 1905, in Freer Papers.
18. Charles Freer to Samuel P. Langley, February 16, 1905, Freer Papers; for the committee's correspondence with Langley see RU 45, Box 108, in SIA.
19. Charles Freer to Frank Hecker, February 25, 1905, in Freer Papers; on the Smithsonian's increasing sensitivity to press accounts supporting Freer, see "Memo for the Secretary, April 17, 1905," in RU 45, Box 108, SIA.

in Detroit was an unmitigated disaster and a bizarre comedy of errors. Freer delighted in bringing out his objects one at a time in a bravura performance that was wasted on the ignoramuses who had come to pass judgment. The committee knew nothing about art and fell back on name calling. They tried to discredit the collection by calling it "impressionist art," as if that stigma would automatically make the collection worthless. Senator Henderson summed up the committee's feeling: "The things were all very well of their kind—but damn their kind." [20] The regents read the papers and understood that pressure was on Freer's side, but they did not know enough to make any meaningful comment on Freer's art. The impressionist label was probably designed to suggest that the art was either foreign, insubstantial, or ephemeral. If any of the committee had understood the meaning of the word they would have completely avoided using it. For anyone who doubts the cultural ignorance of art in early twentieth-century America, the committee's response to Freer's impressive collection should provide ample evidence.

The committee was not content simply to stall. Using Freer's insistence that the collection's unity not be disturbed by additional purchases, Henderson embarked upon a Senate campaign to dissuade his former colleagues from continuing their support.

> I am gradually becoming confirmed in the opinion, that Mr. Freer is either a humbug or a shrewd and unconscionable speculator. I now seriously surmise that he is attempting a new role of advertisement of himself and his collection, at the expense of the Committee or of the Smithsonian, by using some of our picture dealers and the public press to extol the great value of a pretended donation, which he has never made, and which, in my judgement he never intends to make.
>
> I will state the facts and then he may go on with his advertisements without further notice. Leniency is generally not the proper treatment for the mania of commercialism.

The attack was partly successful. Senators Lodge and Hale, convinced that Freer was unreasonable and self-serving, withdrew their previous endorsements. Secretary Langley had tried to calm Senator Henderson's attacks by asking that negotiations remain open and recriminations be kept at a minimum. Henderson was mollified but unrepentant:

20. Aline Saarinen, *The Proud Possessors* (New York, 1958), 136.

"I shall treat [Freer] with that merciful assumption of innocence." Henderson, perhaps the most obnoxious of the opposition, was convinced that Freer's newspaper support was not genuine. The newsmen "either write in ignorance of the facts, or else have an interest in the dissemination of falsehood."[21]

Meanwhile, Freer was confident that acceptance was only a formality. In a letter to Rosalind Birnie-Phillip on "the fourth day of the visit," Freer was confident that only the details and a final report remained unfinished. The day after the committee left, Freer wrote Richard Rice that "the Committee are anxious to accept my offer," and urged Rice to prepare for the vigors of Washington winters as possible curator-designate of the collection. Freer felt that the committee really wanted the collection but was troubled by the details. On March 8, 1905, writing to artist Charles Morse, Freer was much less confident: "There are a great many more things to think about than I knew of at the time the offer was made." Freer's best estimate became "several months."[22]

Freer remained patient: "I shall rest quietly on my oars and let the Regents do whatever hard work may be required in the future." But patience was not the same as confidence. Freer clearly saw the problem: "Think of trying to convince the politicians of America that the fine arts have any virtue." The Freer and Charles Moore strategy was based on the assumption that convincing a small committee was easier than convincing an entire Congress. In March, 1905, the strategy was failing.[23]

In fact the regents were ambivalent. Richard Rathbun, the Smithsonian director who succeeded the ill Langley, became involved with the negotiations only after the committee's visit to Detroit. His first action was to calculate the cost of maintaining the Freer collection. Since the annual maintenance figure of $18,960 was hardly a monumental sum, Rathbun remained willing to negotiate rather than decline the gift. But the parties were so far apart, especially on the question of control, that

21. John B. Henderson to Samuel P. Langley, April 20, 1905, and for Lodge's strong original endorsement, see Henry Cabot Lodge to Samuel P. Langley, March 23, 1905, both in RU 45, Box 108, SIA.

22. Charles Freer to Frank Hooker, February 27, 1905, Freer to Richard Rice, March 1, 1905, Freer to Rosalind Birnie-Phillip, February 28, 1905, Freer to Charles Morse, March 8, 1905, all in Freer Papers.

23. Charles Freer to Rosalind Birnie-Phillip, March 10, 1905, in Freer Papers.

negotiations appeared unpromising. Freer was sure that "it is unlikely that anything more will happen until next fall."[24]

By March, 1905, the dispute had reached the White House. Theodore Roosevelt, perhaps the first man to hear of Freer's unique vision at Senator Alger's Detroit reception in 1902, never hesitated. He knew the difference between Oriental art, Whistler, and impressionism. Roosevelt unequivocally instructed Langley on March 21, "Do not on any account refuse the offer." Roosevelt thought the troublesome point was maintenance (at the time it was the operating excuse). He assured Langley: "I have no question that Congress will appropriate the trivial sum needed to take care of them. They are very valuable." Langley immediately switched gears and replied to the president that Freer's conditions, rather than the cost of maintenance, were the major difficulties. At this point Roosevelt's intervention may have prevented an outright refusal by the Smithsonian, but he could not budge the bureaucracy enough to insure acceptance. The matter simply drifted. The Smithsonian was indeed winning the war of attrition.[25]

The situation had become absurd. The Smithsonian's contention that the collection was of questionable value was patently false and caused resentment in the art community, fanned by occasional pieces in the press. The time had come for the unique talents of Charles Moore to move the battle into its decisive phase. On November 1, 1905, Charles Moore wrote a four-page letter directly to President Theodore Roosevelt setting forth in their entirety the issues in the dispute. Moore's letter was not merely that of an outsider or a citizen interested in art. Moore was the great insider, and even in the address to the president, he revealed his genius for knowing what strings to pull and when. He did not write the president of the United States but rather the president in his capacity as "presiding officer of the Smithsonian Institution." Moore's letter is an impassioned defense of Freer, praise of his collection, and a stunning indictment of the Smithsonian's duplicity in dealing with Freer.[26]

24. "Possible Cost of Maintaining the Freer Collection of Art," February 11, 1905, in RU 45, Box 108, SIA; Charles Freer to Charles Morse, March 8, 1905, in Freer Papers.
25. TR to Samuel P. Langley, March 21, 1905, Langley to TR, March 22, 1905, both in RU 45, Box 108, SIA.
26. Charles Moore to TR, October 1, 1905, in RU 45, Box 108, SIA.

Moore defended his own strategy in choosing the Smithsonian as the recipient of Freer's collection. Moore cited the Smithsonian charter as his primary reason "and also from the fact it is not directly in politics." Freer, Moore told the president, had been encouraged by Secretary Langley to make his formal offer. Moore charged that instead of considering the Freer offer in good faith, the committee tried to talk Freer out of it. The suggestion that the Freer collection would serve as the nucleus of a national museum collection Moore dismissed as absurd: "Mr. Freer's collection is a special one. It can have no possible relations to such a general and indeterminate thing as a National Art Gallery; and had he consented to their proposition the result would have been disastrous, for it would have meant an appeal to Congress, and a campaign on behalf of a project which must require years of agitation to accomplish."[27]

Moore in his appeal to Roosevelt assumed that Theodore Roosevelt understood more about the value and significance of the Freer collection than the Smithsonian. Moore knew first hand of Roosevelt's involvement with attempts to make Washington a cosmopolitan center of beauty to best represent America's new national image. Moore cited other cities' desire for the Freer collection, restrictions and all, and praised Freer's continued patience: "He has been caught by the new spirit for Washington and believes that the proper place for the works of an American genius is the Capital." Moore closed his plea to Roosevelt with a request for the president's immediate intercession in the Freer-Smithsonian debate, a debate that Freer, Moore, and the capital art dealers had kept alive. Roosevelt was now convinced that the delay was not an accident and that the Smithsonian was dragging its feet. On November 3, 1905, the president sent Langley a copy of Moore's letter, a presidential request "that everything possible should be done to secure the Freer Collection," and a query on what the Smithsonian could do to help. "Will you advise the President concerning it at your earliest convenience," the presidential communication reasonably asked.[28]

Langley's formal reply to the president was calmer than his original waspish comments that he decided not to send. He promised that the

27. *Ibid.*
28. *Ibid.*; William Loeb to Samuel P. Langley, November 3, 1905, in RU 45, Box 108, SIA.

board meeting of December 5, 1905, would answer all unresolved questions. Charles Moore, well aware of the importance of the December 5 meeting, orchestrated the pressure from the press through his friend, writer Lelia Mechlin. On November 30, the first of three editorials in the Washington *Evening Star* reiterated the worldwide fame of the Freer collection and called it "valuable, unique and inspiring." The *Star* remarked that "it is difficult to imagine upon what ground this magnificent offer should not be accepted."[29]

On December 2 the *Evening Star* dealt with the weak but persistent Smithsonian objection that the gift was so exclusive it required a separate hall. The *Star* thought gifts so good should have separate halls, and that perhaps acceptance of the Freer gift would encourage other equally good collections, which would also require separate buildings. The movement for a national museum in Washington encouraged by Freer's gift was for some inexplicable reason opposed by the Smithsonian. In its closing editorial, printed on December 3 just before the scheduled and decisive Smithsonian board meeting, the *Star* supported the international scope of Freer's collection as just the right balance for the new cosmopolitan image of the nation and its capital. Freer's gift and its acceptance would offer proof of "the American advance in the arts, professions, sciences, and all practical endeavors of life." Theodore Roosevelt, however, was not willing to leave the fate of the Freer gift to the press. On December 4, 1905, the day before the board meeting, he summoned to the White House Smithsonian secretary Cyrus Adler, Senator Henderson, the most outspoken member of the Regents' committee, Supreme Court Justice Oliver Wendell Holmes to advise on any legal questions, and art dealer Victor Fischer to advise on artistic questions. The Smithsonian was requested to bring all of its papers concerning the Freer negotiations.[30]

Victor Fischer was an influential Washington art dealer who dealt

29. Samuel P. Langley to William Loeb, November 21, 1905, a reply to Charles Moore's letter with the notation "not sent," in RU 45, Box 108, SIA; Charles Moore to Mrs. Richardson, January 9 and January 23, 1906, in Moore Papers; "Freer Art Collection," Washington *Evening Star*, November 30, 1905; "The Capital and Art," Washington *Evening Star*, December 2, 1905.

30. "A Good Reason for Acceptance," December 3, 1905, Washington *Evening Star*; William Loeb to Cyrus Adler, December 4, 1905, in RU 45, Box 108, SIA.

with both Charles Moore and Edith Roosevelt. Moore had given Lelia Mechlin the information for her article of May 20, 1905, in the Washington *Evening Star* about the Freer-Smithsonian controversy. On a later occasion Fischer casually gave Edith a copy of the article on one of her visits to the shop. When Edith gave a copy of the article to Roosevelt, it precipitated the decisive presidential intervention. In the White House meeting of the Smithsonian board and the president, Fischer was present in a dual capacity as representative of the art establishment and as the president's unofficial adviser on art.[31]

Senator Henderson, a determined yahoo, was not intimidated by the White House surroundings. He charged loudly that Whistler was indeed an impressionist, convinced that this charge alone was sufficient to taint the artist even in the grave. The president impatiently dismissed Henderson's nonsense. Whistler, said Roosevelt, was not an impressionist nor were any of the other Americans whose works were included in the Freer collection. Art dealer Fischer pedantically backed up the president and insisted that Whistler, if he was anything, was a positivist. When Henderson refused to budge Roosevelt attacked all the references to Greek and Roman art in the Henderson report. The ignorance of the Smithsonian committee on art was impressive, but no more so than their lamentable legal opinions.[32]

Roosevelt dismissed the Smithsonian objections as nit-picking. "Mr. Freer was an honorable man and meant to do what he said he would do." And in lieu of any formal agreement the president of the United States "would take his word." Roosevelt, who had set the stage rather dramatically, looked at his Supreme Court justice for agreement. Holmes thought that Freer's word was good enough. But this assurance did not satisfy Senator Henderson who asked pointedly whether the Freer proposal was a legal document. Holmes said it was not yet but suggested that the addition of one simple sentence would make it a legal contract. Theodore Roosevelt dealt with the Smithsonian's board as he would a foreign nation. As the political and administrative head of the govern-

31. Annotation for the May 20, 1905, newspaper clipping and Notebook, Freer Folder, in Charles Moore Papers.
32. "Confidential Memorandum of a Conference held at the White House, dictated by Dr. Adler," December 6, 1905, in RU 45, Box 108, SIA.

ment, Roosevelt could probably have ordered the regents to accept Freer's gift on terms the president specified. Roosevelt preferred to practice a more subtle and graceful form of diplomacy. As he did with difficult foreign ambassadors, Roosevelt made his point as forcefully as possible, then backed off to allow the other side to accept its inevitable fate as gracefully as possible.[33]

Senator Henderson made it clear that the Smithsonian would continue to be stubborn, and Roosevelt backed off from a direct challenge that might involve Congress. He felt that he and Freer together now had the upper hand and he turned from toughness to charm while making it clear that Freer's position was fully supported by the president. Senator Henderson might still feel independent, but the other directors on the Smithsonian's board felt the pressure intensely.

Roosevelt told Adler that he felt Freer had made a fine offer and that it "had not been generously met." The president asked Freer to dine with him at the White House and stay overnight, an honor Roosevelt knew would be given maximum publicity by the sympathetic press. Even the obdurate Senator Henderson began to get the point: "Mr. President, you who have settled coal strikes and moved kings and emperors about on the chess board will I hope, succeed in changing some of the details of Mr. Freer's proposition." Roosevelt discussed other government possibilities but more as a means of pressure. Theodore Roosevelt was well aware that a congressional fight on aesthetics was unpredictable at best. He continued to believe that a simple compromise, perhaps a transfer of some of the building money to the maintenance budget, would assuage the Smithsonian's fears. The extraordinary December 4 White House meeting did not solve all of the arguments. But by forcefully supporting Freer against the Smithsonian, Roosevelt made it clear that the Smithsonian would now have to bargain in good faith and not continue its bureaucratic obstructionist tactics.[34]

The regents did not give in at once. They asked Freer to make the correspondence public but softened their tone by also noting their "high appreciation of generosity." The regents invited Freer to choose

33. *Ibid.*
34. *Ibid.*

part of his collection for a temporary exhibit to be held in 1905 at one of the Smithsonian's buildings. Roosevelt's invitation to Freer to visit the White House kept up the public pressure on the newly conciliatory regents.[35]

When Freer returned to Detroit after the December 5, 1905, regents meeting, he was fully optimistic. He told one of his influential Washington friends that he was not only going to visit the president but also to negotiate further with the Smithsonian. "A conclusion is near," Freer confided to Charles Moore. Nor would Freer play the game of compromise himself. He refused the regents' request for public disclosure of all correspondence (a red herring) on the grounds that much of it concerned private matters dealing with the Whistler estate. Freer assured the Detroit *Free Press* that he was well treated by the Smithsonian and the "notion is absolutely wrong" that he was disappointed. On December 6, 1905, the Washington *Evening Star*, reading the handwriting on the wall, proclaimed that the Smithsonian had accepted the gift "in all but formal terms." The *Star* approved of Freer's insistence on a separate building, citing Harvard's Fogg Museum and several European museums as examples, and insisted that a separate "Freer collection establishment would advance not retard the national museum movement."[36]

The Smithsonian with the prodding of President Roosevelt had already entered the fight for establishing a national museum. President James Buchanan's niece, Harriet Lane, had left a conditional bequest to the Corcoran Gallery in 1874 to be moved to a national museum when and if one was established. The Smithsonian had insisted that it was the national museum and legally entitled to the paintings, a matter that President Roosevelt told Attorney General Moody to support fully. After the Freer matter was settled, the Lane litigation came to trial and in 1906 the Washington District Court legally ruled that the Smithsonian was America's national museum.[37]

35. "Abstract from minutes of Board Meeting," December 5, 1905; Richard Rathbun to Charles Freer, December 5, 1905, in RU 45, Box 108, SIA.

36. Freer to Assistant Secretary of the Navy Truman Newberry, December 8, 1905 ("Confidential"), Freer to Charles Morse, December 19, 1905, Freer to Richard Rathbun, December 9, 1905, in Freer Papers; "Relations Cordial," Detroit *Free Press*, December 9, 1905; "The Freer Collection," Washington *Evening Star*, December 6, 1905.

37. Tomlinson, "Freer," 434; Charles Moore, "Makers of Washington," Chap. XIX, p. 223, in Charles Moore Papers; Hellman, *The Smithsonian*, 177–79.

As decisive as the December 4, 1905, meeting may have been, Roosevelt made the government's position even clearer with a detailed public letter addressed to Supreme Court Chief Justice Melville Fuller on December 19, just four days after Charles Freer's much publicized White House visit and conference. The United States should close with Freer's munificent offer as a matter of course, Roosevelt wrote to Fuller. "Mr. Freer's collection is literally priceless; it includes hundreds of the most remarkable pictures by the best known old masters of China and Japan. It also included hundreds of pictures, studies, and etchings by certain notable American artists; those by Whistler alone being such as would make the whole collection of unique value—although the pictures by the Chinese and Japanese artists are of even greater worth and consequence." So much for the piddling objections raised by the Smithsonian on impressionism. In answer to the objections raised by Senator Henderson, Roosevelt answered that "any competent critic can testify to the extraordinary value of the collection." [38]

Roosevelt outlined the Freer offer and suggested consulting other critics if any more expert opinion were needed. The president fully supported Freer's insistence on the integrity of the collection and Freer's condition that only he could add to it. "All that is asked of the Government or the Regents of the Smithsonian now is that they shall accept this magnificently generous offer. Nothing whatever else is demanded at present." Roosevelt pointed out that the collection would remain in Freer's hands until the erection of a building, itself "a gift of great beauty," and only then would Congress need to allocate funds "to take care of what will be a national asset of great value." Roosevelt reiterated that "the gift is literally beyond price" and asked that the Smithsonian "agree to accept on behalf of the Nation the great benefit thus to be bestowed upon the Nation." It was the Smithsonian regents' duty to take the gift, and if they refused Roosevelt threatened to take some other method to "prevent the loss . . . of one of the most valuable collections which any private individual has ever given to any people." [39]

Freer met with the cabinet, the press, and the Congress; he was wined, dined, and feted as befitted a new national hero, albeit a unique

38. TR to Melville W. Fuller, December 19, 1905, in MRL, V, 117–18
39. *Ibid.*

American cultural hero; Freer remained confident that with the president as his active ally he would win the battle. By January, 1906, even the regents' stubbornness was fading. The leaders of the opposition, Alexander Graham Bell and Senator Henderson, had been forced to give up their absurd arguments on the aesthetic merits of the collection. The maintenance cost argument was valid only to a bureaucrat. The Washington *Evening Star* could keep up the public pressure by simply reprinting the more frivolous regents' objections and exposing them to ridicule. Little niggling objections, such as not being legally able to bind a future Congress to provide maintenance appropriations, caused Charles Moore to fear on January 3, 1906, "the back down of the Regents." The regents were in their last gasp of resistance.[40]

Freer remained calm and cautious. He wrote Senator Alger that he still preferred Washington but that "if it should so happen this cannot be cheerfully and comfortably accomplished by all parties interested it would be far better to entrust the collections to some other agency." Freer knew that the pressure upon the regents was intense, and he planned to add to it by coming once again to Washington. On January 9, Moore, writing to his Washington press intermediary, complained of Bell's continued insistence on placing legal obstacles in Freer's path. "How easy it is for Mr. Bell to say 'can't.'"[41]

It was becoming less easy. On January 17, Bell relented and the regents' formal opposition ended. Bell's capitulation came in a telephone call to Langley agreeing to a "single resolution accepting the Freer collection." Not only did Bell give up his main legal objections, but also all of the compromise resolutions attacking the original Freer conditions. Although the formal resolution of acceptance is dated January 24, 1906, Freer had already been informed the day before of the acceptance. The formal agreement was as brief as the dispute was lengthy. It was the first gracious gesture the Smithsonian had offered since the dispute began:

40. Charles Freer to Thomas Jerome, December 23, 1905, Freer to August Saint-Gaudens, December 28, 1905, both in Freer Papers; Freer Folder, in Charles Moore Papers.

41. Charles Freer to Russell Alger, January 4, 1906, in Freer Papers; Charles Moore to Mrs. Richardson, in Charles Moore Papers.

The Board of Regents, recognizing the great value to the people of the United States of the art collection so generously offered by Mr. Charles L. Freer, of Detroit, Michigan,

RESOLVED: That the Board of Regents of the Smithsonian Institution do hereby accept the tender of Mr. Freer to make present conveyance to the Institution of the title to his art collection, and to bequeath to the Institution the sum of five hundred thousand dollars for the construction of a fireproof building in which to house it—under the terms as stated in his communication to the President of the United States dated December 15, 1905.[42]

The victors celebrated immediately. Charles Moore wrote his Washington press confidante and coconspirator: "Mr. Freer has just telephoned me the dispatches he has received announcing the acceptance of the gift on his terms. So the long struggle is happily ended, and you and Miss Mechlin and the *Star* can turn to other fields and pastures now. Now that the deed has been accomplished I shall write to her." Charles Freer remained gracious. He sent appreciative telegrams to everyone including his bitterest opponents. To Theodore Roosevelt, Freer cabled, "Without your good influence it could not have been accomplished." Richard Rathbun, the Smithsonian's new director, had become the acting secretary replacing Samuel Langley. Rathbun would usher in an era of cooperation and graciousness with Freer that eventually healed the wounds of the battle.[43]

Charles Freer not only won his battle, he began at forty-eight a new career that was more pleasing than any of his others. He became an integral part of the Smithsonian's transition into the collecting of art. Freer continued to travel as before, but his new role was as official representative and buyer (with his own money) for the only American national art museum in existence. He added new paintings and objects, annotated the old holdings, and helped with the design of the new building.

42. "Freer Collection," Transcription, January 17, 1906, in RU 45, Box 108, SIA; Charles Moore to Mrs. Richardson, January 23, 1906, in Moore Papers; "Resolution adopted by the Board of Regents of the Smithsonian Institution, January 24, 1906, accepting the tender of Mr. Charles L. Freer, dated December 15, 1905," in RU 45, Box 108, SIA.

43. Charles Moore to Mrs. Richardson, January 23, 1906, in Charles Moore Papers; Charles Freer to Dr. Alexander Graham Bell, TR, Richard Rathbun, and Augustus Saint-Gaudens, January 24, 1906, in Freer Papers.

For Freer, giving was even more rewarding than receiving, and he relished his new role. Both Freer's struggle and his personal rewards were impressive. While his contemporary art philanthropists had made their mark only at the local museum level, Freer became the first industrialist to give his art collection to the federal government. The formal papers between Freer and the government were signed on May 5, 1906. Freer continued to ship purchases from the Orient until just before his death in 1919. The building that was to house the Freer Collection opened in 1921.

How important was the Freer battle? For Charles Freer winning meant that his "Art Collection when established in Washington will open the way to both historical and aesthetic pleasure to the many who are becoming interested in Chinese and Japanese art."[44] Once the gift was accepted Freer changed the emphasis in his collecting. Oriental art became primary, replacing Whistler and the Americans as the dominant focus. Whistler is still spectacularly represented, but the Freer Gallery is primarily an Oriental museum, an irony, since the Freer collection was the first realization of a national American museum. Following the battle over the Freer gift, the Smithsonian accepted more graciously its role as a national museum. Harriet Lane Johnson's gift of thirty-one English oil paintings, the first large bequest, was taken in 1907 after litigation established the Smithsonian as the proper repository. In 1907 William Evans donated 150 American paintings; the newly established Ranger Fund provided for purchases of other American works.

Theodore Roosevelt's role in the Freer struggle is exemplary. His intervention was timely, decisive, and informed. Roosevelt's public letter to Chief Justice Fuller is an enlightened exercise in aesthetic criticism. In an era in which the officials of the only national art repository could challenge the worthiness of an art collection by labeling it as impressionist, as if that single word was universally damning, the president of the United States understood the nature of the gift and could discuss its value with authority and accuracy. By using both the symbolic power of the office of the president, and the presidency's limited domestic power to the fullest degree, Roosevelt won his battle with the bureaucrats at

44. Charles Freer to Professor Frederich Hirth, February 6, 1906, in Freer Papers.

the Smithsonian and struck a vital blow for the growth of American culture and cosmopolitanism.[45]

Indeed, Freer's unique vision of a national rather than an urban showplace for his collection and Theodore Roosevelt's immediate understanding, support, and sympathy make the episode significant in better defining the nature of American nationalism at the time. We are more accustomed to dealing with presidential history in political and diplomatic terms; the Freer struggle shows that cultural matters can be equally significant.

Once one understands the benign nature of Freer's cultural nationalism it may be possible to view other episodes of cultural nationalism in a less critical light. The activities in the Philippines and the history of the Isthmian canal at Panama are examples of an expansiveness in the same vein as the Freer art gift. In all three instances America was not acting under the influence of European imperialism, nor seeking to compete with Europe economically or politically. In each case American actions reflected natural impulses, normal consequences of the new American maturity in cultural as well as diplomatic, economic, and political affairs.

Charles Freer's Oriental treasures were as much a symbol of a new national consciousness as the American protectorate in the Philippine Islands. Neither Freer's museum nor America's Philippine adventure was innocent; nor was either one an indication of a fundamental change in American ideals. America's new awareness of people, nations, and cultures beyond its continental boundaries marked the beginning of America's new place in the world, in a role that was as much cultural as it was diplomatic.

45. For Roosevelt's support of a national art museum, see "National Gallery of Art," Sixth Annual Message to Congress, December 3, 1906, *Works, Nat. Ed.*, XV, 461.

Part II

A New Balance of Power
Foreign Policy in the New Century

For three centuries following the defeat of the Spanish Armada in 1588, English naval power dominated the world. British trade and diplomacy remained virtually unchallenged. But in the decade of the 1890s Britain's dominance faced its most serious test. Two events, both of which occurred in 1890, at once dramatized Britain's historical achievement and the new challenge of post-Bismarckian Germany. In that year, Alfred T. Mahan, an American naval historian and theoretician, published *The Influence of Seapower Upon History*. Mahan's book gave historical credit to the British achievement. He cited the shrewd development of British naval strategy and the use of a large merchant marine as the chief reasons for the small island empire's ability to dominate world trade and politics. Mahan's book was not only a history, but also a guide for other nations to imitate Britain's grand strategy and success. Eventually Mahan's influence would spur the American rise to naval dominance and world power in the twentieth century. However, before America could develop Mahan's theories, Germany, a more advanced industrial power on the European continent, offered the first challenge to British leadership.

Also in 1890, Kaiser Wilhelm II ousted Otto von Bismarck from power in Germany. Bismarck had led a newly reunified Germany to enormous power in two decades of leadership, but his ambitions were much more limited than the kaiser's. Bismarck was content to see Germany as the supreme continental power. Wilhelm II wanted far more for his new Germany, including a direct challenge of Great Britain's domination of the seas and world trade. The kaiser read and admired Mahan and his theories, and from the outset was determined to take Germany further than the enormous victory in 1871 over its chief rival, France. The kaiser envisioned not simply equality with Britain, but military and naval supremacy. Germany under Wilhelm II would shake the foundations of Western diplomacy for two decades. The opportunistic German leader eventually led Germany to its downfall in World War I, and in the process destroyed much of Western civilization in the trenches of Europe. Wilhelm, though shrewd, lacked Bismarck's intellect and tact, and because of Wilhelm's often mercurial temperament, Germany's challenge was unpredictable and frequently terrifying.

For years Great Britain had basked in the security of almost absolute power. In one cruel historical decade, it was heralded as the greatest super power in history and at the same time forced to deal with the realities of a world with new challenges not only in Europe, but also in America, Africa, and Asia. Although Queen Victoria's death in 1901 signaled the end of that decade, the seeds of dissolution of the mighty empire were already apparent. Germany in Europe, Japan in Asia, and America in the Caribbean all challenged the supposedly impregnable British. And although the Marquis of Salisbury, who became Prime Minister in 1895, still remained committed to the customary British posture of grand isolation, he was forced to bend under increasing and varied pressure.

The bending favored the United States, not because Lord Salisbury or the British admired the Americans, but because Britain reserved its most active enmity for the new Germany of Wilhelm II—and with good reason. Wilhelm's challenge was the most direct and the most serious. Like most Britons, Salisbury neither liked nor understood America. The United States had been born in a revolution that totally rejected Britain. Although Salisbury was not openly hostile, he regarded the Americans as a new and distant breed of barbarian. By contrast, the enmity reserved for Germany was born of a respect for a common European culture. Britain was able to make peace with America in the 1890s and with Japan in 1902 much more easily than she could ally herself with France in 1904 or with Germany at any time.

Great Britain bore the early brunt of the new German diplomacy. Kaiser Wilhelm II, only thirty years old when he ousted Bismarck as foreign minister, became an immediate threat to England. The kaiser replaced Bismarck's exclusively continental ambitions with ideas of world domination. For the kaiser any part of the world that he could gull, beguile, cajole, or conquer was fair game. He combined overwhelming ambition with clumsy and frequently inept diplomacy. No one could tell at any given time if the kaiser's gestures were friendly or threatening—they looked the same. Wilhelm II grew more ambitious while Germany, with a rapidly maturing industrial economy, became even stronger and more frightening.

Had Germany not been so powerful, the kaiser's frequent blunders would have been self-defeating. But because Germany was both powerful and unpredictable, and the world was undergoing a complex series of changes, diplomacy was continually on edge in the 1890s and the early twentieth century. The kaiser remained a blunderer on a huge scale; he saw only the present and took any small opportunity when it presented itself, seldom considering the long-term ramifications of his acts. For both Britain and the United States, the kaiser's most decisive blunder occurred in 1896. The United States, in its own way as ambitious and as aggressive as the new Germany, was embroiled in a bitter dispute with Britain over Venezuela's borders. British and American enmity was long-standing, stemming from the American Revolution and later encouraged by the heavy flow of Irish immigrants; in spite of obvious practical reasons for alliance and friendship, there remained a festering prolonged animosity. Had it not been for the kaiser's senseless and gratuitous intervention in the British controversy with the South African Boers in 1896, there is no telling how long the Americans and British would have remained rivals.

President Grover Cleveland in his bellicose message to Congress in December, 1895, shocked the British when he barely stopped short of threatening war over Venezuela. Almost at the same time, Dr. Leander Starr Jameson, an Englishman acting without government sanction, led a group of commandos in an attempt to settle the Boer dispute. When the Jameson raid failed badly and the attacking Britons were taken prisoner to be abjectly displayed in Johannesburg, British pride and morale were at their lowest ebb. For Transvaal president Paul Kruger the victory was monumental, and Britain's defeat gave the kaiser an easy diplomatic victory in Africa.

However, instead of silently enjoying the British embarrassment and using the blow to Britain's prestige as an automatic boost to Germany's standing in the world, the kaiser blundered onto the world stage in one

97

of the great diplomatic gaffes of modern history. Wilhelm congratulated President Kruger by public telegram, promised support if he needed it (which he obviously did not), and infuriated the British. The kaiser privately decided to send an unnecessary detachment of German marines to help in South Africa, but he was forced to abandon the plan when his aides pointed out that there was no way of getting past the British Navy.

In England the reaction to the Wilhelm-Kruger telegram was intense. German merchants' shop windows were smashed and the anti-German hysteria, encouraged by the press, never abated. All possibility of a German-British detente had ended. The British, able to focus on Germany as their principal enemy, now embraced the United States as a friend. The Kruger telegram did not by itself begin the Anglo-American entente, but it helped make it possible.

In the 1890s the world was caught up in the phenomenon of intense nationalism. Alliances were important, even vital, to peace and survival. For the Americans, nationalism was expressed in renewed avowals of national policies such as the Monroe Doctrine. America's Monroe Doctrine, directed at all Europe, was messianic; it denounced monarchy, encouraged the spread of democracy, and declared the Western hemisphere off limits to European political expansion. Prior to the Kruger telegram it was possible, though not likely, that efforts to enlarge the Spanish-American conflict into a European-monarchial versus American-democratic war might have succeeded. But with Britain now wary of Germany and leaning toward detente with America, Europe was no longer united. Neither Britain's break with Germany nor its new alliance with America was complete, but in the struggles ahead, British neutrality, some British diplomatic aid, and the continued mutual interests of the two English-speaking nations helped establish American hegemony in its own waters. The informal Anglo-American detente helped make the Monroe Doctrine a recognized world policy, and eventually ended the threat of German territorial expansion into Central and Latin America.

Germany was not the only newly ambitious world power. Japan, by virtue of a decisive victory in 1895 in her war with China, emerged as a threat in the Pacific. And America, ending her century of continental expansion to the Pacific coast in 1890, began to seek a more active role in world trade and politics. Mahan's book in 1890 and Frederick Jackson Turner's frontier thesis in 1893 offered different forms of cultural nationalism, and were immediately popularized in the new mass market newspapers of Hearst and Pulitzer, as well as in the many periodicals made possible by the new technology of photoengraving.

Populist unrest and a great depression in 1893 through 1897 added to American uncertainty about its own destiny. Americans no longer had the advantage of unlimited land, nor the economic democracy that landed wealth assured. American domestic uncertainty was further disturbed by the sensationalistic news disseminated widely by the new journalism. Intellectuals might read and ponder the lessons of Mahan and Turner; the public was also impressed by journalistic versions of their theories. They read stories of Spanish misrule in Cuba and were stirred by popular old-time resentments against Britain's power, by concerns over France's inability to complete the Panama Canal, and by the increasing world ambitions of Germany and Japan. The Japanese threat to Hawaii especially concerned an already troubled America. Americans tended to be apathetic toward European politics and more concerned over developments in Asia. German expansion into China, new European interest in Latin America, the constant reminders of authoritarian European political philosophy in the Cuban situation, all helped make Americans more eager to assert their own nationalism.

However, it is a mistake to label the new American nationalism as simply expansionist or to confuse it with older European imperialism. With the end of the American frontier and with both Germany and Japan threatening an already tenuous status quo, America had no choice but to alter its traditional stance of disinterest and to relinquish its thinly disguised contempt for the diplomatic games Europe enjoyed playing. Mahan's book offered a blueprint for painless economic expansion without the responsibility of colonies. The threats from existing world powers such as Russia, or the new powers such as Japan and Germany, made it easier for Americans to support naval power.

Theodore Roosevelt was one of the leaders of new American nationalists. Regarded by contemporaries and by later historians as a representative jingo in the English sense, Roosevelt deeply resented the label. Many of the more exuberant American expansionists—Roosevelt,

Lodge, and Brooks Adams—continually overstated their cases, in part to overcome the extreme reluctance of the established older generation to change anything. The anti-imperialists were reluctant not only to support American expansion, but also to acknowledge any changes within American society. They opposed from habit rather than intellect; their confusion encouraged the younger men's frenzy. Roosevelt, Adams, and Lodge indulged in the rhetoric of impatience, but once the intransigence of the opposition eased with the Spanish-American War of 1898, so did the demands of the expansionists. Americans learned from Europe's colonial mistakes. There was no wish in American thought, expansionist or otherwise, for colonization. Indeed, recent scholarship has suggested that even European imperialism was largely accidental—strategic or tactical rather than economic. Jingoism is probably more of a literary phenomenon than a political movement, led not by expansionist statesmen, but by popular romantic poets such as Kipling. In America, imperialism versus anti-imperialism was largely a generational debate, not an ideological confrontation.

Theodore Roosevelt was more fortunate than Kaiser Wilhelm II in one significant respect. Wilhelm began his rule in 1888, just before a decade of change and crisis. He was very young at the time. Had Theodore Roosevelt become president in 1890, or at the age of thirty, he might have made the same immature and inexperienced blunders that plagued the kaiser. By the time Roosevelt had assumed the presidency in 1901, both he and his nation had matured. In 1898 America had already made its almost inevitable decision to become a world power. Once that action was taken, the urgent need for expansionist lobbying was gone. It was Roosevelt's function to refine rather than initiate America's participation in world politics.

Roosevelt's record as diplomatic leader is far more substantial than that suggested by the stereotype of bellicose imperialist. Roosevelt remained an American nationalist all his life, but his nationalism was tempered by a sophisticated sense of world order based on peace. The Rooseveltian world view envisioned a union of civilized nations maintaining the peace and stability of the world against both incursions of developing nations and temptations presented by nations too weak to effectively defend themselves from attack. In Roosevelt's view America's place was with the civilized world powers, and not as either a newly developing nation or, worst of all in Roosevelt's mind, a nation too weak (as China) to defend itself. Roosevelt's diplomatic program was dedicated to making America not simply a world power but the leader of the world powers.

In his first term Roosevelt's main task was to convince Europe of America's seriousness. Roosevelt clearly believed in the balance of power concept by which Europe maintained its tenuous peace. The balance of power assures world stability by maintaining the relative strength of the various powers, thereby making it impossible for any nation to seize control unexpectedly by developing new strength or new allies. Roosevelt's "civilized powers" were obviously the richer nations that had fully developed their industrial economies. His major fear was not the developing nations but the defenseless ones, those who might tempt the civilized powers into hasty and aggressive moves that could lead to war and a subsequent breakdown of world order. The most striking areas of weakness were in Latin America and China.

The first order of business for Roosevelt was American control of the Caribbean to assure that Europe would not be tempted by the obvious weakness of many of the Caribbean countries. Roosevelt sought to make Britain and Germany respect American hegemony in the Caribbean and to establish that America was both willing to undertake responsibility and also able to defend her strategic interests. The battles of the first term—with Britain, with Germany, and later over Panama— were all concerned with the important first step of establishing American control over its own strategic interests. For Roosevelt any foothold by an established European power near the American mainland threatened the nation's vital interests and was unacceptable.

In his second term Roosevelt used the new American strength not for further expansion through an adventuresome foreign policy, but as a force for world stability. He built on the detente with Britain, the understanding with Germany, and the new balance of power in Asia to help avert a world conflict in the settlement of the Russo-Japanese War. In addition Theodore Roosevelt worked to maintain stability in the Caribbean and Latin America while also supporting Latin American efforts, at both the Pan-American and Hague peace conferences, to

101

broaden its role in world affairs. Roosevelt helped maintain European peace by supporting a settlement in the Morocco dispute at Algeciras; he was able to partially control Japan's growing strength in the Pacific by using the Great White Fleet as a symbolic and diplomatic gesture.

Perhaps too much has been made of the personal style Theodore Roosevelt employed in his more dramatic diplomatic confrontations. It is true that he enjoyed dealing with friends such as the German diplomat Speck von Sternberg and the British diplomat Cecil "Springy" Spring Rice.[1] But when the Russo-Japanese crisis developed, Roosevelt immersed himself in Japanese culture in order to better understand a point of view most Western diplomats completely ignored. Roosevelt's personal diplomacy was an attempt to simplify developing problems and head them off before they became formal confrontations. For the most part Roosevelt worked well with the State Department and his two secretaries of state, John Hay and Elihu Root. Hay, Root, and Roosevelt were all indebted to Assistant Secretary of State Alvey Adee who was able to keep his superiors well informed on all significant world developments and to run the State Department with unique skill and intelligence. Because assistants like Adee were experts in their jobs, Roosevelt was free to concentrate his energies on the most significant diplomatic problems.

The transformation of America from a provincial to a world power began in the 1890s. When Theodore Roosevelt took office, the first and most important steps had already been taken. By going to war with Spain and keeping the Philippines in 1898, America had joined the more ambitious industrialized world powers. With the Platt Amendment in 1901, Congress declared to the world its continued independence from European colonial ambitions. In his presidency Roosevelt supported both the expansion that had taken place and the limitations Congress imposed upon it, and never envisioned any further American expansion. He regarded the taking of Panama as a fulfillment of the

1. Roosevelt first met Baron Hermann Speck von Sternberg through his sister Anna around 1890, and Cecil Arthur Spring Rice in November, 1886, while sailing to England for his marriage with Edith. Spring Rice served as best man at the wedding. See Nelson M. Blake, "Ambassadors at the Court of Theodore Roosevelt," MVHR, XLII (1955), 197–206.

most direct American strategic interest, as a way of denying Europe a foothold in Central America, and at the same time assuring full mobility for a two-ocean navy.

Roosevelt's aristocratic class, his European cultural background, and his ability to put events in historical perspective gave him a deeply pessimistic view of the ability of world leaders to maintain peace. Because of the foundations he built in his first term, Roosevelt was able in the second term not only to take America into the company of the "civilized powers," but to assume active leadership of that elite group. In the second term America and Theodore Roosevelt became the balance of power. Roosevelt believed that American leadership prevented war in 1904–1905, by limiting and finally settling the Russo-Japanese conflict, to a lesser degree in 1906 with the Algeciras settlement, and in 1907–1909 with the strategic warning to Japan through the world cruise of the American battleship fleet.

Theodore Roosevelt had cause to be offended with political or journalistic charges that he was simply a warmongering imperialist. Imperialism is a nineteenth-century European buzzword, inaccurate in describing European expansion and unrecognizable as an American phenomenon during Theodore Roosevelt's presidency.

4 / The Legend of Imperialism
Theodore Roosevelt and the Myths of the War of 1898

When the American Asiatic fleet, under the command of Commodore George Dewey, destroyed a formidable Spanish fleet at Manila Bay on May 1, 1898, after just two hours of fighting, the Spanish-American War of 1898 had begun with one of history's most startling and decisive victories. Dewey's victory over the Spanish fleet was hardly an accident. Dewey was a gifted naval leader, and although the two naval contingents were fairly evenly matched, the two countries were not. America was young, exuberant, and developing; Spain was old, tired, and decadent.

The naval outcome, however, was far from inevitable. The American Navy had commanders who could have lost a sea battle to the Spanish as decisively as Dewey had won; indeed, had the Asiatic command followed standard naval bureaucratic procedures, it is possible a desk admiral would have been in charge, with unknown consequences for American history and legend. Perhaps Theodore Roosevelt's most notable achievement as assistant secretary of the Navy was his successful campaign to promote Dewey as fleet commander over other officers higher on the promotion list.

Although Roosevelt recounts that "sound naval opinion was overwhelmingly in favor of Dewey to command one squadron," Dewey's appointment resulted from intense political maneuvering and was in fact a surprise. Roosevelt was unimpressed with Dewey's rival and superior on the promotion list, Commodore John A. Howell, a "respectable commonplace type." When Assistant Secretary Roosevelt learned that Dewey had a friend in the Senate, he urged the naval officer to use his political influence. Dewey's powerful Senate friend, Redfield Proctor

(Republican-Vermont), was close enough to President McKinley to assure Dewey's appointment.[1]

To Roosevelt, Dewey's unorthodox way of dealing with the naval bureaucracy potentially made him a better naval leader. In one dilemma that Roosevelt remembered, Dewey, in command of a warship, was ordered to move his ship to the safer West Coast if the threat of war between Chile and Argentina materialized. However, Dewey was not authorized to buy the coal needed for the move and almost sure to be reprimanded, if, after buying unauthorized coal, the emergency did not develop. Dewey's decision to buy coal impressed Roosevelt: "In a crisis, the man worth his salt is the man who meets the needs of the situation in whatever way is necessary. Dewey purchased the coal and was ready to move at once if need arose." The war did not develop, but Dewey's coal purchase was subsequently approved. For Roosevelt, Dewey had the ideal qualifications to command the Asiatic fleet—"a man who could be relied upon to prepare in advance, and to act promptly, fearlessly."[2]

Dewey's victory at Manila Bay in May, 1898, and America's subsequent victory over Spain in Cuba have assumed legendary proportions in American history. According to most historians, the American victory made the United States the newest world power and marked the beginning of America's entry into imperialism. John Hay called the Spanish-American War of 1898 a "splendid little war," one in which American losses were small and the gains enormous. Journalists and historians have made it the focal point of a fierce domestic political battle between imperialists who favored overseas expansion and anti-imperialists who opposed it. According to historical legend, both popular and serious, it was Theodore Roosevelt's precipitous telegram ordering Commodore George Dewey to attack the Philippines in case of war between the United States and Spain that plunged America from a state of innocence into the role of superpower and conqueror. Much of what is written on the Spanish-American War assumes the decisive nature of

1. TR *Autobiography* (New York, 1913), in *Works, Nat. Ed.*, XX, 216–18; Ronald Spector, *Admiral of the New Navy: The Life and Career of George Dewey* (Baton Rouge, 1974), 36–39; Roosevelt to William Eaton Chandler, September 27, 1897, MRL, I, 691–92; Redfield Proctor to George Dewey, October 16, 1897, in George Dewey Papers, LC.
2. Roosevelt, *Autobiography*, XX, 216–17.

Theodore Roosevelt's cable to Dewey, and many accounts accuse Theodore Roosevelt of single-handedly fomenting a war with Spain to assure that America would embrace his imperial ideas.[3]

It is time to put the legend of Theodore Roosevelt, the Machiavellian imperialist, the man who by some political and constitutional miracle managed to parlay his minor job as assistant secretary of the Navy into that of supreme commander or declarer of war, permanently to rest. Theodore Roosevelt was a good assistant secretary of the Navy, but he never had the power to make a war. He barely had the power to move ships from one port to another in peacetime America. Historians who focus on war and naval battles to explain the changing American society miss the sense of fundamental change that affected all Americans, not just the naval and military planners. Technology helped effect the change. In the 1890s the discovery and use of photoengraving made it possible for printers to reproduce actual photographs, which revolutionized American culture and opened up a dramatic new kind of journalism. Pictures replaced artistic renditions and enabled newspapers to dramatize events not only with words, but with factual illustrations.

The first of the major technological changes in publishing occurred in 1886 with the introduction of the Merganthaler Linotype machine. The combination of Linotypes and photoengraving literally changed the face of publishing and the character of newspapers and magazines. Now able to print quickly and cheaply and to use real pictures, the publishing business attracted a mass market.[4] "Pictures don't lie" was the newspapers' message. By choosing the most sensational subjects, the new journalism reached audiences theretofore undreamed of. Joseph Pulitzer and William Randolph Hearst developed the mass-market newspaper through techniques that used pictures and sensational reporting. The last decade of the nineteenth century ended with more

3. The Roosevelt "plot" to precipitate war can be found in its most blatant form in A. Whitney Griswold, *The Far Eastern Policy of the United States* (New Haven, 1964), 11–16; See also Walter Millis, *The Martial Spirit* (New York, 1965), 112; William A. Williams, *The Roots of the Modern American Empire* (New York, 1969), 425; Foster Rhea Dulles, *Imperial Years* (New York, 1966), 132.
4. For a brief summary of the technological changes see John W. Oliver, *History of American Technology* (New York, 1956), 442–48. See also Frank Luther Mott, *A History of American Magazines* (5 vols.; Cambridge, Mass., 1930–68), IV, 153–54 for photoengraving, and *passim* for the changes in American periodical publishing.

Americans reading newspapers (or looking at the pictures) than ever before.

Not just newspapers, but periodicals of all kinds benefited from the technology and appeal of photoengraving. Printing was cheaper, and more magazines at every level began competing for the American literary market. Henry James, who most certainly did not write for a popular market, found more American magazines than ever before eager to publish his experimental fiction. Captain Alfred Mahan, the naval strategist, had a wide audience both among the intellectuals and in popular magazines and newspapers. Frederick Jackson Turner's thesis "The Significance of the Frontier in American History" became one of the most widely disseminated academic theories ever propounded in America. By 1900 everyone knew about Turner's West, Mahan's battleships, and Theodore Roosevelt's colorful exploits. Andrew Carnegie's gift of public libraries helped increase the reading of books and may have encouraged the advance of American literacy almost as much as Hearst's photographs.

Diplomatic expansion was but a small part of America's change from provincialism to cosmopolitanism, from developing nation to industrial power. To make the overseas incidents the center of American history in the 1890s or early twentieth century overlooks the more wide-reaching American cultural, social, and political changes that were transforming the nation. The chapter on imperialism, historian James A. Field complained recently, is the worst in any American history textbook. Historians tend to overlook all the other changes taking place and explain the events of 1898 and 1899 simply as examples of America's new imperialism. Although imperialism may have been more a literary or journalistic slogan than an authentic historical phenomenon, Americans were careful to avoid any taint of a European phenomenon they held in contempt. But Europe as well as America was changing.[5]

Field is unequivocal: "Much of [American history texts on imperialism] is wrong and most of it irrelevant to 'imperialism' and the events of 1898. The New Navy was . . . a response to the strategic problems of isthmus, Caribbean and eastern Pacific. . . . In the circumstances of

5. James A. Field, "American Imperialism: The Worst Chapter in Any Book," AHR, 83 (1978), 644–83;

the time, such a defensive policy seems quite reasonable." An example of the changing attitude to European imperialism can be found in Oron J. Hale's general history of modern Europe: "One wonders if 'imperialism,' because of looseness of definition, is a word that scholars ought to use." In reviewing the historiographical arguments on imperialism as the main cause of European conflict, Hale rejects it: "The noes have it."[6]

America's war with Spain in 1898 was but one example of a new American sense of the world. Once we reexamine the assumption that the label *imperialism* explains American actions in the McKinley and Roosevelt presidencies, we might find that what we thought to be imperialism is instead a quickening of the spirit in general, and a new sense of identity shared by many Americans. Not only were wealthy millionaires buying art in Europe and Asia, but college athletes were competing in international events for the first time. It is no accident that Americans won sixteen of the twenty-one contests at the Paris international athletic games in 1900, or that Americans sent more exhibits to the Paris exposition of 1900 than any other country. Americans were simply more active, ready to move from the shadows of geographical parochialism into a world that would eventually accept the seriousness of the new American, even at the cost of confrontation—aesthetic, economic, or diplomatic. "An immense elevation" was how one writer described the mood of the new America.[7]

The heart of alleged American imperialism is the dramatic cable Assistant Secretary of the Navy Theodore Roosevelt dispatched to Commodore George Dewey, commander of America's Asiatic squadron based in Hong Kong: "Order the squadron, except the *Monocacy* to Hong Kong. Keep full of coal. In the event of a declaration of war, Spain, your duty will be to see that the Spanish squadron does not leave the Asiatic Coast and then offensive operations in the Philippine Islands. Keep *Olympia* until further orders."[8]

Roosevelt's cable was dispatched on February 25, 1898. The battle it

---

6. *Ibid.*, 667–68; "Imperialism: Myths and Realities," in *The Great Illusion* (New York, 1971), 4–11.
7. Mark Sullivan, *Our Times* (6 vols.; New York, 1927–35), I, 53.
8. Copy in George Dewey Papers, text in TR, *Autobiography*, XX, 220.

supposedly precipitated took place May 1, 1898, over two months later. Even in peacetime the American Navy moves faster than the legend's fanciful timetable suggests. The myth has no factual or historical basis. Dewey on receiving the Roosevelt order did not sail immediately for Manila; instead he followed orthodox American naval procedures and had his ships painted. (Ships in peacetime are white; when going to war they are gray.)

Theodore Roosevelt's order to Commodore Dewey was not an innocent misunderstanding. Roosevelt and the American government were indeed preparing the Asiatic fleet for a naval confrontation. A war with Spain had become a possibility two years earlier when Spanish reaction to Cuban protests had brought the uneasy colony to the point of civil war. A separate revolution for Philippine independence plagued the Spanish in Asia. America could be held partly to blame for the Cuban dispute, since American sugar tariffs enacted in 1894 seriously disturbed Cuba's main source of income—sugar exports to the United States. But the United States was not responsible for the separate Philippine war for independence. Unbeknown to world leaders and the world press, a phenomenon now identified as Third World nationalism had suddenly begun.

Cubans and Filipinos demanded independence from Spain, Boers fought Englishmen, and even in China, where Americans as enlightened as Theodore Roosevelt assumed that nationalism was nonexistent, the Boxer Rebellion in 1900 should have warned Western diplomats that things were not what they seemed. The Third World had begun its protest, a movement it would take the civilized powers three major wars to recognize. Those who still insist on the decisiveness of Theodore Roosevelt's telegram to Commodore Dewey are practicing a history that even for America is unbelievably provincial.

When Theodore Roosevelt sent the fateful cable to Dewey, a war with Spain, though far from inevitable, was nonetheless likely—not in February but certainly, if war was to occur at all, in April before the Caribbean rainy season precluded any military movement until fall. The United States had begun its war alert over a month before Roosevelt's cable to Dewey. On January 17, 1898, the commander in charge of American naval forces in the Atlantic received the first of several war warnings from Washington. The reasons were specific: the Cuban situation had become grave. Two ships were ordered to duty in Paraguay in case of war, and a little over a week later the Americans began assembling a South Atlantic battle squadron. The new arrangement of ships ordered on January 26, 1898, envisaged an eventual attack upon the mainland coast of Spain. The squadron was to assemble at the neutral port of Lisbon to prepare, as did Dewey at Hong Kong, for eventual combat duties should the dispute with Spain turn to war.[9]

The crisis that led to the eventual naval confrontation between the United States and Spain had festered and grown for several years. Americans had little difficulty in actively disliking Spaniards; Spanish autocrats were openly contemptuous of both Americans and their democratic ideals. Spain symbolized the European attitude most Americans detested: the authoritarianism of a smug and powerful monarchy and a firm belief in the superiority of European principles over New World idealism and ambition. Spanish diplomats were as unyielding as the American newspapers claimed. Even after hostilities began, Spain remained convinced that a coalition of European monarchial states would eventually combine to protect Spain and punish the upstart Americans. Spain did not deal in good faith with the American government at any time in the crisis, nor were the Spanish convincing in their crude charade of diplomacy.

The Americans, however, were far from innocent bystanders. In the Cuban problems, Spain was not entirely at fault. The Wilson-Gorman Tariff of 1894 levied new duties on Cuban sugar ostensibly to help American Gulf Coast farmers. The tariff inevitably and predictably raised havoc with the Cuban economy and helped cause the first serious Cuban protests against Spanish rule. The Spanish were not willing to soothe the ruffled economic feathers of their colonial subjects and reacted to Cuban economic unrest with repressive counter measures. The emerging worldwide mood of nationalism fueled the protest in both

9. The best summary of American naval actions is the chronological list of U.S. Naval orders compiled by Captain Arent S. Crowinshield for Henry Cabot Lodge, September 24, 1898, in Henry Cabot Lodge Papers, Massachusetts Historical Society. For specific orders see the U.S. Department of the Navy *Annual Reports of the Navy Department for the Year 1898, Appendix to the Report of the Chief of the Bureau of Navigation* (Washington, D.C., 1898).

Cuba and America and stiffened Spanish resistance to any possible compromise.

By 1896 the crisis between Spain and America was full-blown. In America, mass-circulation newspapers further inflamed the dispute, with Hearst and Pulitzer exploiting every possible incident in Cuba. Cuban patriots with an open line to American newspapers became adept propagandists and provocateurs. In popular accounts of the causes of the war, William Randolph Hearst and Joseph Pulitzer share the responsibility with Theodore Roosevelt in pushing the United States into the conflict. But neither Hearst, Pulitzer, nor Roosevelt fomented a war with Spain; the war was not caused by any single person or group. One man, however, has a far better claim to being the father of the war of 1898 than Hearst, Pulitzer, or Roosevelt. Lieutenant William Wirt Kimball, a naval intelligence officer, wrote the plan that eventually helped decide the war. Although he is overlooked in most histories of the age, Kimball is one of the war's most significant figures.[10]

William Wirt Kimball's low rank should not obscure his importance or the influence of his long career in Naval Intelligence. In the halcyon days before the United States became a world power, promotions in rank were rare and frequently reflected political or social influence more than merit. Kimball, an Annapolis graduate, was one of the first officers in the Navy's new intelligence service in 1882. When he retired from active duty in 1910 as a rear admiral, following a varied and distinguished naval career, Kimball's main achievement was his pioneering work with torpedo warfare and the development of submarines in the 1890s. In the 1880s Kimball worked on the designs of early machine guns and magazine-loaded armaments. He served at sea in the Spanish-American War as the commander of the first American torpedo-boat flotilla. In his last active duty he led the American intervention in Nicaragua in 1909. His more colorful exploits with torpedos and submarines have overshadowed his equally important intelligence career.[11]

10. William Wirt Kimball, "War with Spain, 1896, General Considerations of the War, the Results Desired, and the Consequent Kind of Operations to be Undertaken, June 1, 1896," Records of Naval Operating Forces, in RG 313, Entry 43, Box 11, NA. Hereinafter cited as Kimball, "War with Spain," in RG 313.

11. For Roosevelt's support of Kimball's war plan, see TR to Henry Cabot Lodge, September 2, 1897, in MRL, I, 685–86; on Kimball's new role as commander of Amer-

Kimball was both well known and well respected and had been for a long time. Over a decade before he wrote his war plan in 1896, he was influential in dealing with the American response to the imminent failure of Ferdinand de Lesseps' Panama Canal Company. The French project had run into enormous difficulties from its start in 1880, and by 1885 Congress had become concerned with the ramifications of a possible French failure. Americans were extremely sensitive toward any European incursions into Central America. Since the de Lesseps canal project was a private rather than a government undertaking, the Americans tolerated its presence while keeping a watchful eye on its progress.

In 1885 the Navy Department's Office of Naval Intelligence was asked to report on the status of the French Panama project to the House of Representatives. Kimball was sent to the construction site, and as a shrewd and acute observer, was more impressed with de Lesseps' accomplishments, understanding the magnitude of the attempt as well as the reality of its failure. Because Kimball accurately predicted the imminent French collapse, American naval intelligence recommended an increase in American naval operations in the area. After de Lesseps' failure, the United States was ready to intervene quickly if either anarchy or European intrusions threatened. As the tension increased following de Lesseps' withdrawal, American naval activity also increased. American naval intelligence was active and perceptive and in times of trouble was called upon for advice and analysis.[12]

In 1896 when the threat of a confrontation with Spain became more likely, Kimball was asked, as one of his regular duties in naval intelligence, to work with the Naval War College in writing a contingency war plan for a possible Spanish-American war. Kimball's "War with Spain— 1896" is an exercise in practical intellect that avoids possibly embarrassing political issues, such as imperialism. Kimball treated the war prob-

---

ica's first torpedo boat flotilla, see TR to John Long, August 9, 1897, in MRL, I, 642–43, and TR to William W. Kimball, September 22, 1897, in MRL, I, 687–88; for Roosevelt's acknowledgment of Kimball's importance in planning for war with Spain, see TR to Long, December 16, 1899, in John D. Long Papers, in Massachusetts Historical Society; for Kimball's role in naval intelligence, see Jeffery M. Dorwart, *Office of Naval Intelligence: The Birth of America's First Intelligence Agency, 1865–1918* (Annapolis, 1979), 12–13, 55–57.

12. House Miscellaneous Report 395, 49th Cong., 1st Sess. *Progress on Panama Canal*, Serial 2422.

lem as a purely strategic one, meticulously listing the geographical and military assets of both Spain and the United States before assessing the best strategy. In the process William Kimball wrote the masterpiece of naval strategy for the 1890s—a war plan that began as a theoretical work and eventually became the reality itself.[13]

Kimball was not alone in seeing the need for a contingency plan in case war with Spain materialized. Students at the Naval War College in Newport, Rhode Island, had considered a hypothetical war plan as early as 1894, and by 1895 had completed another plan that was sent to the Navy Department in 1896. As staff intelligence officer at the college, Kimball would have been well aware of these early efforts. Kimball's superiors, Admiral Stephen B. Luce, and Chief Intelligence Officer Lieutenant Commander Richard Wainwright, also saw the need for a war plan.

Kimball's original draft was subjected to intense critical scrutiny, partly because of political rivalry in the naval hierarchy and also from genuine intellectual disagreements among naval administrators. Captain Henry C. Taylor, president of the Naval War College, disagreed with Kimball's conclusion that Spain could be defeated primarily by use of naval forces. In 1897 a naval board headed by Rear Admiral Montgomery Sicard was convened to formulate a final revision of Kimball's plan. The debate was intense and the differences substantial. Captain Taylor and the Naval War College disagreed with Kimball's primary objective. Taylor wanted to substitute the Canary Islands in the Atlantic for the Philippines in Asia as the major objective for American naval diversion. Taylor also insisted on making Cuba the major naval target. In the showdown with the entire naval board, Kimball's choice won out over Taylor's. Strategy and tactics rather than economics and empire were the battleground in the naval debate.[14]

Technically Sicard's revision became the Navy Department's policy. In

13. For the genesis of the Kimball plan and its ultimate fate, see John A. S. Grenville and George Berkeley Young, *Politics, Strategy and American Diplomacy: Studies in Foreign Policy, 1873–1917* (New Haven, 1967), 267–81; David F. Trask, *The War with Spain in 1898* (New York, 1981), 72–79, and Ronald Spector, "Who Planned the Attack on Manila Bay?" *Mid-America*, LIII (1971), 94–102.

14. For the texts of both the Taylor and Sicard plans, see John A. S. Grenville, "American Naval Preparations for War with Spain, 1896–1898," *Journal of American Studies* (Great Britain), II (1968), 33–47.

fact the Sicard plan is mostly Kimball's original plan except for an additional contingency against the possibility of a Japanese attack. Although he called for an indemnity to be wrested from Spain in exchange for the return of Manila, Kimball's plan was entirely strategic. The idea of making Spain pay, both for possible captured American ships and for the port of Manila, was primarily military rather than economic or political. Kimball hoped to limit Spanish naval and military options by making them impossible or too costly. Surprisingly after all the controversy, which remained within the naval hierarchy and did not become public, Sicard's revised plan was almost identical to Kimball's original. When the revised Kimball war plan was approved by the naval board it became the official United States naval policy governing the eventual war with Spain in 1898.[15]

Kimball's war plan directed that if war occurred the primary engagements with Spain should be naval rather than military. A naval war minimized both casualties and cost, eliminated the tactical difficulties presented by Cuba's long rainy season, and gave the United States additional time to increase arms and armies if needed. In addition a naval war would bring the widest and most effective pressure against Spain, while giving Cuba a chance to establish independence prior to conquest by an invading army. In short, Kimball's war plan of 1896 was irresistible. Almost instinctively the Navy Department and the chief executive began to follow the script that promised a stunning victory.

Kimball's strategic conclusion was unassailable. "Both strategy and sentiment point to purely naval operations in a war with Spain arising from the complications on the Cuban question, and that a resort to invasion would be necessary only in case naval operations alone were not effective or required a longer time to be made so." Kimball's plan demonstrated that a naval war against Spain was the most logical strategy, and proposed that the United States assume the offensive in the three designated theaters of war. The three war zones included "Cuba and Porto Rican waters," Spanish waters, "for the purposes of striking at Spanish trade and transport services, and Philippine waters." The Philippine projection was the most detailed and the most effective: "For the

15. For the view that Kimball's primary objective in the war plan was to wrest an economic indemnity from Spain, see Spector, *Admiral of the New Navy*, 33.

purpose of reducing and holding Manila, of harassing trade, of cutting off revenue (especially that due to sugar and tobacco), from Spain, of occupying, or at least blockading the Philippine principal ports so that the release of our hold of them may be used as an inducement to Spain to make peace after the liberation of Cuba."[16]

The Philippines were a primary objective not because they were on the path to the China market or because the Germans or Japanese coveted control of the islands. The key to the Philippines was not the islands themselves, but the use of Manila as the base for the Spanish Asiatic navy. Kimball insisted that the United States, in order to successfully challenge Spain in Cuba, must be able to challenge Spanish naval forces throughout the world. The Spanish controlled the Philippines with their navy, and it was the Spanish navy, rather than the Philippines themselves, that was the main target of the proposed American attack.

By forcing the Spanish fleet to remain in Philippine waters, Kimball neutrálized that fleet and prevented its sailing to help Spanish forces in Cuba. The Kimball plan also attempted to deceive the Spanish by making them believe that the Americans seriously threatened the European mainland. By making the Philippines and Spain itself subject to American attack, Kimball believed that the Americans significantly improved their already substantial tactical advantage in nearby Cuba. The importance of the Philippine economy to Spain made it certain that the Spanish navy would be forced to defend the Philippines and not concentrate all its forces at Cuba. In Kimball's plan the Philippines were seen as a strategic necessity for Spain, and therefore held the key to the winning American tactics in the war.

Many Americans of the time, and even now, might be astonished at the thoroughness of the war plan of 1896. Every Spanish ship, its location, and its specifications are listed in exhaustive detail. In Philippine waters Kimball cited eight Spanish cruisers and twenty-four gunboats, each with its date of launching, weight, armament, maximum speed, and draft. Following the list of Spanish ships is an inventory of American private ships, their location, and their suitability for purchase for conversion to warships in event of war. In addition, a detailed analysis

16. Kimball, "War With Spain," 3–4, in RG 313.

of every major and minor Spanish port with appropriate navigational maps and fortifications is listed. There is even an economic analysis of the Philippine trade that shows, in the years 1888–1892, the source of all Philippine imports, the total value of exports, population, and a revenue projection for 1894–1895. Also given in minute detail is the blueprint for what would become Dewey's eventual attack upon Manila. The major addition to Kimball's original war plan was the military offensive for the invasion of Cuba.[17]

The beauty of Kimball's plan was its practicality. Kimball was not concerned with the most pressing ideological question of the day—the issue of American expansion. His plan avoided the question by treating the problem as a purely tactical naval and military issue. Since members of the anti-war group remained convinced until the very end that Spain was dealing with America in good faith and would go to almost any lengths to avoid a war, they went along with the initial preparations called for by Kimball's plan. Secretary of the Navy John D. Long, a passionate anti-war advocate, remained optimistic, until the week war was declared, that there would be no war. The war group was equally convinced that war with Spain was inevitable. As long as the preparations for war continued along with the debate, the interventionists had no fundamental quarrel with American strategy, outside of a minor impatience at the slowness of mobilization.[18]

The public debate in America focused mainly on Cuba and only peripherally on the Philippines. Americans felt a natural sympathy with the Cubans and a natural distaste for the European authoritarianism that Spain exemplified. Economic interests were not well defined or sophisticated. At first the business community was wholly opposed to any war, and much of the friction between Theodore Roosevelt's strategic faction and business interests as a whole came from this early fundamental disagreement. As the diplomatic deadlock with Spain continued, the hope for an easy solution to the business problems effected by the

17. *Ibid.*, Appendix, 1–48. For the additional plans, see "Plan of Operations Against Spain," December 17, 1896, in RG 38, NA. For Roosevelt's urging of an amphibious landing and his view of the Army's role, see TR to William W. Kimball, November 19, 1897, in MRL, I, 717.

18. John D. Long Journal, in John D. Long Papers.

dispute faded. Businessmen still thought that war was disruptive, disorderly, and expensive, but eventually began to look upon a Cuban war as a necessary evil.

McKinley's hesitation even after the *Maine* incident of February 15, 1898, reflected the business community's initial reluctance to support a war. During March and April, business opinion dramatically changed from insistence on a diplomatic settlement to an eagerness to settle the dispute quickly and by military means. War fever reflected the intense nationalism of the time, but until the business community's shift in March, passion for war was confined to mass popular opinion encouraged by an inflammatory press.[19]

Hope for a peaceful settlement had been unrealistic from the start. Spain remained intransigent and unyielding. Clumsy Spanish diplomacy made the problem worse, but the Spanish were ideologically incapable of reaching a compromise except by force. Political nationalism rather than economic nationalism—imperialism—fanned the flames of discord. Three conflicting nationalisms—Cuban, American, and Spanish—each equally intense, were all based more on emotion, not self-interest. When a fourth nationalism was added to the conflict, that of Filipino independence, the war of 1898 became more a religious war than a conflict for expansion.

It was William W. Kimball, rather than Theodore Roosevelt or William Randolph Hearst, who masterminded the war of 1898 with Spain. Kimball's "War with Spain—1896," written in the avowedly anti-imperialist administration of Grover Cleveland and dated June 1, 1896, is a strategic naval document and not an ideological statement. It became the major naval text of the decade. Captain Alfred Thayer Mahan may have created the theoretical foundations used by a generation of would-be imperialists, but Kimball created a practical blueprint that enabled America, a relatively weak and unprepared nation, to wage an effective and ultimately victorious war with a nation most other world powers considered superior to the United States in ability, in naval preparation, and in the will to fight. Kimball's plan is the decisive cata-

19. Walter LaFeber, *The New Empire* (Ithaca, 1963), 354–406, gives an excellent chronology of the change in American mood from confidence in peace to the inevitability of war.

lyst and elusive first cause of the American victory in the Spanish-American War of 1898.

Even in American domestic politics, the suggestion that the American debate centered on the opposing ideologies of imperialism and anti-imperialism is misleading. The American political conflict is best exemplified by the bizarre relationship between Secretary of the Navy John D. Long and his assistant secretary, Theodore Roosevelt. The two men disagreed on fundamentals from the start. Long was a New England pacifist who hated war. Theodore Roosevelt's position is more difficult to describe. He seemed to exult in the romantic notion of war, eagerly urged war as an effective American policy, and was quick to volunteer whenever a war threatened. Yet Theodore Roosevelt does not fit the mold of the classic imperialist. Not only was he ignorant (and innocent) of the economic basis of imperialism, he was at odds with most of the business community. Roosevelt regarded the businessman as a pacifist too concerned with material and economic matters to be able or willing to defend himself or his country from attack. It can be argued that strategic expansion is another form of imperialism, and Roosevelt is vulnerable to such a charge. But a man as innocent as Roosevelt of economic motivation makes a poor candidate for the role of America's leading imperial spokesman. And John D. Long, his superior and ideological adversary, understood as little about European economic imperialism as Roosevelt.

The two men constantly battled, but not over an ideological concept that remained foreign to American interest at the time. European imperialism was not the issue. Roosevelt did not want colonies, nor did he ever think in terms of trade or markets. He feared European aggression and European nationalism and felt that the new naval technology had eliminated the great natural buffer that had protected America until steel and steam replaced wood and wind in warships. John Long lived in the world of an older generation. His America was provincial; its main interests were domestic. For Long, politics was more interesting, significant, and essential than anything to do with navies or diplomacy.

Neither man was as extreme as he appeared to the other; they worked well together except when the crisis of the impending war with Spain seemed to overwhelm the normal peacetime routine. The two men represented President McKinley's shrewd attempt to neutralize the prowar and propeace factions within his own party and the country. John D. Long, an old Republican politician, a friend of McKinley, and former governor of Massachusetts, was recovering from a serious middle-age illness. Both Long and McKinley saw the post of secretary of the Navy as one that would enable Long to mend his political fences, make new contacts in national government, and recuperate in a government position that was responsible but not overly demanding.[20]

McKinley carefully chose Roosevelt as the Navy Department's second civilian in command. Traditionally the administrative burden of the Navy Department falls upon the assistant secretary, who should be young, eager, vigorous, and willing to do most of the work. Roosevelt was exceptionally qualified professionally and politically. Since becoming a professional politician, loyal to the Republican party in the 1884 presidential election in spite of his early opposition to Blaine's nomination, Theodore Roosevelt was entitled to consideration for appointive positions in any national government headed by a Republican president. When McKinley defeated Bryan in 1896, Roosevelt, who was active in the campaign, was a natural candidate for a position somewhere in the government.

Because Theodore Roosevelt was known as a partisan of expansion and as a colorful leader in the reform wing of the party, McKinley had to choose a position for Roosevelt that was not overly sensitive. Roosevelt, however, who wanted responsibility, was well suited for the Navy Department and used all the political pull he could muster to get the post of assistant secretary of the Navy. Senator Lodge forcefully lobbied with the president, who understood Roosevelt's potential political value as an administration spokesman and officer representing the substantial expansionist sentiment within the party. McKinley insisted as a condition of appointment that Roosevelt not allow his own convictions to interfere with his administrative duties. Roosevelt pledged his loyalty, a vow he honestly fulfilled. The team of Long and Roosevelt functioned well enough together until the debate became a crisis and later a war. Only then did the accommodation of the two men fall apart with considerable acrimony on both sides.

John D. Long was mainly a domestic politician. He cared little and

20. John D. Long Journal, in Long Papers.

knew less about the operations of a Navy and was horrified by the idea of war. For most of the nineteenth century, Long would have made an ideal secretary of the Navy. In 1898 he was close to a disaster. Long consistently refused to take the threat of war with Spain seriously and remained convinced even to the day when war was declared that Spain would back down and grant all American demands. He also felt the Spanish were fundamentally innocent and that newspapers and war advocates like Theodore Roosevelt were responsible for Spain's authoritarian image.

Theodore Roosevelt was convinced the Spanish were not innocent, that they practiced the diplomacy of delay, and that they would eventually go to war with America rather than give in to American demands. Roosevelt feared that if people like Long failed to take the Spanish threat seriously, even a nation as weak as Spain could win a naval war with the United States with disastrous long-term consequences for future American security. Both Roosevelt and Long were completely innocent of the ideas of economic empire that recent revisionist historians suggest as the main cause of the war of 1898. Roosevelt's and Long's arguments were always strategic.

To make the battle between Roosevelt and Long a paradigm for abstract American imperialism and anti-imperialism is absurd. Theodore Roosevelt in his own way was as conservative as Long. Roosevelt's world view also centered upon America. He simply feared that the geographcial advantages of the past were no longer sufficient for the present and future. Roosevelt's ideology involved expansion only as a tactical exercise that would prevent other nations from threatening American interests or taking Americans too lightly. For Roosevelt the best defense was attack—but not for material purposes. Long and Roosevelt agreed that the first priority was America's safety from foreign intervention. They differed in their assessment of American ability to defend itself. Long insisted that the ocean and American goodwill were sufficient defenses. His opinion was grounded in nostalgia and sentiment, and he remained indifferent to the new naval technology that made the old, natural defenses obsolete.

Roosevelt feared that America was not only unprepared to fight, but that the unwillingness to prepare would eventually tempt an opportunistic European power to test American ability and resolve. By then Roosevelt felt the struggle could be lost before it even began. Both sides were shrill, tended toward hyperbole, and predicted doom if the other's policies were followed. The debate was intense and passionate. But it had little to do with imitating European imperialism or with American economic expansion. The most significant discussions, which took place within the naval hierarchy, concerned primary targets in a possible war and the merits and defects of the Kimball, Taylor, and Sicard plans, not potential markets or the advantages or disadvantages of colonialism. The arguments centered on how the changes in naval technology and the obvious intensification of European ambitions and world nationalism affected the United States.[21]

The public political debate over questions of American expansion was not nearly as ideologically neat as our historical summaries make it appear. Neither side made much sense most of the time. Theodore Roosevelt was given to grandiose overstatement and some bloodthirsty whims. In 1886 he looked eagerly to a possible armed intervention with Mexico and in 1891 exulted over the possibility of killing some "dagos" in a threatened war with Chile.[22] Even by the late 1890s when he had achieved some power as assistant secretary of the Navy, Roosevelt's expansionist views frequently tended to be frenzied and confused. Part of the problem for Roosevelt, as for the group that opposed expansion and change, was a naïveté about the possibilities actually open to America at the time, an ignorance of other countries' policies, and a total confusion over the state of the newly aggressive powers of Germany and Japan and Britain's reaction to them.

Both sides of the imperialist and anti-imperialist argument were only in small part ideological. Both adversaries were feeling their way along uncharted waters; American confusion was only a part of the problem. The Europeans were at least as confused. Even world powers such as Britain were terrified at times. Germany and Japan wrestled with possible opportunities, but all of the nations involved were caught up in the

21. See Peter Karsten, "The Nature of Influence," *American Quarterly*, 23 (1971), 585–600, for a better understanding of Roosevelt's role as a leader of the naval intellectuals and the nature of the naval debates of the 1890s.

22. TR to Henry Cabot Lodge, August 10, 1886, in MRL, I, 108; Henry Pringle, *Theodore Roosevelt: A Biography* (New York, 1931), 166–67.

massive confusion that was almost wholly strategic. By 1897 classic imperialism appeared dangerous and overly expensive in terms of competition and administration. Fear of the kaiser's obvious ambitions, China's
weakness, the temptations of seizing more of China or Latin America,
and the arguments in favor of preventing other seizures were more important than the ideological arguments used as rationales for purely
strategic options. The relationship between Roosevelt and Long is one
of the best examples of the confusion over ideological differences.

For years Theodore Roosevelt had pushed for the annexation of Hawaii—not for the sugar, but to prevent the Japanese from taking it. He
feared that if the Japanese took Hawaii other American interests would
be harder to defend and that the initial appearance of weakness might
encourage the Japanese or other nations to make further incursions
closer to America. Only by being able to prevent any nation's seizure of
potentially important strategic areas could the United States hope to
survive in a new and more volatile world. In 1897 Roosevelt wrote
Mahan, "If we refuse those islands then I honestly hope England will
take them."[23] Neither Long nor Theodore Roosevelt even vaguely understood what the other was arguing. Long thought Roosevelt's attempts at preparedness were a form of warmongering and dismissed
them as incitements to war; Roosevelt regarded Long as incredibly
naïve and tried to educate him, to no avail. President McKinley, by listening carefully to both of his aides, was able to reach a better understanding of America's strategic options.

Long's and Roosevelt's major friction developed in 1898 when the
diplomatic crisis between the United States and Spain deepened to a
prospect of war. In 1897 the two squabbled and argued over their obvious differences on the desirability of going to war, but these disagreements did not affect the work of the Navy Department. In his address to
the Naval War College on June 2, 1897, Roosevelt told the naval officers
that "to be prepared for war is the most effectual means to promote
peace."[24] There is no evidence that President McKinley was disturbed,

23. TR to William McKinley, April 22, 1897, in MRL, I, 601, 601*n*; TR to Alfred T.
Mahan, May 3, 1897, in MRL, I, 608; TR to Mahan, June 9, 1897, in MRL, I, 622; TR
to Henry Cabot Lodge, June 17, 1897, in MRL, I, 627; Roosevelt to Mahan, December 9, 1897, in MRL, I, 726.
24. TR, "Washington's Forgotten Maxim," rpr. in *Works, Nat. Ed.*, XIII, 182–99,
182.

or that he regarded what Roosevelt said in public as a breach of Roosevelt's pledge to carry out the duties of his office regardless of intellectual differences with others in the administration. McKinley regarded Roosevelt's views as valid, recognized political support for them within the party and country, and used Roosevelt as an expert adviser on naval strategy and America's preparations for defense.

On September 21, 1897, Theodore Roosevelt conferred with the president over dinner and the two men continued the conversations the next day while horseback riding. If William McKinley did not know of the Kimball war plan before the Roosevelt meetings, he certainly knew about it afterwards. Theodore Roosevelt gave McKinley a thorough summary of the war plan, which constituted official Navy Department policy at the time. In addition Theodore Roosevelt discussed with the president the precise location of every American warship, the availability of other ships for purchase, and gave a thorough endorsement of the major assumptions of attack made by Kimball. The president may still have not known where the Philippines were, as he claimed in his early comments after war had broken out, but he did know that the Philippines were one of the Navy's first targets within reach of a substantial naval force commanded by his own appointee, Commodore Dewey.[25]

Roosevelt was not bashful in advising the appropriate authorities—including Kimball, Long, and the president—of the Navy's strategic and tactical options. Writing to Kimball on November 19, 1897, Roosevelt still was not sure that war was inevitable: "The war will have to, or at least ought to, come sooner or later." He approved of McKinley's "combined firmness and temperateness" in dealing with Spain, and agreed with Kimball's idea that the fleet should "move on Manila at once." Roosevelt's proposed tactical deployment is detailed and well thought out. The point of Roosevelt's letter is the same as all the Navy's contingency planning: if war does come "we should prepare for it well in advance." In December Roosevelt remained doubtful that "those Spaniards can really pacify Cuba and if the insurrection goes on longer I don't see how we can help interfering." But Roosevelt's views were entirely strategic and global. "Germany is the power with whom I look

25. TR to Henry Cabot Lodge, September 21, 1897, in MRL, I, 685–86.

forward to serious difficulty." In listing the advantages of a war with Spain, Roosevelt lists humanity and self-interest. But self-interest for Roosevelt was not a matter of economics, but rather "of taking one more step toward the complete freeing of America from European domination."[26]

McKinley continued to work for a peaceful solution after his meetings with Roosevelt; Roosevelt and the Navy Department continued to implement the details of the Kimball war plan. Roosevelt at no time took over any additional powers that previous assistant secretaries had not exercised. Long and Theodore Roosevelt had worked out their arrangements when Roosevelt became Long's assistant in March, 1897. As in previous administrations, the assistant secretary became the acting secretary when the secretary was out of the office. Long took many days and afternoons off, and Roosevelt, who did most of the administrative work already, simply added the additional secretarial duties (mainly clerical and administrative) to his work load. When a congressman questioned the extent of Roosevelt's new powers, he was assured by Assistant Secretary Howell that "the powers of Mr. Roosevelt do not begin to compare with those possessed by Mr. McAdoo," Roosevelt's predecessor in the Grover Cleveland administration and later Woodrow Wilson's secretary of the treasury.[27]

Before the war crisis put the two men in violent opposition, Long frequently praised Roosevelt's "great ability and usefulness." The sinking of the battleship *Maine* on February 15, 1898, made an already volatile crisis one that tilted toward eventual war. Ironically the sending of the *Maine* to Havana was intended as a gesture of goodwill and the sinking of the ship sent shock waves through the American public. Most Americans doubted that there might be some reasonable explanation for the sinking. For Secretary Long the sinking of the *Maine* changed nothing. He repeatedly wrote in his journal of continued hopes for peace and his faith in Spanish goodwill. And at the same time, Long

26. TR to William W. Kimball, November 19, 1897, in MRL, I, 716–18, and December 17, 1897, MRL, I, 743; for the Naval War College's view that Britain, not Germany, was a potential enemy, see Ronald Spector, "Who Planned the Attack on Manila Bay?" *Mid-America*, LIII (1971), 100–101.

27. William Howell to John J. Fitzgerald, May 1, 1897, Assistant Secretary's Letterbooks, I, 311, RG 80, NA.

began to argue with Roosevelt's execution of naval department policy in Long's absence, suggesting in his journal that Roosevelt somehow was changing policy, rather than simply implementing it in accordance with normal procedure.[28]

The writings of the two men bear witness to the confusion. On February 25, following Theodore Roosevelt's celebrated cable to Dewey, Long questioned Roosevelt's judgment and accused him of going "off very impulsively." On February 26, Long charged that Roosevelt "in his precipitate way, has come very near causing more of an explosion than happened on the Maine." Long cited preemptory orders—ship movements, ammunition disbursements, and suggestions to Congress for additional naval funds—and charged that Roosevelt "had gone at things like a bull in a China shop." Many historians have accepted at face value the charges that Theodore Roosevelt usurped Long's authority and precipitated the war between America and Spain that began two months later. The accusations are nonsensical. Long resented Roosevelt's ability to get things done and reacted to his growing realization that many scheduled matters at the Navy Department received attention only when the secretary was not around. Theodore Roosevelt was a superb administrator and resembled a whirlwind when performing the duties of his office.[29]

Roosevelt's telegram to Dewey sent late Friday could have been countermanded by either Long or the president, and would have been if Roosevelt had actually exceeded his authority. Roosevelt's order to Dewey remained in effect until hostilities did begin, and Commodore Dewey sailed to do battle with the Spanish fleet. Because the Navy had been on war alert since the middle of January, all American squadrons had been apprised, even before the sinking of the *Maine*, that preparations for a war with Spain were serious and urgent. On the very day

28. John D. Long to George Hale, March 23, 1897, in Agnes C. Storer Collection, 1776–1922, Massachusetts Historical Society. The Storer Collection contains some John D. Long letters; Long Journal, in Long Papers.

29. John D. Long Journal, February 25–26, 1898, in Long Papers; for good examples of Roosevelt's initiative, see the detailed tactical plans in TR to John D. Long, January 14, 1898, in MRL, II, 759–63, and January 22, 1898, in Long Papers. One of the best accounts of Roosevelt's administrative ability is in Charles Flint, *Memories of an Active Life* (New York, 1923), 105–107.

following Roosevelt's supposedly incendiary and unauthorized order, Secretary Long himself ordered all American ships, including Dewey's squadron, to "keep vessels filled with the best coal to be had." [30]

Roosevelt's routine correspondence as assistant secretary offers clear evidence that Secretary Long was out of touch with the procedures and operations of his department. Nine days before the cable to Dewey, Assistant Secretary Roosevelt was sending detailed intelligence reports of Spanish vessels in both European and Cuban waters. The correspondence is clearly a routine part of ongoing American war preparations and not an extraordinary war warning or a dramatic departure from procedure. Roosevelt included an intelligence report showing the Spanish view of the relative standing of the two navies (Spain was superior according to the best Spanish intelligence). Roosevelt in an informal handwritten note asks the American commander, "Is there any information you desire about the armor of these vessels?" [31]

The naval bureaucracy was much better at gathering the information than in disseminating it. The Roosevelt letter was received ten days after it was sent. One ONI report of February 26 is marked received on April 6, 1898. But there can be no question that the Americans were serious. Included in Roosevelt's report is an ONI contingency plan for shipping war materials from Europe, through Antwerp, if war with Spain occurred. Secretary Long's surprise at his department's war preparations and the activity of his assistant secretary is at odds with the routine records of the department in Washington and of American naval operating forces throughout the world.

Just one day before the Roosevelt-Dewey order, on February 24, 1898, the press, hoping for an incident that would avenge the *Maine*, objected vehemently to the visit in New York harbor by the Spanish battleship *Vizcaya*. One newspaper offered its readers instructions, verging on incitement, on how to blow up a battleship. In the upper echelons of the Navy Department, Theodore Roosevelt alone worried about a possible attack on the *Vizcaya* by angry citizens; finally after a week of serious pleading he convinced Secretary Long to dispatch a United

30. Henry Cabot Lodge Chronology, in Lodge Papers.
31. TR to Commander in Chief, U.S. Naval Forces, North Atlantic Station, U.S. Flagship *New York*, February 16, 1898, in RG 313.

States naval escort to prevent another incident.[32] Roosevelt, the legendary warmonger, was doing his most to preserve a peace he did not want.

Secretary John Long had become unnerved as the threat of war, always unreal to him, became not only probable but imminent. He became much more querulous and at times irrational. He objected to anything that had to do with war, naval efficiency, or contingency preparations. Most of his neurotic displeasure found a ready target in Roosevelt. But there were others. On March 2, 1898, Long wrote a diatribe against battleships, which he found not "really desirable" and which, he objected, "draw so much water." He went further than mere dislike. He tried to deny the routine request for tugs during the *Massachusetts'* stay in port. There is much wringing of hands and soul searching in Long's journal, along with accounts of meetings with a worried but far more realistic McKinley and, whenever possible, a grasping at straws for any hopeful news from Spain.

The nation had probably begun to see the necessity of war as early as the blowing up of the *Maine* on February 15. When the Germans occupied parts of the Chinese province of Shantung on March 6, 1898, many American businessmen previously opposed to war began to look upon it as an inevitable evil, taking the German occupation as a further European threat to American freedom of trade, since Shantung was the key American access to mainland China. Theodore Roosevelt saw Japanese intervention in Asia and the Pacific as the main threat to American supply lines and strategic interests. Even so, one of the more striking pieces of evidence that Theodore Roosevelt's orders of February 26 were purely routine, and John Long's objections irrational and overstated, is a letter Roosevelt wrote on February 25. Writing in answer to a query addressed to the Navy Department, Roosevelt told a friend, "I don't believe there will be any war."[33] Theodore Roosevelt was simply implementing regular Navy Department policy following the schedule already worked out in conjunction with the Kimball war plan, a plan that was followed not only by Theodore Roosevelt, but by John Long, and the commander in chief, President William McKinley.

32. TR to John D. Long, February 17, 1898, in Long Papers.
33. TR to Dr. F. M. Briggs, February 25, 1898, Assistant Secretary's Letterpress books, in RG 80.

How then did the Roosevelt-Dewey cable get blown out of proportion so badly that most American historians still regard it as the primary cause of the war? The answer is twofold: The Navy Department, after the fact, became embarrassed at how well prepared it had been for the war with Spain—thanks to Kimball's war plan. And Henry Cabot Lodge, the scholar in politics, fabricated a legend to make his history of the war more colorful and to help his political friend Theodore Roosevelt become a legendary national hero.

On the day when Roosevelt sent Commodore Dewey the legendary telegram, Lodge was keeping Roosevelt company at the Navy Department. Lodge knew intimately from Roosevelt the day-to-day routine of the department and was privy as a leading senator in Congress to material that might normally be considered classified; at the time he had not thought his day with Roosevelt would have special historical significance. Only after the war with Spain occurred did Lodge think about the history of the war. *Harper's Monthly* commissioned a two-part series that would subsequently be published as a book. Henry Cabot Lodge's *The War with Spain* is more detailed than most journalistic accounts, partly because Lodge and Roosevelt had long pondered the theoretical possibilities of war. But Lodge had a unique problem in writing his history. Since he had access to inside information as a senator and was present as history was being made, Lodge wanted to tread softly in writing of the historical causes of the Spanish-American War. He desperately needed something other than inside information to buttress his account of the war and make it more like history than political saber rattling or gossip.[34]

The Navy Department also had its problems. The naval war had gone so well that the Navy was loath to admit to the Kimball war plan for fear that the press and the anti-imperialist political activists would suggest that the Navy brought about the war by the thoroughness of its preparations. The argument was plausible enough to make the Navy's reluctance understandable, especially since even most Americans assumed that the United States was still a backward nation and that any Euro-

34. Henry Cabot Lodge to Captain Arent S. Crowninshield, September 21, 1898, in Lodge Papers; Lodge, "War with Spain," *Harper's New Monthly Magazine*, XCVIII, (March, 1899), 512–25.

pean navy should prove a match for nascent American militarism. Lodge himself demonstrates in *Harper's* the relative equality of the two naval forces that eventually engaged at Manila Bay. The Americans won not because they had the better ships or because the Spanish navy was decrepit (it was, but no more so than the American), but because Commodore Dewey was a brilliant tactical commander, the Spanish leader was not nearly as good, and the Americans were both skillful and lucky in making the most of their initial tactical advantage.[35]

In September, 1898, Lodge formally requested the official Dewey order from Captain Arent S. Crowninshield of the Naval War Board, explaining his need for supporting historical documentary evidence. Crowninshield, who had been present with Lodge and Roosevelt on the day the telegram was sent, refused to furnish Lodge with the information and wrote that the Navy Department feared criticism for being overprepared. Lodge then told Crowninshield that he would protect the Navy Department by making Theodore Roosevelt the author of the order. "I will say that the order was sent by Mr. Roosevelt as Acting Secretary, and I have no doubt that the Colonel of the Rough Riders will accept the responsibility of being over prepared with perfect equanimity."[36]

Thus was born the legend of the Roosevelt-Dewey telegram. Lodge, with the approval of the Naval War Board, shifted the responsibility for the Dewey order from the Navy to Theodore Roosevelt. Crowninshield himself was surprised when he looked over the chronology of orders and saw that the preparations had indeed begun even before February 25, 1898. He reiterated the fear of public misunderstanding that it "might look a little too much as if the administration or the Department or both, had made up their minds that they were going to have a fight anyway, whether Spain wanted it or not."[37]

To make sure that the historical implications were not lost in the drama, Crowninshield sent Lodge a chronology that set forth the Navy's impressive preparations for the contingency of a war with Spain. The

35. Lodge, "War with Spain," 522.
36. Captain Arent S. Crowninshield to Henry Cabot Lodge, September 19, 1898; Lodge to Crowninshield, September 21, 1898, both in Lodge Papers.
37. Captain Arent S. Crowninshield to Henry Cabot Lodge, September 24, 1898, in Lodge Papers.

memorandum is still present in the Henry Cabot Lodge Papers at the Massachusetts Historical Society and is confirmed in greater detail in the official records of the Navy in the annual reports of 1898 and 1899, matters of public record. Lodge's history magnified Roosevelt's role in the war of 1898 and made the Dewey telegram a unique communiqué, rather than a routine order in a long series of contingency moves, which would be minor historical footnotes had the United States and Spain been able to settle their dispute diplomatically. The overwhelming weight of historical evidence now shows that the Spanish had no desire to settle the Cuban matter peacefully, that indeed the Spanish were convinced that Europe would bail them out of any difficulties with America. Until the recent scholarship of John A. S. Grenville and George Berkeley Young, Theodore Roosevelt's decisive role as spokesman and fomenter of the war of 1898 has been widely accepted by historians, who often combine that distortion with the image of Theodore Roosevelt as an impulsive bellicose leader, further confusing both Roosevelt's and America's role in the tragic Philippine-American War of 1898–1902.[38]

By the end of March, 1898, Theodore Roosevelt was convinced that a war with Spain was likely if not inevitable. He had already planned to join a local volunteer regiment to fight in the war. When the war began, Roosevelt resigned his position as assistant secretary of the Navy in spite of the determined efforts of all his friends and family to dissuade him. Theodore Roosevelt's exuberance for war and bloodshed have made many historians wary of his human qualities. One must question the apparently unseemly haste, not only of 1898 but in previous American crises—Mexico in 1886 and Chile in 1891—in which Roosevelt wrote almost lyrically of the possible slaying of enemies.[39]

The evidence is clearly given in his letters, which out of context seem to demonstrate a bloodthirsty, insensitive man. But the letters cannot be taken out of context. Theodore Roosevelt was more complex than the

38. See for example, William H. Harbaugh, *The Life and Times of Theodore Roosevelt* (Rev. ed., New York, 1975), 98; Howard K. Beale, *Theodore Roosevelt and the Rise of America to World Power* (Baltimore, 1956), 63; both works are primarily sympathetic to Roosevelt. Pringle, *Theodore Roosevelt: A Biography*, 178, is somewhat harsher.
39. Harbaugh, *The Life and Times of Theodore Roosevelt*, 88–89, gives a good summary.

most pithy comments indicate. Some of the letters, which in isolation would indicate their author to be a war-hungry savage, also show a man driven by a complex sense of duty. Theodore Roosevelt's idea of war also included the idealistic conviction that it was the duty of leaders who promoted wars to also fight in them, that war was not simply a matter for poor people, but a duty to be shared equally in a democratic society.

In 1898 Roosevelt was adamant about his duty. Anyone who advocated a warlike policy, he wrote, must "be willing himself to bear the brunt of carrying out that policy." He saw it as his duty to fight. Politically, Roosevelt's move was dangerous. If he remained in Washington as a leader of the interventionists, and of the now heralded Navy Department, he could make enormous political capital. The likelihood of becoming a hero in a volunteer regiment was slight. Most volunteers wound up drilling in the hot Texas sun for a moment of combat that never came.[40]

William Jennings Bryan, who was also a volunteer colonel in the war of 1898, suffered oblivion, a more common result of war than fame. Bryan is remembered primarily as a pacifist in World War I and not as a hero in 1898. Theodore Roosevelt was well aware that the war could turn out to be a personal fiasco; he was also aware that staying in Washington was preferable to leaving his wife and family. "I am not acting in a spirit of recklessness or levity, or purely for my own selfish enjoyment. I don't want to be shot at any more than anyone else does; still less to die of yellow fever. I am altogether too fond of my wife and children, and enjoy the good things of this life too much to wish lightly to hazard their loss, or to go away from my family." The 1898 decision was a painful one for Theodore Roosevelt; Edith had been seriously ill and for a time there were doubts about her survival. It was a terrible time to go off to a war. Roosevelt felt he had no choice.[41]

John Long, who thought Roosevelt was foolish to leave Washington

40. TR to Douglas Robinson, April 2, 1898, in MRL, II, 809; see also TR to Alexander Lambert, April 1, 1898, in MRL, II, 807–809; TR to William Sturgis Bigelow, March 29, 1898, in MRL, II, 801–803; TR to Paul Dana, April 18, 1898, in MRL, II, 816–18; Joseph B. Bishop, *Theodore Roosevelt and His Times* (2 vols.; New York, 1920), I, 101–107.
41. TR to Alexander Lambert, April 1, 1898, in MRL, II, 808.

just at the time of an enormous political success, later amended his skeptical diary entry with the note that Roosevelt had been right. Roosevelt's going to war led straight to the presidency, Long exclaimed. He was wrong on both counts. Theodore Roosevelt did return as a national war hero, and because of his new popularity, he was nominated for governor of New York. But his victory in New York came in spite of his war record, not because of it; Roosevelt came close to political oblivion in the governor's race and was saved only by a fluke of domestic politics having nothing to do with the war. One political observer was specific and pessimistic: "Teddy will get left, too much Rough Rider business and not enough national issues." But Roosevelt had enlisted because of duty—not politics or dreams of glory. Once he was in the war he acquitted himself well; his legendary charge up San Juan Hill made his choice seem politically logical. But he could just as easily have suffered the same fate as William Jennings Bryan, the forgotten man, or even worse have become a casualty of Spanish bullets or yellow fever.[42]

Many biographers take Roosevelt's exuberance in the war at face value. He did exult in the violence. But Roosevelt's war letters reveal much more than joy at the sight of an enemy's blood. On reading Roosevelt's boast to Cabot Lodge, "Did I tell you that I killed a Spaniard with my own hand," and other equally violent descriptions of personal satisfaction during the war, one historian, usually sympathetic to Roosevelt, regards his actions as desecrations of the human spirit. Perhaps. At the same time Roosevelt talks about killing a Spaniard, he writes despairingly of the suffering of wounded troops, and coolly of comparative historical military strategy. Theodore Roosevelt well understood the uniqueness of the frontal assault upon San Juan, a "deed that European military writers consider utterly impossible of performance . . . to attack over open ground unshaken infantry armed with the best modern repeating rifles behind a formidable system of entrenchments."[43]

Roosevelt's frontal charge up San Juan Hill on July 1, 1898, was in the grand United States military tradition, exemplified earlier by Ulys-

42. For the governor's race, see G. Wallace Chessman, *Governor Theodore Roosevelt* (Cambridge, Mass., 1965); George Lyman to Henry Cabot Lodge, October 18, 1898, in Lodge Papers.
43. Harbaugh, *The Life and Times of Theodore Roosevelt*, 107; TR to Henry Cabot Lodge, July 19, 1898, in MRL, II, 853, 852.

ses Grant's Civil War strategy and later by Dwight Eisenhower's D-day invasion. The charge up San Juan was a calculated recklessness possible, perhaps, only for a volunteer regiment or a group of inspired amateurs, and as Roosevelt himself thought, a tactical triumph in spite of the odds against it. By focusing on either the recklessness of the charge or the exultation following the victory, biographers have made a many-sided man seem like a simpleton; by emphasizing the political success that followed the war, others have made Roosevelt's war performance an exercise in opportunistic politics at least as morally shocking as the apparent truculence.

These explorations of Theodore Roosevelt's motives are historically irrelevant. There is no simple correct answer to the question of whether Roosevelt was a man of war or a man of peace. He was both. But the question may well be as misleading as either answer. Because of Roosevelt's strong statements in favor of war, many historians refuse to take any part of the man seriously. Yet much of Roosevelt's enthusiasm, especially in his letters from the front, were exultations not simply in war itself, but in the fact that America's strength came in part from aristocrats like Theodore Roosevelt who were not afraid to fight or die for their country, and who were unwilling to delegate the nasty business of war solely to the poor.

Roosevelt feared the materialism of most of the businessmen and fellow politicians who shrank from actual fighting. He feared America might be as defenseless as China, which at one time was rich, powerful, and too proud to fight. That a leader in the government could kill an enemy if necessary struck Roosevelt as a more responsible course of action than middle-age pacifism. He could write as tellingly about the terrors of a soldier on a battlefield as he could about slaying a Spaniard. But biographers and historians quote Theodore Roosevelt's gorier words and create the impression that only the blood and killing interested him. Historians picking up the biographer's quotes conclude that the man indeed was a belligerent imperialist, and the distortions of the legend come full circle.

We may never fully comprehend all of the rationales, the real motives, or the consequences of Theodore Roosevelt's decision to fight in the war of 1898, his relationship to war, or his ultimate feelings toward war

133

and peace. But the man is more complex than the myth, and when he became president, Roosevelt became a man of peace, though his utterances still sounded warlike to both friends and foes. The image of Theodore Roosevelt as the irresponsible warrior has persisted in the historical literature of sympathizers and critics alike, distorting the more complex historical reality of Theodore Roosevelt—a man who knew only too well and at first hand the horrors of war, and who during his presidency worked with all his ability to successfully preserve the fragile state of world peace.

5/ The Legend of Anti-Imperialism
Theodore Roosevelt and the Not-So-Splendid War For Philippine Independence, 1896–1902

The war with Spain in 1898 was not the "splendid little war" of John Hay's memory but a brutal and closely contested land and sea war between two untested powers. The United States won the war not because God smiled on President McKinley, or because Theodore Roosevelt was braver than the Spaniards he fought, but because the Americans won the decisive first battle at Manila Bay and remained marginally more skillful and extremely more lucky as the war progressed. Once the Spanish lost in the Philippines, it was unlikely that they could recoup those losses in Cuba, which was closer to the American mainland. The best the Spanish could hope for was a stalemate; with the help of yellow fever they came extremely close to achieving a deadlock. The war with Spain was comprehensible if not splendid. The American war with the Philippines that followed was a miserable and monumental mistake, a war that served no purpose and should not have been fought.

The very strength of William W. Kimball's "War with Spain—1896" was its ultimate Achilles' heel. Because Kimball had not allowed politics or ideology to mar the purity of a tactical and strategic plan, he never went beyond the naval contingencies. When Commodore Dewey dispatched the Spanish fleet at Manila Bay on May 1, 1898, the United States had exceeded the highest hopes of Kimball's war plan. Not only was the Spanish Asian fleet eliminated from any possible harassment of the Americans, it ceased to exist at all.

Unfortunately for the Americans, Spanish civil authority and its power to govern went the way of the sunken Spanish navy. The Americans were now beyond the protective theoretical confines of the Kimball plan. No one had considered the political consequences of a total military victory. Even the victorious Dewey, uneasy with the enormity of his success, kept the news of his smashing victory a virtual secret for over a week, leaving Washington even more unprepared for the political consequences of naval supremacy.

Dewey and the Americans were faced with simple but monumental problems. International law and custom prohibited any help from neutral nations. By law Dewey's vessels were no longer welcome at Hong Kong, the closest friendly port; if Dewey sailed into any neutral port to refuel or to buy supplies, international law required the neutral power to intern the ships and their crews for the duration of the war. Dewey's squadron may have been victorious, but it was also homeless and a long way from a friendly base. Lost in the more dramatic stories of Commodore Dewey's heroic exploits and Theodore Roosevelt's cable is the simplest and most direct cause of America's continued involvement in the Philippines. Once the Spanish were eliminated the Americans could sail off into any Asian port for a peaceful internment, or they could remain in Manila using the Philippines as a new home base. The Americans had no choice but to stay.

The initial decision to attack the Philippines came from the implementation of the Kimball war plan of 1896. Dewey and America, however, quickly discovered that winning one decisive naval victory created more problems than it solved. After Dewey's victory, the Americans had no attractive alternatives. Politically, William McKinley was one of the shrewdest of American presidents. He must have shuddered at the political consequences of simply leaving the Philippines. The newspaper headlines are easily imaginable: "McKinley Turns Tail," and "Americans Leave Filipinos in Lurch." American ideals as well as politics made leaving impossible.

The many Americans who believed that saving the Cubans from an authoritarian Spanish regime was necessary and commendable may have been somewhat naïve in their belief in messianic democracy, but not entirely. The Cubans did need help. The Americans were their only likely allies. But what should be done with Cuba afterwards? Americans were both idealistic and practical. Most businessmen shrank from giving Cuba absolute freedom for fear that Cubans would seize American property or, equally onerous, that revolutionaries would take control of trade relations between the United States and Cuba. Limited autonomy and responsibility were good pragmatic American solutions for maintaining enough control for practical purposes, while avoiding the unattractive administrative and moral costs of outright colonialism. Because the problem of what to do with Cuba after Spanish rule had been well considered, the Americans were not as uncertain when dealing with a total victory over the Spanish in Cuba or, to a lesser degree, in Puerto Rico. But the Philippines remained a complete puzzle. How could the Americans of 1898 realize that there were in fact three separate wars involved in the Philippines. The first was the American naval action against Spain, primarily involving Cuba. But the second, the Filipino war of independence against Spain, was almost unnoticed and certainly unheralded.

When the Filipinos declared war against Spain in August, 1896, they had begun a milestone in modern history, for the Filipino-Spanish war for independence was the first of the Asian colonial wars for freedom in the late nineteenth and early twentieth centuries. The war between Spain and the Philippines appeared to be independent of the "other" war between America and Spain. The Americans could not understand that in Filipino eyes the only war was the Filipino war for independence. Whether the enemy was Spanish or American made no difference. The Americans never came to terms with Filipino culture, Filipino political ambitions, or colonial claims to nationalism. Most Americans, if they thought about such matters, still considered themselves colonial people or even a revolutionary force rather than an imperial world power.

America was somewhere between the two worlds. Americans still cherished their anticolonial heritage, which was recent enough to remain imbedded in historical memory. Because of sympathy for oppressed colonies, the Americans soon developed a feeling that the Philippines could not simply be abandoned. Why save the Cubans and forsake the Filipinos? What kind of logic would excuse the turnaround? Weren't the Filipinos as badly treated as the Cubans and by the same Spanish? How could America argue that fighting to free Cubans from tyranny was different from freeing Filipinos? Indeed, the Asians were even more oppressed. The Filipinos were poorer, less organized, less articulate, and

137

even less capable than the Cubans, it seemed, to effectively govern themselves.

As McKinley agonized, the moral dilemma remained unchanged. No one in America wanted the responsibility of colonies. By 1898 the lesson of the Boers in Africa, the Cubans and Filipinos in the Spanish territories, the hints of other difficulties throughout the world, made absolutely clear that the age of outright colonialism was over. Colonies had become liabilities, not assets, on the twentieth-century diplomatic balance sheet. Although they remained reluctant to the end, the Americans finally decided to stay in the Philippines—not to ensure a stepping stone to the China market, not out of blithe unthinking naïveté, but out of an excess of authentic American idealism mixed with very generous amounts of complete ignorance.

Once the Americans accepted the dictates of their own better natures, which was to retain the responsibility thrust upon them as trustees for the struggling Filipinos, they became satisfied, smug, and impossible to deal with. Given their recent provincial background, how could one expect the Americans to have any sense of the force of Asian nationalism? How could the Americans have known that for Filipinos, their fight for independence did not end with the ousting of the Spanish? All foreign rule was equally (almost) obnoxious. The Filipinos, unpracticed in governing themselves, would have flailed about in a series of bloody civil wars until a surviving military group seized power. And outright civil war was hardly an improvement over Spanish rule.

But the Americans were wrong in assuming that American innocence was obvious to the embattled Filipinos. In Cuba the Americans, by enacting the Platt Amendment and then by implementing the promised withdrawal, may have persuaded some critics that they were still the anticolonialists they proclaimed themselves to be. But skeptics could point to the closeness of the Cuban and American economies and the fact that America still controlled the destinies of their Cuban neighbors simply by being close by. There were no such ties with the Philippines and little time to think or plan.

Time would not have helped. There were no attractive alternatives available. As soon as the Spanish were defeated, the vulnerability of the Philippines became obvious. Theodore Roosevelt feared Japanese interest. Most American diplomats feared Germany. The Americans and Germans had clashed at Samoa in 1889, and when the kaiser occupied China's Shantung province just before the war with Spain, everyone was made painfully aware of German expansionist ambitions. All diplomatic situations involving Germany made the world edgier. The Germans seemed threatening even on innocent occasions. When Admiral Otto von Diederichs and a large German fleet appeared at Manila shortly after the American victory, the Americans would have been hopelessly naïve not to be concerned. Dewey was terrified. The German force was larger than the American, and German naval officers were no more skilled in gentle diplomacy than American sailors. The situation was tricky. The British were also present in force at Manila Bay, ostensibly to keep an eye on things, perhaps to dissuade the Germans from overplaying their hand, or simply because the Philippine situation was so delicate that no one really knew what the outcome would be. Admiral Diederichs' visit to the Philippines was neither innocent nor intentionally threatening. The Germans hoped that the Americans might leave once they had defeated the Spanish, and if they did, the Germans had convinced themselves that the Filipinos would welcome Germany as their savior.

The idea of Germany as patron saint of Philippine independence is preposterous, but only a little less so than the American self-image as liberator of beleaguered Asians. The clumsy German presence transformed a fishing expedition into a world diplomatic problem. The British let it be known that they preferred the Philippines in neutral hands, that is, American; the Germans were not eager nor powerful enough to challenge America, Britain, and Japan for Manila Bay, and finally in early August left peacefully. William McKinley in trying to explain how America found itself with an island empire in Asia cited God as a coconspirator who had urged the president to help the poor Filipino heathens. The white man's burden was already a nonsensical romantic legend unconvincing even as a rationale for colonialism. McKinley, the pragmatic president grasping for straws, willingly invoked Kipling along with God. He really had no idea how the Americans had suddenly acquired a strategic Achilles heel in Asia.

The anti-imperialists assumed that Americans wanted the Philip-

139

pines. How could one explain to a passionate, stubborn, thoroughly provincial Boston Brahmin that the United States did not want the Philippines or Filipinos; America simply wanted to protect them from the Spanish, the Germans, and possibly themselves. The irony is magnificent. Many historians have made our early anti-imperialists modern heroes, opposed to colonialism, American expansionism, and all the bad things of the twentieth century. But the anti-imperialists who opposed expansion were simply racists. They opposed expansion not only because they felt it was morally wrong, but for fear of making Filipinos, Cubans, or other exotics American citizens. Imperialism and anti-imperialism were two sides of the same irrelevant coin. Neither applied to the American situation. The so-called imperialists, however, acknowledged a responsibility to try to patch up matters, rather than leave the islands to whoever decided to fight for them. The war of 1898 had begun as a conscious effort to free Cuba from Spanish persecution. It would have been dishonorable and inconsistent for the Americans to turn their backs on the Filipinos supposedly being freed from the same tyrannical Spaniards. America or another authoritarian power was the only choice. Ironically, the imperialists were trying to do the right thing.

They failed because of the massive mutual cultural ignorance that made any liaison between the Filipinos and the Americans a practical impossibility. Americans understand their own political heritage but have remained remarkably unresponsive to revolutionary and nationalistic ambitions of other peoples. Ignorance was compounded by racism. The Americans regarded the Filipino as a cross between a slave Sambo and a noble but politically ineffective savage unable to govern. If there was anything that the proud Filipino resented, it was the image of being someone's pathetic poor brown brother. It did not take long for the Filipino to hate the American with as much passion as he had hated the Spaniard. And it took even less time for the American to react with the same indignation as the Spaniard upon finding himself despised and hated as an intruder. The Americans expected to be welcomed as New World saviours by the "liberated" Filipinos. Instead the Americans were treated as an occupying army and just another form of Western authoritarianism.

Both sides were dealing in distorted images. The Filipinos cannot be blamed for expecting too much of American political idealism. Even Americans give too much credit to political institutions and not enough to American natural wealth in explaining their success. Many Americans and Filipinos mistakenly thought political reform alone would solve the problem in the Philippines. The Americans thought that their magnanimous gesture of granting independence—eventually—was praiseworthy. For the Filipinos, independence was essential, but not with big brother deciding when they were ready.

Although war is never inevitable, the Philippine-American War that began on February 4, 1899, is as close to inevitable as wars come, and remains one of the most tragic in American history. There were opportunities to settle the conflict before it began, but neither side had the necessary leadership, time, patience, or knowledge. Commodore Dewey was a great naval tactician and a miserable diplomat. Emilio Aguinaldo was a great revolutionary and an equally miserable diplomat. The two leaders met on board Dewey's flagship, *Olympia*, on May 20, 1898, almost a month after Dewey's victory over the Spanish navy. Neither Dewey nor Aguinaldo wanted to fight another war. Neither had the temperament to understand the enormous common ground between the two sides and the senselessness of the future struggle. The real differences between the two men and their two nations were relatively small and unimportant.

But the cultural gulf was too great. The meeting increased the existing tensions and cultural suspicions, and in January, 1899, the Filipinos made it clear that their own struggle had not ended with the expulsion of the Spanish. The Constitution of January, 1899, promulgated the new Philippine Republic and constituted a full warning to the Americans that the situation was critical. Even when formal war was declared and begun on February 4, 1899, the step was far from irrevocable. But the American commander, Major General Elwell S. Otis, was no more of a diplomat than Aguinaldo or Dewey. He misinterpreted Aguinaldo's offer of a cease-fire as a sign of weakness, fell back on military reflex, and insisted on a full and unconditional military surrender. Aguinaldo scornfully rejected such an armistice; although he hated the idea of war with the Americans, he could see no honorable alternative.

141

The Philippine-American War was brutal and bloody. Although President McKinley made an ineffectual attempt to find peace by appointing Jacob G. Schurman, president of Cornell University, to head a Philippine commission of inquiry, both sides had committed themselves to a military solution. By June 1899, the war was in full swing and Schurman's role as peacemaker was disdained by both sides. The United States quickly won the initiative in the formal war and just as quickly lost the advantage when the Filipinos dissolved their formal army on November 13, 1899, and reverted to the successful guerrilla tactics that had worked so well against the Spanish. They worked equally well against an American military occupation that was as inept as it was brutal.

The search and destroy missions, remarkably similar to those practiced seventy years later in Vietnam, produced the same military gains and political setbacks. The Filipinos proved adept at underground government by gaining virtual control of the northern part of the islands through civil servants ostensibly working for the Americans. By 1900 the United States had committed seventy thousand troops; the major results were increases in atrocities, angry news stories in American newspapers, and a frustrated American government.

At no time did the Americans envision an Asian empire, nor permanent possession of Philippine colonies. The main American goal was to end the fighting and to restore order. As the Americans became more knowledgeable about the Philippine situation, they began to compare the status of the Filipinos with that of the Cubans. The Cubans seemed more capable of self-autonomy and were not troubled by minorities as significant as the Moros, which constituted about 9% of the Philippine population. The Moros were Muslims and opposed both the native population, predominantly Catholic, and the occupying American forces. Fear of Moro violence was one of the main American concerns. Perhaps no irony is more compelling in the entire Philippine-American problem than Protestant America's attempt to protect a Catholic populace from Muslim revolutionaries. Had the Moro complication not existed, the Filipinos might have appeared comparable to the Cubans. The Americans, in that case, would have been less reluctant to leave.

In America the anti-imperialists and the imperialists were in complete agreement on ends—no Philippine colony. The means to this end caused violent disagreement. Anti-imperialists wanted independence now; the government insisted that immediate independence would dishonorably abdicate American responsibility. Economics rarely entered the dispute and never in a meaningful way. Even the shrewdest American could see no balance-sheet advantages in holding the Philippines.

Before becoming president, Theodore Roosevelt's chief connections with the Philippines were his intellectual views. He belonged to the group of expansionists who saw the Philippines as a necessary American base. When he was governor of New York, and engaged in a life-and-death struggle with Boss Tom Platt for political survival, Theodore Roosevelt coveted the Philippines as a personal administrative opportunity. He longed for the job of governor general and envied William Howard Taft's appointment as the first civilian leader of the islands. But Roosevelt never wanted the Philippines as a territory, colony, economic stepping stone, or for any reason other than strategic necessity—not even in his most bellicose days: "While I have never varied in my feeling that we had to hold the Philippines, I have varied very much in my feelings whether we were to be considered fortunate or unfortunate in having to hold them, and I most certainly hope that the trend of events will as speedily as may be justify us in leaving them."[1]

Roosevelt joked (perhaps) about James Wilson's suggestion that the Philippines be traded to Britain for Canada. Roosevelt was unequivocal even before he had the power to make the ultimate decisions in foreign policy: "We do not want to expand over another people capable of self-government unless that people desires to go in with us—and not necessarily even then."[2]

Roosevelt's entire imperial policy is summed up in one statement: "It can never be our duty to take a foot of soil; it may of course possibly become our duty; though I cannot now conceive of circumstances under which we would do it, unless, for instance, we have to take some small island, or some point on the mainland, from considerations of naval or

1. TR to Cecil Spring Rice, December 2, 1899, in MRL, II, 1103; TR to Frederic René Coudert, "Personal, not for publication," July 3, 1901, in MRL, III, 105.
2. TR to James H. Wilson, July 12, 1899, in MRL, II, 1032; TR to Frederic René Coudert, July 3, 1901, in MRL, III, 105.

military policy only."[3] Roosevelt never regarded the Philippine intervention as anything more than a strategic necessity. He was frustrated by
the complaints of the anti-imperialists with whom he agreed in principle. As president he could not publicly agree with the dissidents
for fear of undermining the American position in the Philippines.
Roosevelt might have calmed some political waters by making his own
personal views known, but he felt obliged to support the program begun by President McKinley.

For Roosevelt, as for McKinley, the continued occupation of the
Philippines was a necessity rather than a matter of choice. Privately
Roosevelt confided to anti-imperialist Louis R. Ekrich as early as March,
1902, his own personal wish to leave the Philippines as soon as possible.
Roosevelt was troubled by the anti-imperialists' appeals for immediate
Filipino independence. Such arguments he regarded as either insincere,
impractical, or an attempt to politically embarrass the administration.
When Senator George F. Hoar, one of the leading anti-imperial spokes-
men, publicly appealed for immediate Filipino independence in June,
1902, Roosevelt privately promised to do all he could. "I am striving
my best, doubtless with many shortcomings . . . with sincerity and ear-
nestness . . . to hasten the day when we shall need no more force in the
Philippines than is needed in New York. . . . I do not want to make a
promise which may not be kept." Roosevelt feared that a vague promise
of Filipino independence in the future would do more harm than good
and would serve a political rather than a practical function. He declined
to take the easier political option even though the anti-imperialists
seemed at the time more influential than they actually were.[4]

As the guerrilla war continued, the atrocity stories and public pressure increased. When Roosevelt investigated the worst atrocity stories,
he found that "nine-tenths of the cruelties have been committed by
the native troops." But Americans were as deeply involved as the anti-
imperialist lobby suggested. The president pledged to Bishop William
Lawrence and Josephine Lowell on May 9, 1902, that "no provocation

3. TR to Frederic René Coudert, July 3, 1901, in MRL, III, 105.
4. Louis Ekrich to Moorfield Storey, March 11, 1902, Red Box 1, in Moorfield
Storey Papers, LC; TR to George Hoar, June 16, 1902, in MRL, III, 277.

however great can be accepted as an excuse for misuse of the necessary severity of war, and above all not for torture of any kind or shape."[5]

Guerrilla wars with revolutionaries are seldom free of atrocities. The problem was not incidental episodes of cruelty, but the bitterness the revolutionary war engendered on both sides. Knowing that the war was in its closing stages, Roosevelt tried to play down the flagrancy. He talked about investigations but did not pursue them. In a Memorial Day speech on May 30, 1902, Roosevelt defended Secretary of the Army Root's policies and minimized the extent of the atrocities. As long as a civil war raged with no single controlling faction within the islands, the talk of self-government seemed self-defeating to the president.[6]

If the Americans had withdrawn in 1902, the Filipinos would have had no recourse but to continue fighting until one faction emerged from the civil wars as a new authoritarian government. The Roosevelt administration was caught in a cruel political dilemma. It could end American involvement and yield to the demands of the vocal anti-imperialists. That course would plunge the islands into greater bloodshed and chaos. Or Roosevelt could continue the unrelenting war until some form of order was restored, and then try to work with the natives toward an orderly form of self-government. The latter course is often mistaken for imperialism.

Suddenly the war began to end. On March 23, 1901, Aguinaldo himself was captured. The first major battle during Roosevelt's presidency, September 28, 1901, witnessed a major massacre of Americans at Balanga. On April 16, 1902, organized Filipino resistance ended with the surrender of Malvar. By July 4, 1902, the president could announce the end of formal hostilities in the Philippine-American War. The war had been a disaster in every respect. Even the tragic insight the Americans gained about the futility of fighting colonial wars was lost in the bitterness of the moment. When the war ended, Roosevelt and the

5. TR to William A. Wordsworth, May 7, 1902, in MRL, III, 259; TR to William Lawrence, May 9, 1902, in MRL, III, 259; TR to Josephine Shaw Lowell, May 9, 1902, in Theodore Roosevelt Papers, LC.
6. Second Annual Message to Congress, December 2, 1902, in *Works, Nat. Ed.*, XV, 155–56; TR to Elihu Root, May 9, 1902, in MRL, III, 260.

Americans felt relief but still faced the same problems that had been present from the start. American casualties were considerable, especially for a nation not accustomed to foreign war. But the American casualties of about 4,200 dead and 2,800 wounded were dwarfed by the Filipino losses —over 18,000 military and from 100,000 to 200,000 civilian deaths.

William McKinley had appointed William Howard Taft as civil governor of the Philippines, a role that well suited the man who would become one of Theodore Roosevelt's most trusted associates. Roosevelt left the major policy decisions to Taft and Secretary of War Elihu Root with the understanding that Taft handle the civilian problems and Root the military. Until recently the Philippine-American War has remained blurred in many historical accounts. If the conflict is seen more as a domestic political struggle between imperialists and anti-imperialists at home, the war itself can easily become merely a symbol. The anti-imperialists' influence has been vastly overrated as has their intellectual weight. More a vocal elite of older professionals connected mainly with writing and universities, the anti-imperialists opposed all expansion, all war, and all change. They were mostly hysterical, made little sense, and in retrospect resemble little more than a shrill and articulate interest group, perhaps the last gasp of the old Boston Brahmin influence upon American life and culture. The anti-imperialists were not just wrong; they were irrelevant. No one in power disagreed with their ultimate aims.

The entire anti-imperialist argument depended upon the use of straw men to scare other intellectuals or the electorate. The main support the anti-imperialists could muster was the existing war in the Philippines, its continued brutality, and the accompanying atrocities. But the anti-imperialist solution—to simply leave the islands—would have been an unthinkable act of cruelty committed in the name of idealism. To force the factions in a nation that had never governed itself to fight to the end as a means of finding political leadership was both ineffective and barbaric. Yet, outside the unpleasant role of peacemaker, that was the only other choice open to the Americans. That the conduct of the American troops in the Philippines was also frequently barbaric does not mean that unilateral withdrawal was a responsible solution.

Because the anti-imperialists were able to clothe their protests in

146

moral terms, they precluded any intelligent debate about colonial alternatives. The president was virtually helpless in dealing with the two most pressing Philippine problems after the war finally ended. Once the cloud of war had passed, Roosevelt and Taft faced an incredibly complex problem concerning the Catholic friars, who had ruled the Philippines as representatives of both the civil government and the Catholic church. America had to deal with the anomaly of a people, 91% of whom were Catholics, who resented the Catholic church and its friars for having unjustly appropriated Filipino land.

American interference in church politics remained abhorrent to American political traditions. Taft and Roosevelt had to tread very lightly even to negotiate the matter. The negotiations with the Vatican on behalf of the majority of Filipinos were patient, shrewd, and ultimately effective. But even the admission that an American government was dealing diplomatically with the Catholic church was politically damaging. Taft's and Roosevelt's persistence in working out a compromise acceptable to the Catholic hierarchy and the Filipino nationalists should be hailed as one of the high points of American diplomacy. Instead it is buried in the footnotes of a debate that for too long has centered on the shrill but peripheral anti-imperialists.

The anti-imperialists did not cause Congress to balk at effective economic relief for the proposed new Filipino state, but they did not lend any support to the administration's desperate pleas for relief. Opposition Democrats in Congress could easily align with anti-administration anti-imperialists regardless of the issue. Tariff and currency were volatile domestic political issues in America. But Roosevelt insisted that relief from the most restrictive American economic regulations was necessary to enable Cuba, Puerto Rico, and the Philippines to become economically independent. He was not asking for direct assistance, but for shelter from America's most burdensome foreign trade restrictions. Congress had no ideological reason for denying such aid.

But domestic politicians sensed the administration's vulnerability on a matter which, though actually a part of foreign affairs, had to be dealt with through domestic appropriations. Congress stubbornly refused to concede the needed power to the president, or to make desperately needed economic concessions to the Philippines. Roosevelt finally man-

147

aged to convince senators like Lodge and Speaker of the House Cannon to support his program for economic independence for the Philippines. Even Cannon's power was only partly successful. The Congress finally passed currency reform but refused to budge on reducing the tariff.[7]

During all that time, the anti-imperialists were waging a propaganda campaign in favor of political freedom for the Philippines. Theodore Roosevelt was aghast at the intellectual weakness in arguments made by men as distinguished as Charles Eliot, president of Harvard University. He tried to point out to Eliot that rebuilding a nation that had already suffered badly from three centuries of poor colonial rule must precede any program of effective self-government. But Eliot insisted that immediate freedom was the only solution. Roosevelt told Eliot, "Any promise of independence, any expression by us of our belief that they will ultimately get their independence (though personally this is my belief) [is] too remote . . . to solve the problems of the actual present. . . . We are far more necessary to the Filipinos than the Filipinos are to us." Roosevelt, furious with the hypocrisy of the anti-imperialist arguments, attacked southern Democrats who decried the lack of Philippine freedom while denying the most minimal political rights to southern Negroes.

"Reading Rousseau in the closet," Roosevelt declared, is not a substitute for studying the individual case. He insisted that Cuba was more prepared for self-government than the Philippines. Roosevelt pointed out that Cuba, under American rule for four years, had developed a prosperity greater than comparable Spanish American republics. Roosevelt refused to placate the anti-imperialists with future promises he felt were empty gestures. Unless a statement of independence proposed only a short delay, it would cause more harm than help. The president compared the historical plight of India, Egypt, Algiers, and Turkey in support of his refusal to jeopardize stability with future promises of change, even if change brought theoretical democracy with it.[8]

For Roosevelt the Philippine situation was not nearly as bleak as

7. See MRL, III, 428*n*; TR to Elihu Root, February 16, 1903, in MRL, III, 428; TR to Nelson W. Aldrich, February 24, 1903, in MRL, III, 433–34; TR to Charles W. Eliot, April 4, 1904, in MRL, IV, 770.
8. TR to Charles W. Eliot, April 4, 1904 (unmailed), in MRL, IV, 767–70, June 20, 1904, in MRL, IV, 839. TR to Eliot, October 19, 1904, in MRL, IV, 986–87.

his critics insisted. "They are being given a larger measure of self-government than they ever had before, or than any other Asiatic people except Japan now enjoys. They have immeasurably more individual freedom than they ever enjoyed under Spain, or than they could have under Aguinaldo or any other despot." But Roosevelt was adamant: "The Filipinos are not fit to govern themselves." One can accuse Roosevelt of simply reiterating the white man's burden apologia that Western nations use as a rationale for colonialism. But Roosevelt's shadings are finer, his historical analysis more complex and sophisticated. And his reasons were real. Roosevelt would have done anything to be rid of the Philippines and their problems. The Philippines were America's Achilles heel, he declared. "The possession of the Philippines renders us vulnerable in Asia."[9] Roosevelt's arguments were sound at the time. In historical retrospect they are still sound and reasonable. But as long as Theodore Roosevelt can be dismissed as a mock imperialist waving big sticks at the world and his political antagonists, no one will take his rational Philippine argument as seriously as it deserves to be taken.

Roosevelt's long letter to Charles Eliot is a measure both of the president's frustration and his frequent caution. Deciding not to mail the letter to Eliot, since "after consultation with Root and [Secretary of the Navy] Moody I came to the conclusion that it would not be worthwhile to send it," he sent it as an enclosure to Arthur Twining Hadley, an economist whose recent book was the basis of Roosevelt's unmailed letter. It served Roosevelt's purposes well. He could blow off steam and also leave a tangible historical record in a "posterity letter," a means by which Roosevelt could assure his views were clearly on record. By sending a copy to an influential author, Roosevelt could also have the pleasure of publicly berating the president of Harvard, who was a leader of the anti-imperialists, without giving him a chance for immediate rebuttal. Roosevelt did mail his next letter on the Filipino issue to Eliot, a much briefer note than the unmailed letter. Although Eliot remained at odds with Roosevelt on the Philippines, he supported him for reelection in 1904.[10]

9. TR to Arthur Twining Hadley, April 6, 1904, in MRL, IV, 772 (with enclosure of Eliot letter); TR to William Howard Taft, August 21, 1907, in MRL, V, 761–62.

10. *The Relations Between Freedom and Responsibility in the Evolution of Democratic Government* (New York, 1903); TR to Charles W. Eliot, June 20, 1904, in MRL, IV, 839.

Theodore Roosevelt pleaded with the more articulate anti-imperialists not to ask for government promises that would raise the level of Filipino expectations simply to relieve the immediate domestic political pressure. "The Christian Filipinos could not live six months in peace if there was not some strong government over the Moros." Roosevelt insisted that the United States could not simply choose one faction to govern, that the Filipinos had to work out their own destinies, and that the anti-imperialists wanted self-government too soon. For Roosevelt the anti-imperialist timetable spelled anarchy; staying in the Philippines until the people had some experience at self-government struck Theodore Roosevelt as the only responsible course.[11]

Roosevelt always felt that the American occupation of the Philippines stemmed from strategic or military necessity and that continued occupation was a humanitarian duty. Some recent historians suggest that the Americans themselves benefited dramatically, if unexpectedly, from the Philippine occupation. Political experiments first tried in the Philippine occupation, and found to be effective, became part of the American domestic reform program we now call progressivism. How ironic it would be if even *some* American domestic reform resulted from the so-called imperialistic seizure of the Philippines. Certainly the Philippines never produced wealth for American business, nor did any American business group view the islands as an economic boon, even potentially. Roosevelt later acknowledged that the Americans in 1898 took the islands in the excitement over the war with Spain. "I don't see where they are of any value to us."[12]

America's involvement in the Philippines in the first decade of the twentieth century is not nearly as bleak as we have come to believe. The war with Aguinaldo was a tragic mistake, bringing with it the wave of atrocities and the usual barbarisms of revolutionary and colonial wars. But after the fighting ended, America fulfilled its responsibilities nobly. More schools, better medical facilities, and a sounder economy all re-

11. TR to Josephine Shaw Lowell, August 1, 1904, in MRL, IV, 875.
12. See John Morgan Gates, *Schoolbooks and Krags: The United States Army in the Philippines, 1898–1902* (Westport, Conn., 1973), and Glenn Anthony May, *Social Engineering in the Philippines: The Aims, Execution and Impact of American Colonial Policy, 1900–1913* (Westport, Conn., 1980); TR *Works, Nat. Ed.*, XV, 536–39; TR to William Howard Taft, August 21, 1907, in MRL, V, 761.

sulted from the American occupation. Better schools did not dramatically raise the literacy level, nor did a better economy end Filipino poverty. But the Americans tried. And while the improvements did not match their expectations, the attempt marked the first steps to help a colonial people rise from abject poverty to self-responsibility. The American initiative went deeper than just words. In spite of constant domestic opposition, both in America and in the Philippines, the Americans did improve life, liberty, and property for the Filipinos without any motive for exploitation. Not even strategic gain was involved in the American effort during Taft's and Roosevelt's Philippine administration.

Ironically the American government dealt better with the poor Filipino than with the poor American. Social engineering, idealism, new progressive ideas and experiments, were first unveiled in the Philippines. Poor Filipinos felt the first wave of American liberalism and in many ways offered a blueprint for future social programs in mainland America. But the Americans cannot claim all the credit. The American involvement in the Philippines was almost wholly accidental from the start. There was no deep-seated economic plan, no shrewd diplomacy. The Philippine-American involvement remains an accident of history.

Eventually, after the drama of war had receded from the front pages, American public interest waned so badly that the president found little political support for even the most rudimentary economic concessions. Philippine tariff battles remained bitter, reflecting America's basic disinterest in its new possessions. Roosevelt even feared that the American people would soon tire of defending the islands if they were attacked. Roosevelt refused to the end of his presidency to set a timetable for American withdrawal and Philippine independence. The Manila *Times* reported on April 21, 1908, that the president had a plan for Philippine independence in twenty years. In 1913 Roosevelt reiterated, "I do not believe that America has any special beneficial interest in retaining the Philippines."[13]

In the New York *Times* in 1914, Roosevelt publicly advocated Philippine independence. In 1915, embittered both by his failure to regain political power and his deep disagreements with President Woodrow

13. TR, *Autobiography* (New York, 1913), rpr. *Works, Nat. Ed.*, XX, 492.

Wilson's foreign policy, Roosevelt appeared to advocate the unilateral abandonment of the Philippines. Roosevelt, however, was using heavy-handed irony, basing his abandonment argument on the American unwillingness or inability to defend the Philippines against Japanese attack.[14]

The American acquisition of the Philippines had come full circle. The Americans may have blundered into a colonial problem; however, in spite of the unfortunate American-Filipino war, the Americans acquitted themselves honorably. There was no profit in the Philippines in any economic sense, present or future. By remaining, the Americans eliminated the islands as a prize in the fierce European imperial rivalry, then at its most volatile stage in Asia and the Pacific. By taking the Philippines, the Americans prevented either a European or an Asian contest that could have precipitated a world war. The major powers were content to have the Philippines in the relatively neutral hands of the Americans, who of all of the powers had the least interest in China and represented the least threat to existing European holdings. The Americans in essence maintained the status quo, at best an uneasy balance of power.

In the process of possession the Americans, with few exceptions, dealt honorably with a people who had been oppressed for centuries. A major irony of the Philippines occupation is the more favorable disposition, of both the American government and the American people, toward the Filipino brown brother over the the native American Negro. To call the American occupation of the Philippines in 1899 economic expansion, or imperialism in the pejorative sense, is to confuse America's problems, ideals, and politics in 1900 with the far different culture, economy, and outlook of the European powers and Japan.

The occupation of the Philippines was a strategic necessity and, though tragic, probably a political necessity as well. All the rhetoric about freedom and independence is worthless in the face of grinding poverty institutionalized for centuries. To the Americans' credit they remained in the Philippines even when the vision of strategic or economic

14. New York *Times*, November 22, 1914, p. 1; William Howard Taft to Mabel Boardman, July 14, 1915, in Mabel Boardman Papers, LC. See also TR to Hiram Johnson, November 16, 1914, in MRL, VIII, 846–47; TR to W. Cameron Forbes, January 4, 1915, in MRL, VIII, 869–70.

gain had failed to materialize. Neither the Americans nor the Filipinos were farseeing enough to understand where their best interests lay, and both fought furiously against those interests—the Filipinos for a premature independence, the Americans for a burdensome occupation.

But in both cases the struggles were extensions of the original revolutionary idealisms of both peoples. One cannot make a historic success out of the Philippine-American conflict. But there are enough bright spots to offer some historical solace to both sides, in this first confrontation of a Third World people with the older revolutionary United States.

6 / Great Britain
A New Detente with an Old Enemy

Theodore Roosevelt had one perfect solution to two of his most pressing problems: "Hand the Philippines over to England, if she would leave this continent." Coming in July, 1899, when he was governor of New York, Roosevelt's idea was pure diplomatic fantasy. Even had Roosevelt been president, with the power to reinforce his disingenuous scheme, neither the Canadians nor the British would have given the exchange a moment's consideration. Britain had as much desire to "give up" Canada as America had to relinquish Texas. Roosevelt did understand, however, the major remaining point of friction threatening the newly developing Anglo-American friendship; Britain would go to great lengths to keep America as her new ally in the world balance of power. Canada was the problem. "The relations between Canada and England always tend to bring on friction between us and both of them," Roosevelt observed. To work out a continuing alliance between the newly emergent Americans and the suddenly cautious British, in the face of Canadian uneasiness, was a major challenge to the McKinley and Roosevelt administrations.[1]

Although Roosevelt often talked of holding Canada hostage if Britain did not behave properly, he was indulging in meaningless bravado. Historically, American and Canadian destinies had never shown the slightest inclination of meeting even halfway. Even during the American Revolution, Canada, though it was more French than English, rejected an alliance the Americans always took for granted. Resisting serious American invasion attempts in 1776 and 1812, Canada wanted no part

1. TR to James H. Wilson, July 12, 1899, in MRL, II, 1032.

154

of American protection, independence, or occupation. To the Canadians, America seemed the chief foreign threat. Had the Americans seemed less aggressive, Canada might have chosen independence, rather than dominion status with Great Britain.

Irish immigrants, who hated England and came in large numbers to America, gravitated to the troubled border area and helped keep the Canadian-American border in a state of constant turmoil during the 1850s. Turmoil became outright invasion on May 31, 1866, when a Fenian "army" from the United States actually invaded Canada. The invasion was easily repulsed by the Canadians, and the incident should have remained a minor episode in Irish folklore. But Canadian fear of its avaricious and aggressive American neighbor pushed an ambivalent Canada into a long-postponed affiliation with Britain, primarily as insurance against any other wild schemes originating from America.

The Canadians were not the only ones worried by future American intentions. In 1872 one of Britain's most perceptive diplomatic minds, Benjamin Disraeli, accurately predicted that America was "throwing lengthening shades over the Atlantic," and in time would become "a vast and novel element in the distribution of power." Disraeli had reason to be fearful. Secretary of State William Seward in 1865 declared, "I know that nature designs that this whole continent, not merely these thirty-six states, shall be sooner or later within the magic circle of the American Union." Just before Seward purchased Alaska in 1867, Queen Victoria took note of the American danger in her diary: "Talked of America and the danger which seems approaching, of our having a war with her as soon as she makes peace; of the impossibility of holding Canada; but we must struggle for it."[2]

Canadian relations settled down after the Canadian-British alliance. A minor disturbance between Britain, the United States, and Germany in 1889 over rights to a naval coaling station in Samoa was settled peacefully. Britain's most serious concern in America was the continued political threat posed by the free silver movement, which if successful would seriously devalue extensive British investments in America.

2. H. C. Allen, *Great Britain and the United States: A History of Anglo-American Relations, 1783–1952* (London, 1953), 522. George E. Buckle, ed., *Letters of Queen Victoria*, Second Series (3 vols.; London, 1930–32), I, 550.

Britain, along with everyone else, was ignoring the danger signals from America. For the first time, Americans seemed to want to be taken seriously. They had never thought of themselves as colonial provincials, as the British and other Europeans saw them, but with their complete absorption in settling the West and dealing with their own sectional problems, the Americans paid little attention to the world's cpinion of their culture. American self-absorption did not change, but around 1890 it shifted direction dramatically. The ending of the frontier announced in the 1890 census is an obvious turning point. But the building of the great White City in Chicago, part of the centennial celebration of Columbus' discovery voyage in 1492, was the most significant indication of fundamental change in America's view of itself.

Chicago was not alone in sending America's message to the world. The United States sent the same message in the strongest possible diplomatic terms. In 1893 the United States changed the ranking of its diplomats from ministers to ambassadors; American legations throughout the world became embassies. The American diplomatic change was as fraught with nationalist symbolism as the Chinese Boxer Rebellion of 1900, in which outraged Chinese seized foreign embassies.

Unfortunately neither America's gentle gesture nor the Chinese warlike efforts made much of an impression on an increasingly smug and insular Europe, content with the cultural pattern that excluded outsiders like Americans, Asians, and Africans. But the Americans went further. In 1890, Congress included for the first time a reciprocity clause in a tariff law, a sure sign that increased international activity was contemplated. And as if to underline the possibility, the same 1890 Congress appropriated money for the building of America's first three battleships. The Americans were sending signals to the world: Take us more seriously.

The world, and especially Britain, ignored both the changes and the messages. The indifference did not discourage the new American spirit. It enraged it. When the Venezuelan border dispute with Britain occurred in 1895, the Americans chose the occasion to make their message and their new image unmistakably clear. President Grover Cleveland and his Secretary of State Richard Olney threatened to go to war if Great Britain, then the most powerful nation in the world, did not agree to America's new policy. The new policy—in fact an old one, the Monroe Doctrine—insisted that all of South America was symbolically and diplomatically a part of America's borders, and that the dispute between Venezuela and Britain was a domestic North American problem that could be solved only by international arbitration sponsored by the United States.

Cleveland's pronouncement was shocking and his bellicose manner offensive. Britain, still secure in its unchallenged power, looked upon the Americans as a negligible and backward people—a poor enough attitude in itself, but one that became insufferable when undisguised by even the pretense of diplomacy or tact. Secretary of State Olney clearly explained why he took such an aggressive posture with the British: "In English eyes the United States was then so completely a negligible quantity that it was believed that only words equivalent of a blow would be really effective."[3] Olney and Cleveland fired the first salvo not in a diplomatic battle but in a cultural confrontation.

Olney's and America's dilemma was a real one. No nation could be taken seriously diplomatically if it were not taken seriously culturally. Defeating Spain in the war of 1898 helped the American image in European eyes. But war was an expensive way to gain respect. Theodore Roosevelt well understood the main battle lines between America and Britain. Somehow the British must be made to grant Americans the respect they wanted and deserved; the patronizing attitude powerful Englishmen displayed to Americans was more damaging than any dispute over Latin American borders. Eventually the Americans won the cultural as well as the diplomatic battle.

At the time of the Venezuelan dispute, some of America's most persuasive expatriates were already narrowing the cultural gap. James Whistler, the artist, Henry James, the writer, John Hay, a writer and a diplomat, all helped to build a common ground of mutual understanding and respect. Eventually the cultural ties of a common language, the patient and careful diplomacy of a dedicated group of American Anglophiles, and pressure from the outside upon British insularity promoted a detente that was both cultural and diplomatic and stabilized relations

---

3. Allen, *Great Britain and the United States*, 534.

between the former revolutionary foes. Even though Theodore Roosevelt became the most important leader in the new movement toward detente, without President Grover Cleveland's bombastic thundering against England in 1895, the enmity and the distrust might well have remained permanent, in spite of the natural inclination of the two peoples toward cooperation, and their obviously mutual interests in a volatile and changing world.

The key to the new American sense of destiny is best expressed in the Monroe Doctrine, much more significant as a symbolic expression of American nationalism than as a rational or intelligent diplomatic policy. Even in 1823, when the Monroe Doctrine was first announced and America was simply a distant revolutionary irritant with little power and no influence, Prince Metternich of Austria was outraged at the American vision: "They lend new strength to the apostles of sedition, and reanimate the courage of every conspirator." Metternich worried that "if this flood of evil doctrines and pernicious examples" persisted, it would endanger "that conservative system which has saved Europe from complete dissolution."[4] Between 1823 and 1900 neither American nor European attitudes had changed. The Americans still saw themselves as unique political saviours, and Europeans as corrupt and unprincipled despots. What had changed was the relative power of the two peoples. Europe was less secure; America was much stronger. European indifference or arrogance no longer would be tolerated by the Americans. The European nations to first understand that American arguments about the Monroe Doctrine had little to do with law, international policy, or anything but national pride had the best chance of settling minor differences with the new Americans and winning their friendship. In a world in which alliances were essential to maintaining peace, or winning a war, America could no longer be taken lightly.

The history of the Monroe Doctrine, regarded purely as a diplomatic phenomenon, can be puzzling. Americans waxed and waned on the idea and throughout the nineteenth century seemed to ignore many of its provisions. President Grover Cleveland seems the least likely American leader to attempt to reestablish an aggressive and messianic Ameri-

4. Dexter Perkins, *A History of the Monroe Doctrine* (Boston, 1955), 56–57.

can foreign policy. Cleveland was avowedly anti-imperialistic and almost wholly concerned with domestic rather than foreign politics. Indeed, the most plausible explanation for Cleveland's saber rattling is the grim state of his domestic political fortunes in 1895. Cleveland had failed to deal with the serious American depression, the demands for free silver from the West, and indeed the anguish of a domestic economy that was on the verge of complete failure.[5]

How tempting it was to create a diversion by pulling the lion's tail and provoking a war scare with Great Britain. There is no question that Cleveland's tactics were more concerned with domestic political matters than with the principle of international arbitration or the sanctity of Venezuela's border. Nonetheless, that a fervid anti-imperialist such as Cleveland could use foreign policy as a political device was itself a new development in American history, indicating that the American image was no longer that of a self-contained isolated country, but rather that of a nation aware of its growing influence and potential power. Grover Cleveland was not an imaginative man. If the changes in America were apparent to him, they were profound indeed.

But if Cleveland's actions were significant, the sweeping words used by Secretary of State Richard Olney were nothing short of monumental. The actual border dispute between Britain and Venezuela was inconsequential. The British regarded the entire matter as frivolous. For the Venezuelans the dispute centered around new discoveries of gold, which, though well within British territory, offered tempting possibilities for compromise, since the border was ill-defined and unsurveyed. Who could tell what an international arbitration commission would find? Venezuela had nothing to lose. Neither the gold, the arbitration, nor the actual dispute concerned the Americans. Now was the time for the Americans to make a hemispheric earthquake out of a diplomatic ripple, and put the world, and especially the world's most powerful nation, on warning that there was indeed a new America and that it refused to be ignored.

5. For the political motivation of Cleveland's strong messages to Britain on Venezuela, see John A. S. Grenville and George Berkeley Young, *Politics, Strategy, and American Diplomacy: Studies in Foreign Policy, 1873–1917* (New Haven, Conn., 1967), 158–60; Allen Nevins, *Grover Cleveland: A Study in Courage* (New York, 1932), 633–46; Horace Samuel Merrill, *Bourbon Leader: Grover Cleveland* (Boston, 1957), 201–202.

Cleveland and Olney had chosen their ground well. Nothing could better dramatize the extent of the American vision than the sweeping claim Richard Olney made in his manifesto of American influence. Olney was quick to disabuse both Britain and Venezuela of their relative importance in the dispute. Wherever the border was, it was clearly not a problem for either of the two nations most directly involved. The border was not Great Britain's or Venezuela's problem. All of the border, all of Venezuela, all of Latin America was indeed a part, incredibly, of the United States. "The States of America, South as well as North, by geographical proximity, by natural similarity of governmental constitutions, are friends and allies, commercially and politically of the United States."[6] In 1883 an earlier secretary of state, James G. Blaine, had claimed all the rivers and coastlines in Latin America.

It is too easy to ridicule Olney's message. Obviously, palpably, logically, and even historically, everything that Olney claimed in his sweeping pronouncement was false. The United States was not a commercial ally of Latin America, the cultural and geographical gulf between North and South America was prodigious, and the similarity of governmental constitutions was merely a reflection of fashionable political rhetoric. South America was not a bastion of effective democracy.

Theodore Roosevelt was one of the few men in America or Britain who understood what the argument was about. Still a relatively insignificant New York City police commissioner in 1896, and certainly no friend of Grover Cleveland in temperament, intellect, or politics, Roosevelt saw the Monroe Doctrine issue as the symbol of newly emerging American nationalism—not law or diplomacy, but an expression of cultural principle. Roosevelt wrote: "The Monroe Doctrine is not a question of law at all. It is a question of policy. . . . Lawyers, as lawyers, have absolutely nothing whatever to say about it. To argue that it cannot be recognized as a principle of international law, is a mere waste of breath. Nobody cares whether it is or is not so recognized, any more than one cares whether the Declaration of Independence and Washington's Farewell Address are so recognized."[7] In essence Roosevelt was making the

6. Richard Olney to Thomas Bayard, July 20, 1895, in FRUS, 1895, I, 545.
7. TR, "The Monroe Doctrine," *Bachelor of Arts,* March, 1896, rpr. in *Works, Nat. Ed.,* XIII, 169–81.

Monroe Doctrine a part of American political poetry—myth, legend, an expression of destiny—not a policy of *Realpolitik* or statesmanship, but simply a national metaphor that became the central symbol of the new America of the early twentieth century.

The new America was not expansionist. Olney and Cleveland had absolutely no desire for any part of Latin America, neither the disputed border nor the gold that might be discovered. The Americans were still thinking in terms of their own revolutionary idealism and saw Europe as the old as well as the new enemy, the perennial aggressor. The message from Olney—and it could have come just as easily from Theodore Roosevelt—was a message about American expectations, not about a South American border crisis. "The age of the Crusades has passed," Olney astonishingly told the British, who must have wondered what kind of historical enchantment affected the Americans that they could possibly connect the medieval crusades to the strange American Monroe Doctrine. Olney was perfectly willing to explain: "It is not to be tolerated that the political control of an American state [one must read South as well as North in this marvelous elision] shall be forcibly assumed by a European power." Thus was the Mohammedan Kingdom of Venezuela made safe for democracy by President Grover Cleveland.[8]

With Olney's and Cleveland's bellicose statements, a new era in American diplomacy began, which reflected the enormous economic and cultural growth that had already transformed America into an increasingly ambitious cosmopolitan people. In 1896 the United States was still not a world power, but it was also no longer a passive provincial. America's main defense continued to lie in the safety of its geographical isolation. But intelligent Americans already saw that startling new advances in naval technology had diminished the natural geographical barriers. Until the United States could defend itself from possible European threats, it tried to buttress its safety with words. Reflecting their own revolutionary heritage, the Americans remembered their traditional European enemy and made the warning a combination of both ideology and strategy.

Grover Cleveland's rhetoric in 1896 and Theodore Roosevelt's rheto-

8. Richard Olney to Thomas Bayard, July 20, 1895, in FRUS, 1895, I, 545.

ric in 1901 were both based on the words Americans had used effectively since the American Revolution. More impressive, however, is the similarity in the policies of the two strikingly dissimilar presidents. Grover Cleveland's policy in 1896 and Theodore Roosevelt's in 1901 were identical: European influence in any part of Central America, the Caribbean, or nearby Latin America must be neutralized by whatever means possible: political persuasion, metaphorical excursions into history, bluster, bombast, and even force if necessary.

Ironically, world events favored the timing and the brashness of the Americans. Had Cleveland ventured his warlike gambit a year, or even several months, earlier, he would have failed. But at the end of 1895, the British had their hands full with the Boers in South Africa and the Germans in both Europe and Asia. Britain, once supreme, was faced with threats from all over the world. France was threatening Britain in Siam as well as Africa; the Russians coveted Constantinople and even India. It was no time for the imperious British to take on a new enemy. Diplomatically it was clear that the Venezuelan dispute was minor and that the United States—if one overlooked its provinciality and the bitterness of past feelings—could be a useful ally, if only for its geographical advantages. Cultural preferences aside, the Americans, now that they had become troublesome like the other "mature" nations of the world, could be useful, allowing the British to concentrate on their preferred enemies like the Germans, who were both closer to home and more of a direct threat than the distant Americans.

The British, however, had to make some serious adjustments. They actually had to concede to the Americans the practical wisdom of the hated Monroe Doctrine. They had to give up their imperial expectations in Central America and the Caribbean. And perhaps worst of all, they had to learn how to suffer the Americans as allies. Diplomatic alliance was relatively easy; cultural alliance was not. If a true detente were to prosper, the British could no longer regard every American as a barbaric provincial. The newer breed of American leader—John Hay, Theodore Roosevelt—was insufferably sensitive to any of the slights the Englishman imposed on colonials, Indians and Americans, around the world. The transition was not easy but tolerable.

Lord Salisbury dropped his strong but irrelevant (and insulting) diatribe on the legal basis of the Monroe Doctrine. In the war with Spain, Britain worked well, if informally, with the Americans and effectively prevented the possible, though minor, threat of a concert of Europe allied with Spain. In the aftermath of the war the British gave the Americans moral support, the appearance of strategic help in the Philippines, and at the same time encouraged American suspicions about the ambitious Germans. But enormous obstacles still remained that could threaten the new spirit of detente.

Great Britain still had to relinquish formally any hopes for joint participation in a Central American canal; Britain also had to give up control of, and ambitions for, Central America. These were not onerous requirements. Central America had ceased to be one of Britain's favored areas either economically or strategically. And American willingness to assume responsibility assured that no other European nation would win control. But habit dies hard. After centuries of almost unchallenged supremacy, the British, though willing to give up actual power in the region, were loath to confirm their formal withdrawal in words. The British hoped to save face. A few concessions would satisfy them. Unfortunately the new American mood precluded even the hint of concessions. The Americans wanted complete control not only in substance but in symbol. The Monroe Doctrine had become a matter of belief in America; for the Americans, sole ownership and control of a canal were as important as the building of the canal itself.

The French failure of Panama had stiffened American resistance to any European incursion and whetted the Americans' ambition to build their own canal as quickly as possible. But the British, sensing the American impatience, thought they had found a diplomatic opportunity in which they could gain a compromise. By using the unhappy Canadian dispute with America over Alaska, they hoped to win concessions either in Central America, Canada, or both. The Canadians were sensitive about their secondary status with both America and Britain and made a *cause célèbre* over a newly significant boundary running through an unexpectedly prosperous area between Alaska and Canada. The Canadian boundary dispute was a diversion from the start. The Canadian claim had no legal or moral justification and became an issue of expediency, a means of putting another issue on the table to force concessions either in Alaska or in Central America. Only the new prosperity of the former wasteland called Alaska made the disputed area valuable. But the maps and surveys taken when Alaska was owned by the Russians unequivocally supported the American boundary lines; the Canadian case was a prime example of Canadian nationalism frustrated by American success and Alaskan gold. It had nothing to do with justice or legal boundaries.

The Canadian dispute had even less to do with Britain's diminished capacity in Central America. But the British, unwilling to simply concede everything, were determined to link the Canadian and Isthmian issues and perhaps win something from the resurgent Americans. Given the shape of history, which the British as a declining power were unable or unwilling to see, the British had picked the wrong time and the wrong argument for a diplomatic showdown with the Americans. The Americans held all the cards, and knew it.

The Anglo-American detente that slowly developed at the beginning of the twentieth century worked so well, in retrospect it almost looks inevitable. But the final settlement was a diplomatic cliffhanger. There were two major issues. The formal treaty, which would remove Britain from participation in an American canal in Central America, was easier to negotiate than the compromise of the spurious border dispute with the hypersensitive Canadians. The credit for the success of the new alliance must be shared. Without Grover Cleveland's threats, the opportunity for detente would never have occurred; without the meliorating influence of John Hay, who convinced English diplomats that not all Americans—especially cultivated Anglophiles like Hay—were barbarians, there could have been none of the necessary transition between the crude diplomacy of Grover Cleveland and the finesse of Theodore Roosevelt. Without Theodore Roosevelt's determination, understanding, and diplomatic skill, the British might well have won the struggle, and in winning, lost a friendship and an alliance that transcended the relatively petty issues of the moment.

The Americans won resounding victories in both the Central American and Alaskan disputes because they proved to be tougher in diplomatic infighting than the more experienced British. The Americans were also more determined. But there were still many opportunities for the brash new nation to make a fatal misstep in the complex negotiations.

John Hay, American gentleman from Illinois, a respected poet, novelist, wit, and patron of the arts, secretary to President Lincoln during the Civil War, and Anglophile extraordinary, became the cultural and diplomatic mediator between the two major English-speaking countries. In 1897 John Hay was appointed President McKinley's ambassador to Great Britain. He was on intimate terms with Henry James, the American expatriate writer living in London, and with the most upcoming of the newer breed of English gentleman diplomats. As William McKinley's, and later Theodore Roosevelt's, secretary of state, as well as Roosevelt's close friend and a regular at the White House, Hay understood the close natural ties that existed between Britain and the United States. To Hay fell the task of eradicating the many years of bitterness between America and Britain. One of the most gifted men of his age, one of the most sympathetic to English culture and society, even John Hay at times miscalculated the fierce cultural tensions that troubled the potential friends, even while the diplomatic difficulties were being resolved.

Both sides had to mend some fences. If Grover Cleveland, the brawling Buffalo, New York, politician, was clumsy and destructive in diplomatic relations, then Britain's imperious Lord Salisbury, who disdained the Americans, was at least as much of a liability. Cleveland and Salisbury, both products of a passing age, were stubborn, unyielding, and imperfect leaders at a time when new cultural and national alliances had to be forged. Cleveland's temper was never as volatile as when he had to deal with Salisbury's patronizing arrogance. Salisbury's successors, Lord Lansdowne and later Arthur Balfour, both good friends of John Hay, were more sympathetic to American problems and further benefited from knowing and liking Americans like John Hay and Thomas Bayard, who were as literate as the better educated English diplomats.

Lord Salisbury, the British prime minister, would have been correct in his response to Grover Cleveland's tirade had he been dealing with the old America. Salisbury was judicious, careful, insulting, and totally ineffective as a diplomat. After taking his time in replying to the Cleveland demands, Salisbury neatly disposed of the legal and historical arguments behind the Monroe Doctrine. His arguments were correct, but all he did was infuriate the very Americans who were most likely to be friendly toward Britain, and who were willing and able to prevent needless enmity or a pointless diplomatic crisis. All that Salisbury's cool logic accomplished was to encourage further wild fantasies about Canada by frustrated and sensitive Americans such as Theodore Roosevelt.

Roosevelt despised Salisbury's obdurate stance. Even in anger Roosevelt could speak sensibly about the mutual destinies of the two English-speaking nations that had remained historical enemies. "We do not wish to be misunderstood. We have no feeling against England. On the contrary we regard her as being well in advance of the great powers of Continental Europe, and we have more sympathy with her. In general, her success tells for the success of civilization, and we wish her well. But where her interests enlist her against the progress of civilization and in favor of the oppression of other nationalities who are struggling upward, our sympathies are immediately forfeited."[9]

In that reasoned response lies the basis of American policy during Roosevelt's presidency. Eventually the cooler heads on both sides of the Atlantic prevailed. Bayard and Hay worked with shrewder and more sensitive English diplomats like Arthur Balfour, and the fuss over Venezuela died down. When Britain gave America important direct and indirect support in the war of 1898, the new friendship prospered. The British postponed taking possession of Mirs Bay off the Chinese coast to allow Commodore Dewey's fleet to use it as a "neutral" port en route to the battle at Manila Bay. The British also convinced the Egyptians to deny Spain the use of their ports for refueling a fleet intended to counterattack the Americans at Manila Bay. Britain expelled Spanish agents in Montreal but allowed Americans to continue limited espionage in Gibraltar. When Dewey seemed threatened by the German fleet at Manila, the British presence calmed a potentially explosive situation and made a lasting impression on the beleaguered Americans. The Americans were ready to bend as well. Hay told Washington in July, 1898, that the "British Government prefer to have us retain the Philippine Islands." The wish became the deed.[10]

9. TR, "The Monroe Doctrine," *Bachelor of Arts*, March, 1896, rpr. *Works, Nat. Ed.*, XIII, 176.
10. For the details of British help, see Bradford Perkins, *The Great Rapprochement* (New York, 1968), 43–47; for the change in British policy, *ibid.*, 34–39. The misunderstandings of British actions in the naval maneuvers at Manila are in Thomas A. Bailey, "Dewey and the Germans at Manila Bay," AHR, XLV (1939), 58–81; John Hay to William R. Day, July 28, 1898, in Hay Papers, LC.

The new sense of friendship went beyond official acts. The British press, unhappy with the Germans, openly adopted the Americans and spoke of a union of the two English-speaking peoples. John Hay told the Lord Mayor's banquet in London on April 21, 1898, that the "good understanding is based on something deeper than expediency."[11] Nonetheless, the two peoples still badly underestimated each other. Britain thought it had acquired a new imperial partner. It had not. America was as fiercely independent of Britain and Europe as ever and would resist any suggested status as a junior partner, no matter how helpful the British navy appeared to be. John Hay was right. Expediency was not at the root of the new American attitude toward Britain. The British were more likely allies than the continental Europeans because of the common background and language they shared with the Americans. But Britain was still a part of Europe in most Americans' eyes.

Even more misleading was the solidarity suggested by Rudyard Kipling's famous imperial poem, "The White Man's Burden," first published in *McClure's*, an American magazine, in February, 1899. (Were British readers tiring of imperial exhortation?) Many literate readers have exaggerated the significance of Kipling's poem, perhaps intended to encourage cultural and diplomatic solidarity. Racist America wanted no part of the European white man's burden, the difficulties of colonies, or reminders of how much trouble the old European style of colonialism could cause the mother country. Britain's anguish with the Boers and America's absolute insistence on freedom rather than annexation for Cuba demonstrated not solidarity with European imperialism, but conviction for the original American ideas of anti-colonialism.

In the rush of new patterns, changing alliances, and cultural confusion, even the most acute observer could make a major blunder in assessing how Britain and America could best coexist as friends. To John Hay fell the dubious distinction of making the first major mistake—albeit with the best intentions.

Standing in the way of a Central American canal built and controlled by the United States was a minor diplomatic obstacle: the old Clayton-Bulwer Treaty with England, negotiated in 1850, giving both countries

11. Allen, *Great Britain and the United States*, 581.

an equal partnership in any future canal. Clayton-Bulwer served its purpose well. The British were satisfied enough with their own economic dominance in Central America and in 1850 did not need a canal. Neither the Americans nor the British wanted competition from other powers; the treaty tended to discourage other ventures and held the area intact until the Americans were ready for their own canal. By 1898 the time had come. The increased pressure of the war of 1898 dramatized the American disadvantages in a two-ocean war; when the flagship *Oregon* sailed from the West Coast bound for Cuba, the twelve-thousand-mile voyage around South America took so long that the American ship almost missed the war.

On the surface British abrogation of their rights in Clayton-Bulwer should have been easy. John Hay and British ambassador Julian Pauncefote were friends. The British government had reassured Secretary of State Olney, and later Hay, that it had no objections to an American canal, planned at the time for Nicaragua, an area dominated by the British. The Hay-Pauncefote Treaty promised to be routine, and John Hay, seeing no potential problems, graciously delegated the details to his British colleague. What neither Hay nor Pauncefote understood was the growing nationalism within the United States: not simple expansionism with which the phenomenon is often confused, but a more complex and all-encompassing feeling within the whole society.

America was emerging from its early historical development. It had reached the end of its continental frontiers in 1890. Its artists and writers were producing literature and art that its wealthy industrialists had the leisure to buy and enjoy. America was on the move, but not in the narrow imperial or political sense. The nation's pace and self-image had changed. The change was reflected in the war of 1898, the building of the White City in Chicago, the unwillingness of the new America to remain a second-class nation or to avoid any challenge.

What rights the British already enjoyed came from the power of the Royal Navy. For John Hay, the diplomat, there could be no danger in formally spelling out in great detail advantages Britain already enjoyed through the implicit power of her navy. Hay, Roosevelt, and any intelligent American knew that without British protection and friendship the Americans could not hope to defend a Central American canal. Hay's mistake was not in the substance of the agreement with Great Britain, but in the very words. They were correct, but superfluous.

Indeed, to many Americans the wording of the Hay-Pauncefote Treaty was abhorrent. Important Americans, including Theodore Roosevelt, were uncomprehending. The United States Senate was both incredulous and incensed. In anguish Theodore Roosevelt, then governor of New York, pleaded with Hay: "Oh how I wish you and the President would drop the treaty and push through a bill to build *and fortify* our own canal!" Roosevelt and the Americans were shocked at the very features that Hay found harmless. An unfortified canal, Roosevelt objected, would fetter the American fleet. And in inviting joint ownership with other countries, Roosevelt claimed, Hay had undermined the principle of the Monroe Doctrine. "If Germany has the same right we have in the Canal across Central America, why not in the partition of any part of Southern America? To my mind, we should consistently refuse to all European powers the right to control, in any shape, any territory in the Western hemisphere which they do not already hold."[12]

Although Theodore Roosevelt and Grover Cleveland were both New York–based national politicians, governors of New York, and presidents of the United States, their dissimilarities were substantial. History labels Cleveland a parochial, stubborn politician more concerned with domestic than foreign affairs, and an avowed anti-imperialist. Roosevelt and his aggressive foreign policy are the apotheosis of the legendary American imperialist. Cleveland, a Democrat from a working-class Buffalo background, and Roosevelt, an aristocratic Long Island and Manhattan Republican, agreed on very few things. Yet on this crucial issue both men, in echoing their own convictions, bellowed the same message for the world to hear: America is no longer content to play second fiddle to Europe. American geographic and strategic interests were much more broadly defined in hemispheric rather than national boundaries, a characteristically bold American move. America under two completely different presidents—different in style, ideology, and party—made a clear case for a larger role in the pecking order of nations.

12. TR to John Hay, February 18, 1900, in MRL, II, 1192.

Theodore Roosevelt's impassioned letter to John Hay was kinder and milder than the United States Senate's reaction to Hay's international treaty with Britain. Deeply shocked and depressed by the wave of protest, Hay insisted on resigning as secretary of state. McKinley wisely dissuaded him, and Hay endured the Senate's almost obscene destruction of the hated diplomatic document. The Senate did not just refuse to approve the Hay-Pauncefote Treaty. It mutilated it and added gratuitous insult to the British. The Senate gleefully rewrote the treaty and gave the United States the sole right to fortify and build the canal, removing any international participation, and to make sure that John Bull got the full message, added a clause that simply and unilaterally abrogated the original Clayton-Bulwer Treaty. The Senate passed its own treaty on September 20, 1902, by a 55–18 vote, knowing full well that even a lesser power than Great Britain could not sign it and retain any measure of self-respect.

Gestures are important. When Richard Olney and Grover Cleveland thumbed their noses at powerful Britain, the British eventually got the message. They got the Senate's message even more quickly. Lord Lansdowne, successor to the Marquis of Salisbury, immediately rejected the Senate's insulting draft. But it was clear to the British that the Americans could simply abrogate the old treaty and build a canal any time they chose. Indeed, the Americans had ignored their legal obligations as early as 1884, when they first made a deal with Nicaragua for a possible canal route. In 1900 Roosevelt had warned Hay, and through Hay the British, of the American temper: "A treaty can always be honorably abrogated—though it must never be abrogated in dishonest fashion."[13] Roosevelt did not make clear the distinction, and the British were hard pressed to find one. But Americans did not shrink from abrogation, and the British, faced with the American determination, looked for something to salvage from the mess. Although the British tried to link saving face in Central America with concessions for their Canadian allies in an unrelated border dispute, the British eventually capitulated completely.

The rewritten Hay-Pauncefote Treaty II gave the United States the right to fortify the new canal, and as a face-saving gesture included a

---

13. *Ibid.*

clause that prohibited blockading the canal and other acts of overt hostility. Theodore Roosevelt, now vice-president, worked hard behind the scenes to convince his English friends that the issue of fortification was irrelevant:

> I felt that it would be criminal in this nation to allow the canal to be used against it in time of war, or not to use the canal in its own interest during such a crisis. As I have said before, this consideration in my mind did not apply to England at all. England's navy would render it absolutely certain that whether the canal was fortified or not, and no matter what treaty stipulation should exist, it would immediately fall into her hands in case there was war between her and the United States. As a matter of fact, if the possibility of war between England and the United States were all there was to consider, it would be wholly to the advantage of the United States to have outside powers guarantee the neutrality of the canal in time of war. But in the event of war with any power of continental Europe, I have felt that such neutrality would be a great disadvantage to our country.[14]

Roosevelt understood that the Americans and the British had become allies in fact if not in words, and that the two nations shared powerful and compelling mutual interests. Neither wanted German expansion in the Western hemisphere, neither wanted Russian expansion in Asia, and each would benefit from American responsibility in the Caribbean, which would free the British fleet for action in the rest of an increasingly troubled world. Hay had known this when he negotiated the first treaty. But he had underestimated the new sense the Americans had of themselves.

Hay had no difficulty coming to terms with the new spirit in America; he remained an effective diplomat, able and willing to negotiate forcefully with his English friends. But the British, though they came around eventually, were less eager. Cultural prejudices and habits die hard. Roosevelt disliked Lord Lansdowne, the new British prime minister, for his refusal to understand the new relationship that existed between the two English-speaking powers.[15] Even in the growing mood of detente, the Americans continually battled the condescending British

14. The text and chronology of Hay-Pauncefote Treaty II is in FRUS, 1902, pp. 513–17; TR to Arthur Lee, April 24, 1901, in MRL, III, 64–65; see also Lee to TR, April 11, 1901, in Theodore Roosevelt Papers, LC.
15. TR to Henry Cabot Lodge, March 27, 1901, in MRL, III, 32.

attitude toward America, an attitude that drove Theodore Roosevelt to near apoplexy, and even shook old Anglophiles like John Hay and the new American ambassador to Britain, Joseph Choate.

But the British needed American help more than the Americans needed the British, and diplomacy could not undo the changing destinies of the two nations. Before the final passage of the revised Hay-Pauncefote Treaty, Theodore Roosevelt had become the new American president. The new treaty won overwhelming Senate approval, 76–6; when Theodore Roosevelt signed it on December 26, 1901, he did so with immense personal satisfaction. Not only was the final Hay-Pauncefote agreement the kind of treaty Roosevelt had wanted even when he was governor of New York, it was fittingly the first treaty Roosevelt signed as president. In the Hay-Pauncefote Treaty II, the Americans won all their demands and gave no real concessions.

But President Theodore Roosevelt did not gloat over his hard-won triumph. Instead he took the trouble to point out to his friend and personal confidant in British affairs, Arthur Lee, that the treaty was not simply an American victory: "I must say how pleased I was by the ratification of the treaty. Really I think it is as much to your interest as to ours."[16] Roosevelt encouraged the sense of growing detente by his conciliatory attitude. But it remained apparent that though a detente was clearly in the American interests, the direction of that detente would be firmly in American hands. The most serious threat to the new friendship was the long-simmering Canadian-Alaskan boundary dispute. Not only firmness and patience, but shrewd and tough diplomacy would be necessary to preserve the new and still tenuous alliance.

16. TR to Arthur Lee, December 31, 1901, in MRL, III, 214.

7 / Theodore Roosevelt and the Alaskan Boundary Dispute

The Preservation of the
New Anglo-American Detente

Even before he assumed the American presidency, Theodore Roosevelt held strong opinions on the continuing Canadian-American dispute over the Alaskan boundary: "I have studied that question pretty thoroughly," Roosevelt told his English confidant, Arthur Lee, "and I do not think the Canadians have a leg to stand on." The Canadian claim was as silly as if the Americans had arbitrarily claimed a part of Newfoundland. Furthermore Roosevelt resented the fact that "Canada did not in the least share England's good will towards us in '98."[1] There was no love lost between the Canadians and Americans. Both were caught up in the intense national fervor of the times.

A prospering America added to the Canadian frustration. Having to depend on a distant mother country for support was difficult enough. Worse was the continuing evidence that Canada's neighbor to the south was better situated geographically and becoming more prosperous and powerful with each passing year. Theodore Roosevelt did not really covet Canada, though during the Alaskan boundary dispute he frequently talked offhandedly of holding it hostage to insure responsible British behavior. His attitude toward the Canadians was one of measured contempt. The boundary dispute seemed to Roosevelt to be a completely artificial issue, designed either to help the Canadians gain territory and concessions they were not entitled to, or to salvage for the British some minor consolation from their unsuccessful diplomatic

1. TR to Arthur Lee, March 18, 1901, in MRL, III, 20, 21.

173

battles with the resurgent Americans. Both objectives struck the sensitive Americans as offensive and made dealing reasonably with the British more difficult.

The original boundary between Alaska and Canada, drawn in a treaty between Great Britain and Russia in 1825, was both a convenient abstraction and a geographical absurdity. The boundary was drawn to parallel one of the most irregular coastlines in the world. The diplomatic purpose of the apparent confusion is clear. Russia, which owned Alaska, insisted on denying Great Britain access to the coast or the use of its navigable waters. At the time, the land and adjacent waters seemed valueless, and the British did not contest the Russian position. Later when the value of the area changed, the boundary did not.

When the United States acquired Alaska through the Alaskan Purchase Treaty of 1867, America also retained the Russian boundary and access rights. Increased resources of fish, lumber, and eventually gold changed the area from wasteland to cornucopia. Suddenly denied a priceless tidewater and coastline, the Canadians rebelled. Ironically, most of the gold was found on Canadian land, though access to it was through American territory. The Americans made the situation worse with inflexible coastal shipping regulations and an aggravating lumber tariff.

The intense nationalism of the 1890s—Canadian and American—compounded the friction. Some of Canada's problems were eased when British Columbia became a part of the dominion in 1871, but soon the Canadian disputes became British problems and threatened the spirit of the new Anglo-American detente. A joint high commission failed to solve the problem in 1899. After that failure and the rejection of the first Hay-Pauncefote Treaty, Britain tried unsuccessfully to link the renegotiation of the Clayton-Bulwer Treaty of 1850 with the Alaskan border dispute between the United States and Canada.

Even John Hay, who regarded the dispute as an irritant and a threat to the increasing friendship with Britain, and not a strategic necessity for the United States, thought the Canadian border case entirely spurious. The British aggravated the Americans when they attempted to use the Cleveland-Olney demand for arbitration over Venezuela as a precedent for the Canadian dispute. Hay ingeniously suggested a commission of six members, three from each side, which, though it resembled arbitration, insured that with the three Americans voting together, the United States could not lose. In effect the commission simply extended the negotiations, hoping for an eventual settlement; Hay's device successfully separated the Alaskan boundary dispute from the Isthmian issues.

From the start, the Canadian cause was realistically and diplomatically hopeless. Britain would have willingly sacrificed even genuine Canadian interests to keep the United States as a needed ally in 1901; it was obvious that the Canadian case had been manufactured to take advantage of the opportunity offered by the strong American desire for a Central American canal. The British and the Canadians were grasping at diplomatic straws. The British, by linking a Central American canal to the spurious argument, hoped to ease the real cause of the Canadian-Alaskan boundary dispute—Canada's frustration. Shut off from the wealth of a suddenly rich timberland, and unhappy with the growing contrast between America's prosperity and her own still relatively undeveloped economy, the Canadians hoped to gain some satisfaction through diplomacy.

The British were caught in the middle. They sympathized with the Canadians, but there was little Britain could do to help. The British were more and more dependent on the new American goodwill, which gave the empire a desperately needed informal ally in the unstable Caribbean, while freeing Britain to fight its more pressing imperial battles in Asia and Africa. But although the United States was in the better tactical position, Americans could not act with impunity. To properly defend a Central American canal after the monumental engineering task of building it, the Americans needed the protection of a friendly Great Britain—or at least a neutral British navy. The Americans could remain secure in their splendid isolation, their mainland fairly safe from foreign attack, without British friendship. But enlarged trade with other nations, the result of successful American industrial expansion, was impossible without increased naval power.

Until the Americans could build their own navy, they needed all the help they could get. Friendship with Britain, as Theodore Roosevelt realized from the start, was essential. With Britain's informal support, though it was far short of a formal alliance, the United States could bluff and bluster its way to the status of at least a marginally great power, protect its rights to a Central American canal, and assert its own hegemony in nearby Caribbean waters. An implicit alliance with Britain protected American strategic interests and prevented permanent European incursions in nearby Latin America.

The Americans and the British needed one another. By 1901 their leaders understood the importance of the two nations' mutual interests. Canada, however, remained the odd man out, the colonial stepchild caught between the distant mother country concerned with world politics, and the aggressive and irritating emerging power to the south. The United States had been a cultural and political irritant for over a century. Although the Canadians remained an undeveloped nation and no match for the dynamic United States economically, in national zeal the Canadians were easily the Americans' equal. Canadian nationalism, fanned by frustration and bitterness, became an increasing and serious threat to the tenuous and still developing detente between America and Britain.

Although the eventual solution of the Alaskan boundary dispute seemed to be the result of international arbitration, the struggle was actually resolved by direct diplomatic negotiation. Arbitration was a subterfuge, a face-saving device to give what was a *fait accompli* the look of a more reasonable procedure. The Americans from the start refused to arbitrate the Alaskan boundary dispute. They never changed their position, though at times they appeared to waver by accepting arbitration.

As a compromise President Theodore Roosevelt agreed, on the surface, to submit the matter to arbitration; but he always made clear that arbitration was merely a gesture of compromise and that the United States reserved its rights, regardless of what an arbitration commission decided. Roosevelt has been accused of using big-stick diplomacy throughout the Canadian boundary dispute, of being insensitive to the wishes of a weaker neighbor, and of simply bullying the British and the Canadians to concede to American desires. Since Roosevelt and the Americans won all their points, the charges have a degree of plausibility. But as Roosevelt pointed out from the beginning, since the Canadian legal and moral case was without merit, American self-interest demanded that the United States remain firm and not agree to arbitrate a national interest that was not subject to compromise or any kind of arbitration.

International arbitration was at the height of its brief vogue during the Canadian-American dispute, and America strongly supported it as a solution to difficult international problems that did not involve either party's vital interests. Roosevelt explained (semiprivately) to Arthur Lee why the United States would not arbitrate the Alaskan dispute: "There are cases where a nation has no business to arbitrate. . . . This Canadian claim to the disputed territory in Alaska is entirely modern. Twenty years ago the Canadian maps showed the lines just as ours did." Roosevelt argued that the instances where the United States supported arbitration were completely different. The Canadians "have no such *prima facie* case as the Venezuelans had. You did not arbitrate the Transvaal matter, and I do not very well see how you could have arbitrated it."[2]

Roosevelt's diplomacy was far from big-stick intransigence. He remained opposed to arbitration on the Alaskan boundary dispute in principle and practice, but he was willing to appear to yield. If the other side wished the settlement to appear to be an arbitration arrangement, President Roosevelt was willing to go along with the useful fiction. In his final instructions to Secretary of State John Hay, Roosevelt made it clear that there were strict limits to the American concession: "I will appoint three commissioners to meet three of their commissioners, if they so desire, but I think I shall instruct our three commissioners when appointed that they are in no case to yield any of our claim."[3] Roosevelt eventually relented somewhat by seriously negotiating a compromise settlement and, as the talks proceeded, agreed to additional American concessions. But there always remained a point beyond which Roosevelt was unwilling to budge.

He was not bashful in using a show of force. Secretary of War Elihu Root gradually strengthened the American garrisons in the disputed area, mainly to insure that the Americans could prevent the isolated disorders, common to any mining frontier, that might further inflame a touchy situation. The British, who were as anxious as the Americans to

2. TR to Arthur Lee, April 24, 1901, in MRL, III, 66.
3. TR to John Hay, July 16, 1902, in MRL, III, 294.

keep the Klondike calm, had warned about possible new insurrections. The Canadians obviously had the most to gain by disruption and disorder, and Roosevelt was vehement in his distaste for Canada's opportunist diplomacy. He complained bitterly of the "spirit of bumptuous truculence which for years England has resisted." Roosevelt traced the Canadian tactic with "this wholly false claim. They now say as they have got the false claim in, trouble may come if it is not acted on." Roosevelt saw the Canadian tactic as big-stick diplomacy. His reaction was firm but not overly belligerent: "I feel a good deal like telling them that if trouble comes it will be purely because of their own fault; and although it would not be pleasant for us it would be death for them."[4]

The Canadians were the aggressors in the dispute, a fact that in the heat of the diplomatic maneuverings that followed many observers tended to forget. Instead of simply ignoring the Canadian claim, which was frivolous from the start, the Roosevelt administration treated it respectfully and diplomatically. By not responding in force immediately, the Americans ignored the patent provocations and maintained a tenuous diplomatic order, the exact opposite of mythical big-stick diplomacy. Diplomats Hay, Pauncefote, and Roosevelt worked together to minimize the possibility of a Canadian-American confrontation. Even the Canadian police, afraid of violence, cooperated in exchanging important information on possible disorders. Roosevelt assessed the situation in February, 1902, as not serious but one which could add friction to the dispute. On March 29, 1902, Roosevelt had Secretary of War Elihu Root send "additional troops as quietly and unostentatiously as possible so as to be able promptly to prevent any possible disturbance along the disputed boundary line."[5]

4. See John Hay to Elihu Root, November 23, 1901, and George Cortelyou to Root, May 27, 1902, in Phillip Jessup, *Elihu Root* (2 vols., New York, 1938), I, 391–92; TR to John Hay, July 16, 1902, in MRL, III, 294–95.
5. Of the writers who use Roosevelt's actions in the Canadian border dispute to distort the actual diplomacy, Pringle is probably the worst offender. By omitting the final phrase "to prevent any possible disturbance along the disputed boundary line," he makes the Root order appear more ominous than it was. Henry Pringle, *Theodore Roosevelt: A Biography* (New York, 1931), 290. For a discussion of Pringle's distortion, see MRL, III, 294n and Jessup, *Elihu Root*, 390–91. For other similar historical distortions, see Frederick Marks, III, *Velvet on Iron: The Diplomacy of Theodore Roosevelt* (Lincoln, Nebr., 1979), 110, 126n45.

The stage was set for one of the most dramatic diplomatic show-downs in modern American history. All three principals accepted John Hay's original proposal of equal representation for both sides, American and British-Canadian. (The proposal had been rejected by Britain in 1899 but in 1903 was eagerly accepted as a way out.) Roosevelt publicly made it clear to everyone that he did not regard the proceedings as an arbitration tribunal. Such a designation he insisted was absurd. And to make sure that no one misunderstood the position of the United States, he went out of his way to give George Smalley, an English journalist with whom Roosevelt frequently clashed, a not-so-veiled threat of force. When Roosevelt told Smalley of his willingness to "send up engineers to run our line as we assert it . . . and send troops to guard and hold it," Smalley objected to the president's tone. "I meant it to be drastic," Roosevelt told the writer. Roosevelt was adamant. "In the principle in-volved there will of course be no compromise."[6]

Roosevelt told the commission that they could draw boundaries, but that the only boundary question was whether the original treaty boundary was right or wrong. The boundary specified in the original American-Russian treaty had been honored by everyone—Americans, Russians, and British—for sixty years. The Canadians alone demanded a change. Roosevelt barred a compromise: "It is right in its entirety or wrong in its entirety," Roosevelt declared. And further, if the British failed to agree with the American position, Roosevelt would be forced to assume bad faith on Britain's part. He left no doubt how the United States would deal with British bad faith: He would ask Congress "for an appropriation so that we may run the line ourselves." Roosevelt thought that course was inadvisable but felt the United States would have no choice.[7]

Once he became involved in the negotiations that concerned strategic national interests, Roosevelt was unrelenting, using every diplomatic and political weapon at his command. The most ingenious involved the employment of Supreme Court Justice Oliver Wendell Holmes as a spe-

6. Henry Cabot Lodge, Journal, March 8, 1902, in John Garraty, *Henry Cabot Lodge* (New York, 1953), 244.
7. TR to Commissioners Root, Lodge, and Turner, March 17, 1903, in MRL, III, 449; TR to John Hay, June 29, 1903, in MRL, IV, 507.

cial emissary. The briefing Roosevelt gave to Holmes is an impressive legal and diplomatic document and a brilliant if unprecedented example of international legal pressure. Roosevelt asked Holmes to talk to Britain's foreign minister Joseph Chamberlain "privately and unofficially" on Roosevelt's view of the matter. He reiterated the threat to run an American boundary unilaterally, calling the Canadian claims analogous to their claiming Nantucket Island near Cape Cod. Roosevelt agreed that a Canadian case for the Portland Canal islands existed, though insisting that the American case was better. Roosevelt basically gave Holmes and the British the same message: settle or else. Roosevelt was convinced in retrospect that Justice Holmes's intervention was one of the decisive elements in the eventual American victory.[8] With three Americans, two Canadians, and one Briton on the commission, it became obvious that the British member would decide the dispute.

The British representative, Chief Justice Lord Alverstone, was regarded by everyone as a man of integrity and principle. For the Americans, however, doubts still remained on what the official British position might be. If the British favored the Americans, as they might for diplomatic reasons, or if they remained neutral, as they might for judicial reasons, the Americans were confident they would prevail. Hay, writing to American consul Henry White on May 22, 1903, assessed American chances as dependent on "whether Lord Alverstone goes on the bench with an imperative mandate or not. If he goes there with an open mind, we consider our case as won."[9]

The Americans at times verged on paranoia but never failed to use any means at hand to influence a decision in their favor. Ambassador Choate carefully placed the lovely Nannie Lodge next to the chief justice at the first dinner in London, with hopes of charming Lord Alverstone. Lodge's wife, one of the most celebrated women of her time, was, as always, successful. Meanwhile Lodge himself talked with every British politician of note.[10]

Roosevelt refused to take anything for granted. He told Hay on July

8. TR to Justice Oliver Wendell Holmes, July 25, 1903, in MRL, III, 529–31; TR to Holmes, October 30, 1903, in MRL, III, 634.
9. John Hay to Henry White, May 22, 1903, in Henry White Papers, LC.
10. Garraty, *Henry Cabot Lodge*, 247.

29, 1903, that if Britain did not agree, the United States would act in a manner that would wound English pride. Roosevelt used Root's dual role as secretary of war and "impartial jurist" to deliver an ultimatum, which severely compromised Root's own difficult role but left no doubt that compromise was out of the question. Once again Roosevelt threatened to establish enough posts on the disputed islands to give the United States "actual occupancy." He would then ask Congress for money for at least a partial survey.[11]

Roosevelt fretted that his own commissioners, finding themselves in a judicial setting, might weaken and become neutral arbitrating commissioners, rather than diplomatic representatives of the president. Roosevelt's pressure on Lodge and Root never relented, and the Americans remained single-minded. The British were assailed on all sides by persistent Americans and Canadians.

The formal meeting of the boundary commission began in London, September 3, 1903, with the main hearings scheduled for September 15. The British (Canadian) case was carefully worked out with legal arguments. The Americans continued their unrelenting campaign of personal diplomacy. Lodge and Root met frequently with Lord Alverstone, even though such meetings really constituted a form of blatant political pressure. The Americans wavered between cool confidence and wild paranoia. The only consistently confident American was the senior diplomat Henry White, who remained calm and optimistic throughout the proceedings. Roosevelt kept up the pressure, frequently repeating past threats or alternatives, or, as on September 26, 1903, asking a new representative to deliver an old message. Henry White passed on to the appropriate British officials Roosevelt's promise that the United States would take matters in its own hands and not enter into any other negotiations if the current talks failed to solve the problem to the complete satisfaction of the Americans.[12]

11. TR to John Hay, July 29, 1903, in MRL, III, 533; TR to Elihu Root, August 8, 1903, in MRL, III, 546.

12. Henry Cabot Lodge to TR, September 5, 1903, and September 13, 1903, in Henry Cabot Lodge (ed.), *Selections from the Correspondence of Theodore Roosevelt and Henry Cabot Lodge, 1884–1918* (2 vols.; New York, 1925), II, 53–57; Henry White to TR, September 19, 1903, and TR to White, September 26, 1903, in Theodore Roosevelt Papers, LC.

John Hay and Henry White frequently softened Roosevelt's direct threats by personal contact and large amounts of charm and reassurance. The Americans, from Roosevelt on down, continued to threaten the Canadians but not the British, making it clear that Great Britain's self-interest would be better served by aligning with America rather than Canada. The main American worry was the possibility that Lord Alverstone would make a political rather than a legal decision. If Alverstone stuck to his legal guns as expected, the American case was airtight. The fear remained that if he wavered, sentimental sympathy for Canada might temper the judicial process. If politics did enter the deliberations, the Americans were determined that pressure from Canadians would be matched by that of Americans in Washington and on the scene in London.

As the proceedings neared a conclusion, it became apparent that American fears over Lord Alverstone's ambivalence were justified. He began to waver wildly, considering arbitrary compromises that would enrage the Americans. Roosevelt had feared that any procedure resembling arbitration might, in the end, result in a political rather than a legal solution. Not all compromises were equally bad. The trick was to preserve America's original strong legal case and somehow not make Canada's resentments more volatile. In spite of his previous tough talk, as the time for decision approached the president was eager to compromise. Roosevelt told Lodge to yield on the Portland Canal islands, the Wales and Pearse islands, and other minor areas, providing he held the line on the main American principle. Roosevelt was willing to compromise specific elements to avoid a deadlocked tribunal, which would leave the main issue still unresolved.[13]

From the American standpoint a stalemate was as bad as a decisive defeat. When it became clear on October 12 that Lord Alverstone was perilously close to a political compromise favoring Canada, even the usually circumspect Elihu Root decided to warn the British in no uncertain terms. Root, in a delightful instruction, told diplomat Henry White to threaten Foreign Secretary Arthur Balfour with dire consequences if the Americans were denied what they considered right.

13. TR to Henry Cabot Lodge, October 5, 1903, in MRL, III, 616; TR to John Hay, September 15, 1903, in MRL, III, 601.

Somehow White had to manage to deliver that message without saying anything that "might be misconstrued as being in the nature of a threat."[14]

Henry White, a magnificent old-school American diplomat, could and did accomplish the impossible assignment with aplomb. As a personal friend of Arthur Balfour, White talked with the English leader at Balfour's country home and found that the British were as concerned as the Americans over Canadian pressure. The White-Balfour conversations on October 12 were probably decisive. The British officially dropped any further pretense at alliance with the Canadians or the appearance of impartiality. In an unprecedented action during a supposedly independent arbitration decision, Balfour openly consulted Lord Alverstone and shared with him the mutual American-British misgivings. Alverstone still resisted. He wanted to give the Canadians some compromise. The Americans persisted, indicating that they would compromise by accepting a final decision on five questions while continuing to negotiate the remaining two, a stand that the Americans would have completely rejected earlier. Even more compelling was the American decision to accept a boundary compromise, though it would dilute the entire principle the Americans had insisted upon from the beginning.[15]

By October 15 the arbitration proceedings had given way to intensive diplomatic negotiations between the principal diplomats of both nations. American ambassador Choate met with Lord Lansdowne and reached an agreement between the two countries. Lansdowne called in Alverstone and worked out the terms of the compromise that would be acceptable to both the Americans and the British.[16] At this crucial juncture in the proceedings, the Canadians were without an ally. The ultimate decision was not based on the boundary disputes, but on the need to maintain the spirit of detente between America and Britain.

From the beginning, the Canadians had been adept at the fierce political infighting that characterized the frequently brutal diplomacy, but in the end the Canadians succumbed to equal American pressure and

14. Elihu Root to Henry White, October 2, 1903, in Henry White Papers.
15. Henry White to John Hay, November 20, 1903, in Henry White Papers; Henry Cabot Lodge to TR, September 24, 1901, Lodge, ed., *Selections*, II, 57.
16. John Hay to Joseph Choate, October 16, 1903, in John Hay Papers, LC; Garraty, *Henry Cabot Lodge*, 254.

superior American inducements. The Americans made clear that any British support of the Canadian position would be costly. The British were not prepared to pay a considerable diplomatic cost simply to show their support of a dominion, especially since the Canadians had neither a strong legal nor a strong moral case on their side. The Americans had all the advantages: a strong legal, moral, historical, and diplomatic stand and a persuasive presentation.

Even though the private negotiations had resolved the dispute by October 15, 1903, suspense remained high until Lord Alverstone agreed to the political settlement and the British officially announced a final decision. The Americans realistically feared that their victory could be snatched away by a sudden and capricious reversal. On October 17 Alverstone finally agreed to the American boundary line and in spite of three days of intense Canadian objections, on October 20, 1903, the decision was formally announced.[17] The announcement ended one of the most frenetic episodes of modern international politics. Historical retrospect has been no less frenzied than the original events.

The Americans had won a major victory in the Alverstone decision. But although the decision carefully followed the original legal logic of the dispute, historians have regarded the episode more as an example of irresponsible Rooseveltian big-stick diplomacy than as a benchmark demonstration of shrewd, patient, and effective power diplomacy. Theodore Roosevelt used far more of a velvet glove than a big stick and successfully resisted the real big-stick tactics of the Canadians, who were the original and continuing aggressors throughout the dispute.[18]

The Americans never wavered in regarding the matter as closed to arbitration. They knew that the main issue was Canadian nationalism rather than a valid border dispute, and that the main diplomatic problem was maintaining cordial American-British relations in the face of a volatile but irrelevant challenge. For the Americans the main goal of the Canadian-Alaskan boundary dispute was to find a way to allow the British to save face with their Canadian dominion without penalizing American self-interest or endangering the new Anglo-American friendship. In the Alaskan dispute, the Canadians, Americans, and British

17. Text of the decision is in FRUS, 1903, 543–44.
18. The best revisionist argument for Roosevelt is in Marks, *Velvet on Iron*, 108–11.

worked out mutual diplomatic problems, each side using as much diplomatic pressure as it could muster. The Americans won because Theodore Roosevelt understood the balance of interest and strength involved, and because he was entirely correct, legally and morally, in assessing the Alaskan boundary dispute as a manufactured complaint. The American position was strategically the strongest. Roosevelt was supported by his cabinet, the Senate, prevalent public opinion, and eventually by a British chief justice.

Roosevelt, recounting his own reluctance to even pretend to use arbitration, wrote afterward to his son of how pleased he was with the final result. He also revealed the strategy that he used consistently. thoughout the struggle: "I . . . would trust to the absolute justice of our case, as well to a straight-out declaration to certain high British officials that I meant business." If the commission did not work out as expected, Roosevelt would draw the line and refuse any further negotiations. For Roosevelt the firmness of the American diplomatic initiative and the justice of the case were equally decisive in winning the significant diplomatic settlement.[19]

At first the Canadians were unhappy with the decision and issued charges of big-stick diplomacy and unfair political pressure, charges that were erroneous at the time and have remained a part of the historical distortion in spite of overwhelming contrary evidence. The Canadians charged Alverstone with yielding to political influence, a charge he consistently denied. Roosevelt was not nearly as unyielding as he appeared to be during the proceedings. He gave up Pearse Island and Wales Island, which were much larger and more well-developed than the two islands America retained. The Canadians calmed down after a while, and in 1908 even named one of their mountains after Lord Alverstone.

American relations with Britain were strengthened. By conceding to the Americans virtually every point concerning Central America and the Isthmus, the British made a firm friend, if not an ally, in North America; the friction between Canada and America was lessened, though not eliminated. As Roosevelt had insisted from the start, the settlement favoring America in Alaska and in Central America was in

19. TR to Theodore Roosevelt, Jr., October 20, 1903, in MRL, III, 635.

the best British interests. Roosevelt continued to assure the British that American nationalism expressed through the Monroe Doctrine was not directed against the now firm Anglo-American understanding, but against common enemies.

By 1903, the United States and Theodore Roosevelt had consolidated with Great Britain the informal alliance that had started so stormily in 1895 when Grover Cleveland and Richard Olney stunned the world by making Venezuela a matter of American strategic interest. Roosevelt could put into words and policy what Cleveland and Olney felt intuitively. The Alaskan settlement was not an exercise in big-stick diplomacy but a sound continuation of a new American policy that reflected America's growth and inevitable influence in a changing world.

Epilogue / Theodore Roosevelt and Henry James
Cultural Nationalism versus Imperialism in Modern America

Henry James, the expatriate novelist who was a guest at the White House in 1905, is a far better symbol of the Theodore Roosevelt era than the Panama Canal. James's novels about sensitive Americans losing their innocence—with dignity—in sophisticated Europe are more germane to America's relationship with the world in Theodore Roosevelt's presidency than the usual symbols of imperialism and the big stick.

To make even Panama the *bête noire* of the Roosevelt presidency requires extensive stretching of historical evidence. Historians who accept the Panamanian episode as an example of a belligerent, bellicose, or imperial presidency must ignore Colombia's specific condition in 1902 and 1903. Although undisputed, Colombia's revolutionary chaos is usually not emphasized. Also ignored, or not emphasized, are the illegal seizure of power by Colombia's acting president José Marroquín, Panama's tradition of independence and revolution, and the older French motives for building canals as symbols of modern civilization and works of art and technology. Instead, Panama is reduced to a stereotyped example of American imperialism, or Roosevelt's big stick, and most of the historical questions, which remain open, are simply ignored. Panama dominates much of the history of the Roosevelt presidency for the wrong reasons. In addition, Panamanian-American history is often inaccurate and badly distorted.

The Panamanian Revolution was justified by Panama's own history and often predicted by Colombia's own diplomats, who had worked out several agreements with the United States and France for a canal at Panama. It was Colombia and its leader Marroquín that made a settlement impossible, and it was Marroquín who Colombia's citizenry blamed after the news of the Panamanian revolution became known. Not until the Latin American newspapers picked up the partisan columns of the Democratic, anti-Roosevelt press, did Theodore Roosevelt emerge as a possible villain in Panama. But arguments by Democratic senators like John T. Morgan made in the heat of the political moment, by journalists like Hearst and Pulitzer looking for sensational issues, and by Latin American nationalists looking for anti-American slogans should not become the permanent historical record of a misunderstood and inaccurate legend.

But Panama is only one example of the wrong legend and the wrong history. Theodore Roosevelt's interventions in the Dominican Republic in 1905 and in Cuba in 1906 are also seen as hallmarks of the new imperial America. Yet, the Americans did not stay in either place; nor did they envision colonies in the Caribbean. In both instances, governments on the verge of anarchy and chaos asked the United States for help in restoring order. In the Dominican Republic the American occupation restored order and served as the occasion for proclaiming the Roosevelt Corollary to the Monroe Doctrine. The Dominican intervention was not an imperialistic seizure in the Caribbean but an assumption by the United States of responsibility for debts incurred by poorer Latin American nations. The Roosevelt Corollary was designed to prevent European interference or intervention in Latin American affairs, whatever the pretext or reason. In the Dominican Republic both the actual American intervention and Roosevelt's principle worked well. The Dominican debt was reduced and finally settled; the Americans not only restored order but built schools, roads, and hospitals. And when the debt was settled, the occupation ended. If anything, the intervention was an example of anti-colonialism and anti-imperialism at its best.

In 1906 Cuba was in equally dire straits. The American intervention lasted just long enough to stabilize the government. Once again the Americans left as soon as they could. And the Americans would have left the Philippines just as quickly had it been strategically or humanely possible. The other grand example of Roosevelt's big stick, the sailing of

188

the Great White Fleet in 1907–1909, occurred as part of a settlement between the United States and Japan, ending the worst instances of racial discrimination against Orientals in California. Roosevelt settled the real grievances of the Japanese in California, and then used the fleet to assure the world that the Americans had not been pressured by a superior Japanese navy. The fleet's goodwill mission began with a triumphant visit at Rio de Janeiro and ended with a festive reception by the Japanese at Yokohama.

Ignored in the convenient imagery of the big stick and the slogan of imperialism is Theodore Roosevelt's close work with the Hague Convention of 1907 and the World Court for arbitration of international disputes, the inclusion of Latin America's Drago Doctrine—no forced collection of debts—as part of the Roosevelt Corollary, and Roosevelt's diplomacy in moving Latin American countries to full participation in international law tribunals. Theodore Roosevelt also worked with both the kaiser and the tsar to prevent the spreading of the Russo-Japanese conflict. When the kaiser's opportunistic diplomacy threatened Europe's precarious peace in 1906, Roosevelt supported the Algeciras talks, which helped maintain the European balance of power and peace.

Roosevelt himself encouraged the image of the big stick as an effective diplomatic tool. In 1905 the kaiser hesitated joining Russia because of the promise from Roosevelt of swift American intervention. The kaiser, who had already tangled with Roosevelt in the Venezuelan dispute of 1902–1903, took Roosevelt's messages seriously. In letters to the tsar he indicated an awareness of the American diplomatic presence. Roosevelt and historian Tyler Dennett were convinced that Roosevelt's intervention helped prevent Germany from intervening on the side of Russia. The kaiser told the tsar, "If anybody in the world is able to influence the Japanese and to induce them to be reasonable in their proposals, it is President Roosevelt." Influence and reason were hallmarks of Roosevelt's diplomacy, not belligerence. The big stick was more a useful image than a historical reality.[1]

1. Tyler Dennett, "Could T. R. Have Stopped the War," *World's Work*, XLIX (February, 1925), 392–99; TR to Cecil Spring Rice, December 27, 1904, in MRL, IV, 1087; William II to Nicholas I, March 6, 1905, in Isaac Don Levine and N. F. Grant (eds.), *Letters From the Kaiser to the Tsar* (London, 1920), 189.

We are more accustomed to viewing American history in political terms, or lately with New Left revisionists in economic and diplomatic contexts. Until the myths and inaccuracies of Panama are finally sorted out, Panama is a poor symbol of anything except perhaps historical hysteria. A better symbol than big sticks and imperialism is the role of Theodore Roosevelt as a gentleman aristocrat, a man who shunned a standard career in business and corporation law to exercise political power and responsibility. Indeed, America and Americans did not go from innocence to corruption in one imperial decade, as some older diplomatic histories suggest. Although imaginary, a much better and a more accurate explanation of American society existed in the already published novels of Henry James.

In literature, art, politics, industry, and diplomacy, Americans were reaching out, looking for a new place in the world and a new set of accomplishments. The Americans of 1900 were following Victor Hugo's plea to Ferdinand de Lesseps to astonish the world with peaceful feats. Americans were also following the advice artist Little Bilham (a fictional James Whistler?) gave to Lambert Strether, the hero of James's novel *The Ambassadors* (1903): "Live!" Strether lives by discovering the wonders of Paris and French civilization without losing his own American identity. Although Paris and France are a revelation to the middle-aged American writer, Strether vows of his new consciousness that it must not spoil him. For Strether, the paradigm of a moral American, there could be no pleasant exile in Paris; the innocence is ended, but Strether insists, "Not, out of the whole affair, to have got anything for myself." Strether's principle is consistent with Theodore Roosevelt's own ideas of duty.[2]

Theodore Roosevelt wanted nothing from his enlistment in the war of 1898, though others insisted that he had planned it for the national political prominence that followed. In extricating Americans from Caribbean interventions, the Russians and Japanese from their disastrous war, the Europeans from entanglement over Morocco at Algeciras, Roosevelt is a model of the Jamesian idea of the good American. Both

2. Leon Edel, *Henry James: The Master, 1901–1916* (Philadelphia, 1972), 375; Henry James, *The Ambassadors* (New York, 1903; rpr. Boston, 1960), 365.

James's characters and Theodore Roosevelt grew up with the times. In James's 1877 novel *The American*, Christopher Newman was a callow, well-meaning, and wealthy innocent; the 1903 version of Newman, Lewis Lambert Strether, is still innocent, but compared with the earlier American, he is a sophisticated quick learner. In 1877 Newman remains a puzzled outsider in Europe; in 1903 Strether is master of both worlds: he has charmed the French, has two women in love with him, remains uncorruptedly the American—no longer innocent but still free of European materialism—and he is the moral balance of power in the complex Jamesian novel.

Theodore Roosevelt and Henry James had much more in common than either thought possible. Both were close personal friends of novelist, poet, and diplomat John Hay, the Henry Cabot Lodges, and diplomat Henry White. Both were vigorous walking companions of Jules Jusserand, who walked with Henry James in the Paris of the 1880s and, as the French ambassador to the United States, with President Theodore Roosevelt in Washington's Rock Creek Park. When James and Roosevelt met, the epithets they had thrown at each other were forgiven; they were gentlemen. Forgotten was Roosevelt's opinion that James was "a miserable little snob" whose "polished, pointless, uninteresting stories about the upper social classes of England make one blush to think he was once an American." James thought Theodore Roosevelt "the mere monstrous embodiment of unprecedented resounding Noise." But at the dinner for James at the White House on January 12, 1905, the two men managed famously. Henry James was accorded a seat of honor almost next to the president and was impressed. "Theodore Rex," as James referred to him, was "a wonderful little machine: destined to be overstrained perhaps, but not as yet, truly, betraying the least creak. It functions astonishingly, and is quite exciting to see. But it's really like something behind a great plate-glass window on Broadway."[3]

3. TR to James Brander Matthews, June 29, 1894, in MRL, I, 390. Roosevelt's early assessment of James was a response to a collection by writers in England, *The Yellow Book*, which in 1894 carried two of James' stories, "The Death of the Lion," and "The Coxon Fund"; Henry James to Dr. J. William White, November 14, 1912, in Percy Lubbock (ed.), *The Letters of Henry James* (2 vols.; New York, 1920), II, 283; Edel, *Henry James: The Master*, 266.

Much of the later acrimony between the two men came from the unfortunate dispute over John Hay's role as secretary of state in his dying days in 1905. When Roosevelt directed the Russo-Japanese diplomacy, Hay received the credit, and was later the target of Roosevelt's resentment when Hay's friends suggested that he, not Roosevelt, helped bring about the peace that won Roosevelt the Nobel Peace Prize. Roosevelt struck back and intimated that Hay had been virtually useless and that Roosevelt had acted as secretary of state when Hay was ailing. Attacks on both sides were exaggerations, but once the acrimony started, friends and partisans made it a part of the permanent legacy that clouded the original and splendid Roosevelt-Hay collaboration.[4]

Although there were some disagreements between the two men on policy, they were not serious, were easily resolved, and did not interfere with the good personal relationship the men enjoyed. The biggest difference was generational: Hay was an older man and tended to see Roosevelt as a more energetic youngster, which accounts for Hay's paternal (rather than patronizing) attitude toward Roosevelt. Although Hay, the witty frail man of letters, and Roosevelt, the inexhaustible man of action, seem worlds apart in temperament, they liked one another and worked very well together. When Hay's letters were printed in 1909, Roosevelt took exception to some of Hay's remarks. Hay's friends (like James) resented Roosevelt's denigration. The so-called feud has continued, though it is almost wholly a posthumous war of words.[5]

Theodore Roosevelt did not care for Henry James's dense literary style nor for his expatriation; James was at once attracted to and repelled by power. But the two men were both symbols of the new America. James published his three great works, the dense complex novels of "the later James," during Theodore Roosevelt's first term. *The Wings of the Dove* in 1902, *The Ambassadors* in 1903, and *The Golden Bowl* in 1904 were excellent examples of the newly emerging formal revolution in the novel that took place throughout the world. Virginia Woolf in England, Marcel Proust in France, and James Joyce in Dublin were innovators

4. The best assessment of Theodore Roosevelt and John Hay's relationship is in Kenton J. Clymer, *John Hay: The Gentleman as Diplomat* (Ann Arbor, Mich., 1975), 190–212.

5. TR to Henry Cabot Lodge, January 28, 1909, in MRL, VI, 1489–98; Edel, *Henry James: The Master*, 266.

who, like Henry James, were writing intense novels about civilized cities using new fictional techniques. The new novel was the literary counterpart of the new painting of Picasso, Cézanne, Matisse and others that comprised the widespread imaginative avant-garde that shocked and excited Europeans in the same decade. James, an American, was one of the first of the growing avant-garde and one of the best.

And although James's expatriation offended American nationalists—like Theodore Roosevelt—no one understood or more passionately cared about the American character than Henry James the novelist. Much of his work deals with innocent Americans discovering awareness in the civilization of Europe. In the later James, heroes like Strether are much more ready and able to shed their ignorance and are eager to assume a sophistication they regard as rightfully theirs. Strether resembles Theodore Roosevelt in his concern for duty and selfless morality. However, he is even more compatible with Woodrow Wilson, the Staunton, Virginia, intellectual who became president and in almost Stretherian terms proclaimed that World War I should end as a peace without victory, an idea that capped the entire age of American idealism beginning with Roosevelt and ending only with Wilson's failure to achieve a League of Nations.

James and Roosevelt came together over World War I. James, living in Rye, a coastal town south of London, was outraged in 1914 when America refused to come into the war on the side of Britain. James found himself, almost alone, on the side of interventionist Roosevelt. "Mr. Roosevelt is far from being dear to me, but I can't *not* agree with his contention that the U.S.'s sitting down in meekness and silence . . . constitutes an unspeakable precedent, and makes us a deplorable figure."[6] James's tone is almost Rooseveltian. James also admired, like Roosevelt, the work of Rudyard Kipling, to the extent that he contributed an introduction to Kipling's *Mine Own People* in 1891. However, no historians belabor James for being an imperialist, in spite of his fondness for Kipling and his truculence toward American neutrality and the world war.

Neither should Theodore Roosevelt be encumbered with the label of

6. Henry James to Mrs. William James, February 20, 1915, in Lubbock, *The Letters of Henry James*, II, 466.

imperialism or the oversimplified legend of the big stick. Americans, even those as mild as Henry James, talked assertively when their country was involved. The new American age of self-awareness had begun when Grover Cleveland launched his tirades against Great Britain in 1895. Assertiveness became a part of the new American awareness. America and Americans were becoming aware of their power, their numbers, their gifts, and their unique view of the world. The unique American character owed its origins and traditions as much to the luck of geography and the inherent wealth of the land as to American genius. When America had been born in the Enlightenment, Jean Jacques Rousseau had envisioned the new land as a kind of Enlightenment utopia, a vision further encouraged by the Hudson River school of painters, the monumental transcontinental railroads, and the vastness of the land itself. In the 1890s Americans were coming of age. America's initial industrial and economic development was completed; the frontier period had ended. The Americans had also served their cultural apprenticeship in the civilizations of Western Europe, where Henry James's wealthy Americans came to terms with culture, and in Asia, whose civilization fascinated the early transcendentalists, the China clipper traders, and later American art collectors like Charles Freer. Americans were ready for grander leaps in 1900, and Theodore Roosevelt was ready to lead the new consciousness.

In Philadelphia, Robert Henri began the first modern American painting movement of urban realism, with former newspaper artists who had been replaced in their original profession by the new technology of photoengraving. The unemployed photojournalists, experienced in the images of gritty cities, ignored the painterly artistic revolutions of Europe and instead painted realistic scenes of American cities. Derisively called the Ash Can school, John Sloan, George Bellows, and Robert Henri were using the gray palette of Philadelphia while Monet and Pissarro were perfecting the impressionist palate of France; both schools offered exciting new ways of seeing the world. Americans Leo and Gertrude Stein lived in Paris and actively took part in the revolutionary development of the Fauves (wild beasts) and cubists. The Steins encouraged Picasso and were integral parts of the aesthetic revolution that shocked Frenchmen in the 1905 and 1906 salons and later amazed and shocked Americans at New York's Armory Show in 1913.

James Whistler discovered Oriental art at the same time that Matisse, Cézanne, and Gaugin became fascinated with it. Charles Freer collected both Whistler's works and Oriental art for the first national American art museum, and in 1912 Ernest Fenollosa, also an American, wrote one of the best books on Oriental art. America was expansionist. But it was not land or economic opportunity but cultural adventure that beckoned. Henry James's American character in search of European culture found not only the culture but the sense of self that comes with it. In 1879 James wrote, in explaining the shortcomings of American novelist Nathaniel Hawthorne, there was "no State, in the European sense of the word, and indeed barely a specific national name. No sovereign, no court, no personal loyalty, . . . no literature, no novels, no museums, no pictures, no political society." For James "history, as yet, has left in the United States, but so thin and impalpable a deposit." How could anyone, James argued, have written in the cultural and historical vacuum that existed in Hawthorne's America?[7]

By 1904 history was no longer a problem. In 1893 Chicago had celebrated Columbus' historic trip. In 1904 the Louisiana Purchase Exposition in St. Louis, honoring the acquisition of the Louisiana territory in Thomas Jefferson's presidency, became the second American world's fair in a single decade to celebrate a unique event in the American past. Americans now had history; they had art; they were as assertive in aesthetics as President Theodore Roosevelt appeared to be in diplomacy.

The assertiveness was universal. Americans transformed the static French inventions of the cinema and the internal combustion engine into the monumental cultural institutions of the movies and the automobile. In Chicago, where beaux-arts architecture had been given a second life in the 1893 world's fair, indigenous American art forms—the skyscrapers of Louis Sullivan, the ranch houses of Frank Lloyd Wright—were also flourishing. In 1910 it seemed that everyone was writing in verse, and poetry competitions were commonplace. In 1912 Harriet Monroe inaugurated *Poetry* magazine, which became the leading poetry journal in the world, publishing William Butler Yeats, T. S. Eliot, as well as the distinguished school of Chicago poets, Carl Sandburg, Edgar Lee

---

7. Henry James, *Hawthorne* (London, 1879; rpr. Edmund Wilson, *The Shock of Recognition* [Garden City, 1943]), 460, 436.

Masters, and Vachel Lindsay. In 1914 *Poetry* celebrated its growing stature by inviting the Irish poet Yeats to Chicago. Yeats warned Chicago— in person—that it was not yet the center of the cultural universe. But Chicago was closing the gap.

While Americans were taking in Europe and Asia, Europeans and Asians were also coming to America. The trickle of immigration in 1880 became a torrent by 1910. The cultural transformation was incalculable. And it worked both ways. The Jews who came to New York's East Side abandoned Hebrew, their official language, and adopted Yiddish, an almost obsolete folk tongue because its colloquial nature fit in well with the spirit of their new country and its improvisational genius. Yiddish became an American language, and the East Side Jews became a potent American force with a new culture, part old world, part new world—American and Eastern European at the same time—and as unique as the Chicago efflorescence of Theodore Dreiser, Edgar Lee Masters, Carl Sandburg, and Vachel Lindsay. Europe was also in the grip of a great cultural awakening.

Because of the new American awareness, many of the great works of modern European art were finding their way into American museums. Georges Rouault's *Two Nudes* painted in 1905 and Pablo Picasso's *Les Demoiselles d'Avignon*, one of his first blue paintings, are hung in different New York city museums. Picasso's *The Old Guitarist* (1903), one of the first great works by the Spanish painter, is in the Chicago Institute. One could make a better case for imperialism in art than in diplomacy. The Europeans brought their love of music to their new country, and soon many American cities had symphony orchestras playing a repertoire of primarily romantic European music. The ultimate merging of old and new culture is symbolized by Platon Brounoff, a Russian musician, who emigrated to the United States in 1891. Brounoff's elaborate Yiddish opera *Ramona*, performed in New York City, was based on Helen Hunt Jackson's book about American Indians.

No opera was written to celebrate the construction of the Panama Canal, as there was for the Suez Canal, but the internationalization of American culture has no better example than Giacomo Puccini's *Madame Butterfly*, originally a story by American writer John Luther Long. The successful American producer David Belasco made it into a play, which opened in New York in 1900. Puccini liked the stage version and had two Italian librettists adapt the American story. The finished opera opened at La Scala, Milan, on February 17, 1904.

The 291 Gallery in New York brought together the photographic art of Alfred Steiglitz and the Ash Can painters and ultimately led to the New York Armory Show of 1913, which brought the new European art to America for the first time. It was fitting that former president Theodore Roosevelt visited the Armory Show and reacted in as perplexed a fashion as most Americans, and as most Europeans, on seeing the wonderful new world of cubism, Fauvism, and expressionism for the first time. What was significant was not that Theodore Roosevelt had little empathy with the new art, but that virtually every journal quoted his remarks and gave modern art even more publicity.

Roosevelt's article on the Armory Show is more sensitive than his out-of-context yahoo remarks that are more often cited. He does compare his bathroom Navajo rug to Duchamp's painting (the Navajo wins) and makes fun of the Cubists ("Knights of the Isosceles Triangle" might be as good a name, Roosevelt suggests). Roosevelt also cited the show as an example of the lunatic fringe in art. Yet Roosevelt also wrote "they have helped to break fetters" of the past and helped "to shake off the dead hand, often the fossilized dead hand, of the reactionaries." Matisse he assessed as a merit, but not a high merit. Roosevelt mentioned a number of pictures he found worthy, objected to some omissions from the display, and ended by "trying . . . to point out why a layman is grateful to those who arranged this exhibition."[8]

Roosevelt's presence made the new art at least acceptable, if not familiar. An American president promoting new European art was taken by most Americans as normal. It was in fact unique, but America had changed so much in the eight years of Roosevelt's presidency that things unheard of at the start of the century were everyday conversational items in 1913. The advent of the world war obscured the enormous changes that had taken place in America in a little over a decade. In 1916 when Theodore Roosevelt addressed the National Institute of

8. "A Layman's Views of an Art Exhibition," *Outlook*, March 29, 1913, rpr. in *Works, Nat. Ed.*, XII, 148–51.

Arts and Letters in New York he warned, "If we do not develop a serious art and literature of our own, we shall have a warped national life." Roosevelt incudes a number of conflicting ideas in his talk, but he ends with a plea for internationalism—the best of all art, no self-conscious straining for nationalism, and a willingness to absorb all art of value, while creating original art that is unmistakably American.[9]

America had grown: in art, in economics, in diplomacy, in wealth, and in influence. The nationalism that accompanied the growth was benign. America with its enormous influx of immigrants, its consciousness of vast new aesthetic cultures, had become not only national but international. Americans had not lost their identity. Henry James pleaded from London for America to join the Europeans in the world war. Theodore Roosevelt had already demonstrated that the new America *was* the balance of power. And when America did enter World War I, its participation was decisive. The balance of power worked. The difference in 1917 from 1900 was that the new America was stronger, more aware, and was willing to try to impose upon the world through Wilsonian idealism the idea of a peace without victory, or in Henry James's words, "Not, out of the whole affair, to have got anything for myself." Such a view is as far from imperialism as it is possible to be.

It is time to put aside the inadequate explanations of the new American expansiveness based upon outmoded legends of European imperialism and the imperious big stick. Instead we should examine the change that engulfed American culture at the start of the century, which better accounts for the new American expansiveness in all endeavors: art, intellect, diplomacy, technology, and culture.

9. "Nationalism in Literature and Art," *Works, Nat. Ed.* XII, 325–36, 329, 336.

Bibliographical Essay

Introduction

PUBLISHED SOURCES

A recent psychohistory useful in explaining Roosevelt's popularity is Kathleen Dalton, "Why America Loved Teddy Roosevelt/Or Charisma Is in the Eye of the Beholder," in Robert J. Brugger, ed., *Our Selves, Our Past: Psychological Approaches to American History* (Baltimore, 1981), 269–91. For the Roosevelt legend, see Richard H. Collin, "The Image of Theodore Roosevelt in American History and Thought, 1885–1965," Ph.D. dissertation, New York University, 1966. The basic Theodore Roosevelt bibliography is contained in Pt. I; European imperialism is discussed in Pt. II, and American imperialism in Ch. 4. The strategic necessity argument is summarized best in John A. S. Grenville and George Berkeley Young, *Politics, Strategy, and American Diplomacy: Studies in Foreign Policy, 1873–1917* (New Haven, 1967).

For a discussion of the change in the concept and usage of the word *imperialism*, Richard Koebner and H. D. Schmidt, *Imperialism: The Story and Significance of a Political Word, 1840–1960* (Cambridge, England, 1964), is invaluable. Roosevelt's claims of postponing World War I for at least a decade are discussed in Tyler Dennett, "Could T. R. Have Stopped the War," *World's Work*, XLIX (February, 1925), 392–99. For the transformation of the 1920s and the bitterness of artists toward the war, see Frederick Hoffman, *The Twenties* (New York, 1955). For the blaming of Pearl Harbor on TR see Howard K. Beale, *Theodore Roosevelt and the Rise of America to World Power* (Baltimore, 1956), 332–34.

The muckraker speech delivered on April 14, 1906, is in *Theodore Roosevelt: Presidential Addresses and State Papers* (8 vols.; New York, 1910), V, 712–24. The best cartoon and caricature collection is Albert Shaw, *A Cartoon History of Roosevelt's Career* (New York, 1910). For the Roosevelt-*World* libel case, see *The Roosevelt Panama Libel Case Against the World and Indianapolis News* (New York, 1910), Clyde Pierce, *The Roosevelt Panama Libel Cases* (New York, 1959), and *The Story of Panama: Hearings on the Rainey Resolution Before the Committee on Foreign Affairs of the House of Representatives* (Washington, D.C., 1914). French cultural motives are summarized in David McCullough, *The Path Between the Seas* (New York, 1978). See also Phillipe Bunau-Varilla, *Panama: The Creation, Destruction, and Resurrection* (London, 1913). For two modern views of the canal, see Walter LaFeber, *The Panama Canal* (New York, 1979), a sensitive treatment of post-Rooseveltian canal diplomacy; the best defense of Roosevelt is in Frederick Marks, III, *Velvet on Iron: The Diplomacy of Theodore Roosevelt* (Lincoln, Nebr., 1979). Henry Adams' life is in his *The Education of Henry Adams* (Boston, 1918).

For a critical view of Henry Pringle and a review of Theodore Roosevelt historiography, see Richard H. Collin, "Henry Pringle's Theodore Roosevelt: A Study in Historical Revisionism," *New York History,* LII (1971), 151–68. For the revisionist assessment of expansion, see Walter LaFeber, *The New Empire: An Interpretation of American Expansion, 1860–1898* (Ithaca, N.Y., 1963). William Appleman Williams, the father of New Left history, has written several books on American diplomacy and empire, the most useful of which is *The Tragedy of American Diplomacy* (Cleveland, 1959). Williams is one of the few historians, old or new, who cites the importance of Roosevelt's aristocracy.

Part One

MANUSCRIPT SOURCES AND THE ROOSEVELT COLLECTIONS

The largest collection of source materials for the study of Theodore Roosevelt is the Papers of Theodore Roosevelt, LC. This enormous collection, originally fifteen series, now sixteen, began with Edith Kermit Roosevelt's donation to the Library of Congress in 1929, made at the express wishes of the late president. The collection includes letter-books, original letters received, scrapbooks, and documents, and is especially strong on Roosevelt's Washington years and the postpresidential years. The Papers of Theodore Roosevelt have become part of the Presidential Papers Series, LC, a mixed blessing for scholars. Beginning in the 1960s the TR papers have been microfilmed on 485 reels and indexed in the *Index to the Papers of Theodore Roosevelt* (3 vols.; Washington, 1971). The reels are available for purchase by or loan to libraries or private parties and make Roosevelt's papers much more accessible than before. But the original papers themselves are no longer available even at the Library of Congress. The scholar must be content with the clumsier microfilm version, a system incorporated to protect the originals, and perhaps as a gesture toward democratic scholarship.

For those of us who worked with the originals the new system is more difficult. The old series numbers from 1 to 15 (now 16) have been retained, but whereas before one could tell at a glance the nature of the material—a letterbook or a box of correspondence—and be able to compare the letters received with those sent, the reels have a logic of their own, a similarity in appearance, and a numbering system that makes the old series identifications less useful. As is almost always the case with massive microfilming, a few papers in the original collection have either been lost or misplaced. Tracing a difficult reference to a paper one has previously had in hand through 485 reels of microfilm is frequently unsuccessful.

Nonetheless, because of its superior indexing system the microfilm edition is in general easier to use than the originals. The difficulties of research in Theodore Roosevelt lie not in the system but in the weight of materials. The Roosevelt period marked the beginning of the modern era of the typewriter. The typewritten word was highly valued, and the result is an enormous cornucopia of documents. Roosevelt produced at least a hundred thousand extant letters, twenty-six volumes of prose (of which only a fraction are government documents), and received, if not a hundred thousand letters, a number close enough to that to occupy a scholar's attentions for many years.

For the origins of the Presidential Papers legislation and a good bibliographic history of the LC collection of the Papers of Theodore Roosevelt, see *Index to the Papers of Theodore Roosevelt*, I, iii, v–xii. Continuing acquisitions are listed regularly in the *Quarterly Journal of the Library of Congress*.

For the Roosevelt scholar, the edition containing ten thousand of Theodore Roosevelt's best letters, Elting E. Morison, John Blum, and Albert Chandler, eds., *The Letters of Theodore Roosevelt* (8 vols.; Cambridge, Mass., 1950–54), offers an excellent selection. All the letters reprinted are complete. The editors' annotations, footnotes, appendixes, and chronologies have made the collection a necessary supplement to the papers themselves. The major flaw with the Morison collection is the absence of incoming letters. One has only Roosevelt's original letter or response, and although the editors are meticulous in annotating the questions raised by the letters, there is no substitute for the missing piece of correspondence. When it exists, the printed version of a Roosevelt letter in MRL is used. MRL gives the manuscript source of each letter.

Morison's edition does reproduce most of the important Roosevelt letters. Howard K. Beale argued with the Morison selections in his reviews in the *American Historical Review*, LVII (1951), 184–87; LVIII (1952), 998-1002; LIX (1953), 159–63; and LX (1955), 918–21. In each of the reviews Beale cited a number of Roosevelt letters omitted that Beale considered essential to a just interpretation. Beale, at the time, was preparing his own biography of Roosevelt, a project ended by his untimely death, and his collection of letters by Roosevelt on most topics was prodigious. Going through the files of rejected letters from the Morison manuscripts that are a part of the Theodore Roosevelt Collections, Harvard College Library, I expected to find a substantial number of omitted letters of value. I found almost none. In each instance the editors had carefully annotated the rejected letter, giving the reasons for rejection, generally because it closely duplicated another printed letter or it was of a routine bureaucratic nature.

One must put Beale's criticism in perspective. As a scholar who had painstakingly amassed his own enormous collection of Roosevelt letters, it must have been heartbreaking to see most of his labors duplicated in printed form. Beale had no choice in amassing the letters as he did his research. Scholars beginning now, however, would be foolish not to use

Morison's edition. They should, of course, supplement the Morison letters with research in the Roosevelt Papers. Based on the evidence of a complete use of the LC collection of the Papers of Theodore Roosevelt, MRL, and the file of letters chosen and rejected at the Harvard College Library, I feel safe in recommending the Morison edition as an even more useful starting point in Roosevelt research than the LC or Harvard collections. What one gives up in completeness one gains in clarity, an essential virtue in a subject with almost overwhelming source materials.

The Harvard College Library collection of Theodore Roosevelt is enormous and more complex than that of the Library of Congress. Most of the original Harvard material was a donation from Roosevelt House and the Roosevelt Memorial Association, and comprised mostly prepresidential materials and enormous amounts of family papers from Roosevelt's sons and daughters and their many relatives. Harvard expanded the original collections and added a vast library of printed materials. Its collection of papers on the presidency is second to that of the Library of Congress, but its collection on the prepresidential years is in many ways superior. Included in Harvard's papers are many useful subcollections, such as the Morison letters reject file and Henry Pringle's notes and research transcripts for his 1931 biography, the first after Joseph Bishop's authorized biography to use the Papers of Theodore Roosevelt. The papers are housed in the Houghton Library, the Theodore Roosevelt Collection in the Widener Library under the supervision of a curator. See Wallace Finley Dailey, "The Theodore Roosevelt Collection at Harvard," *Manuscripts*, XXIX (1977), 147–54, a detailed overview by the Harvard Roosevelt Collection curator.

PUBLISHED SOURCES

Besides the Morison *Letters* several collections are still useful, though most of the older collections have been superseded by both MRL and the microfilm edition of the LC papers. Roosevelt's authorized biography, Joseph Bucklin Bishop's *Theodore Roosevelt and His Times* (2 vols.; New York, 1920) is an old-fashioned combination of biography and letters. Bishop's work includes parts of letters as well as whole ones, and is ardently partisan but still useful.

Henry Cabot Lodge's *Selections from the Correspondence of Theodore*

Roosevelt and Henry Cabot Lodge, 1884–1918 (2 vols.; New York, 1925) must be used with some care, since Lodge was not above changing or deleting historically embarrassing originals. The collection is chronological, and for insight into matters on which Lodge and Roosevelt were particularly close, the Lodge collection is valuable. However, Morison reprints virtually all of the Roosevelt letters included in the original Lodge text, so the collection is more useful for continuity than for originality. Also mostly duplications are the special family letter collections, *Letters from Theodore Roosevelt to Anna Roosevelt Cowles* (New York, 1924); Will Irwin, ed., *Letters to Kermit* (New York, 1946); Theodore Roosevelt, *Letters to His Children*, in *The Works of Theodore Roosevelt*, Memorial Edition (24 vols.; New York, 1923–26), XXI. For a fuller listing of other printed letter collections, see Edward Wagenknecht, *The Seven Worlds of Theodore Roosevelt* (New York, 1958), 304–305. See also *Journal of the Theodore Roosevelt Association, passim*.

The *Works of Theodore Roosevelt* was published by Scribner's in two editions, the Memorial Edition (24 vols.; New York, 1923–1926) and the National Edition (20 vols.; New York, 1926). A comparison of the differences in the two sets can be found in Albert Bushnell Hart and Herbert Ronald Ferleger, eds., *Theodore Roosevelt Cyclopedia* (New York, 1941). The *Cyclopedia* is a selected concordance to Roosevelt's writings from *Works* and occasionally other sources. The Memorial Edition includes the two-volume Bishop biography as its last two volumes; both sets include extensive bibliographic notes on the original versions of reprinted material.

Not included in either edition of *Works* are additional speeches in Theodore Roosevelt, *Presidential Addresses and State Papers* (New York, 1910), and Ralph Stout, ed., *Roosevelt in the Kansas City Star* (Boston, 1921). Bibliographies that include all of Roosevelt's speeches and articles are in the Theodore Roosevelt Collection, Harvard University Library. Revised typescripts, with extensive hand editing, are in the Theodore Roosevelt Papers, LC.

The Theodore Roosevelt Collection at Harvard University, a collection of books, journals, and meticulously preserved articles from contemporary journals, is housed in a corner of the Widener Library stacks. Nora Cordingley, the card cataloguer for the Roosevelt collection when it began, is primarily responsible for the essential Roosevelt bibliography, *Theodore Roosevelt Collection: Dictionary Catalog and Shelflist* (5 vols.; Cambridge, Mass., 1970). Harvard's *Shelflist* is invaluable for both primary and secondary materials listing articles in both original and reprint editions. The collection closed about 1958; the newly active Theodore Roosevelt Association, Oyster Bay, New York, and the Theodore Roosevelt Collection at Harvard are bringing both the collection and the bibliography up to date. For the latest additions, see Wallace Finley Dailey, "Theodore Roosevelt in Periodical Literature, 1950–1981: A Supplement to *Theodore Roosevelt Collection: Dictionary Catalogue and Shelflist*, Harvard University Library, 1970." *Theodore Roosevelt Association Journal*, VIII (Fall, 1982), 4–15.

The earliest bibliography, John Hall Wheelock, *A Bibliography of Theodore Roosevelt* (New York, 1920), is now obsolete, superseded by the Harvard *Shelflist*. Nora Cordingley's "Extreme Rarities in the Published Works of Theodore Roosevelt," *Papers of the Bibliographic Society of America*, XXXIX (1945), 20–50, is peripheral. Dewey W. Grantham, Jr., "Theodore Roosevelt in American Historical Writing, 1945–1960," *Mid-America*, XLIII (1961), 3–35, is the best assessment of scholarship from the end of the Pringle era through the centenary celebration in 1958. See also Richard H. Collin, "The Image of Theodore Roosevelt in American History and Thought, 1885–1965," Ph.D. dissertation, New York University, 1966, for a critical analysis of Roosevelt historiography.

Henry Pringle's *Theodore Roosevelt: A Biography* (New York, 1931), in spite of its interpretive eccentricities, remains the most useful source on Roosevelt's life. William H. Harbaugh's *The Life and Times of Theodore Roosevelt* (Rev. ed.; New York, 1975), a revision of *Power and Responsibility* (New York, 1961), is mainly a historical synthesis rather than a biography from primary sources. Edmund Morris, *The Rise of Theodore Roosevelt* (New York, 1979), the first of a multivolume biography, takes Roosevelt to the presidency.

Chapter One

MANUSCRIPT SOURCES

The best single source for the restoration of Theodore Roosevelt's White House is the Charles Moore Papers, LC. The most useful parts are contained in Box 3 and Box 22. In Box 3 the correspondence between Moore and Charles McKim is carefully preserved. Of interest as well are the letterbooks containing Senator James McMillan's official correspondence until his death in 1902. Perhaps most valuable of all is Moore's unfinished and unpublished long fragment of a proposed book, "Makers of Washington." The rough chapter drafts are in Box 22 and provide an insider's account of the politics of aesthetics as seen by one of its prime movers and historians.

Charles Moore was also responsible for the Charles McKim Papers, LC, a useful but less monumental collection. Some McKim papers are duplicated in the Moore collection. McKim's papers supplement Moore's own collection on the White House project and also include useful other material on the aesthetic and political history of the time, especially the founding of the American Academy at Rome.

PUBLISHED SOURCES

The most useful history of Washington is Constance Green's *Washington* (Princeton, 1967). Green deals with politics, race, and aesthetics with equal grace. Philip Jessup, *Elihu Root* (2 vols.; New York, 1938), is useful on the architectural changes in the capital that were the responsibility of the War Department when Root was secretary of war. See also John Reps, *Monumental Washington: The Planning and Development of the Capital Center* (Princeton, 1967). For a study of the White House, William Ryan and Desmond Guinness, *The White House: An Architectural History* (New York, 1980), is recent, scholarly, critical and well illustrated.

For the work of the McMillan committee and the Park Commission in applying the national City Beautiful Movement to Washington, see *Senate Reports*, 56th Cong., 2nd Sess., No. 191, Ser. 4064, Commission to Consider Certain Improvements in the District of Columbia; *Senate Reports*, 57th Cong., 1st Sess., No. 166, Ser. 4258, Charles Moore, ed., The Improvement of the Park System of the District of Columbia; *Sen-*

ate Reports, 57th Cong., 1st Sess., No. 982, Ser. 4261, Union Railroad Station at Washington, D.C.; *Senate Documents*, 57th Cong., 2nd Sess., No. 220, Ser. 4430, Federal and Local Legislation Relating to Canals and Steam Railroads in the District of Columbia, 1802–1903.

On the change in American cultural consciousness and the new interest in art, Aline B. Saarinen, *The Proud Possessors* (New York, 1958), is the essential starting point. Saarinen shows how widespread the American taste for art had become by focusing on the individual collectors who were mainly responsible for the new American urban art museum collections in the late nineteenth and early twentieth centuries. More general is Charles C. Alexander, *Here the Country Lies: Nationalism and the Arts in Twentieth Century America* (Bloomington, Ind. 1980). An older and invaluable guide to American cultural change is Henry F. May, *The End of American Innocence* (New York, 1959; rpr. 1964), especially invaluable in assessing the influence of Chicago as a national pioneer in art and culture after the 1893 World's Fair. See also Larzer Ziff, *The American 1890's: Life and Times of a Lost Generation* (New York, 1966). Two newer assessments combine economic and cultural history: Emily Rosenberg, *Spreading the American Dream: American Economic and Cultural Expansion, 1890–1945* (New York, 1982), and Alan Trachtenberg, *The Incorporation of America: Culture and Society in the Gilded Age* (New York, 1982).

Chicago's World's Fair of 1893 has a growing and perceptive historiography that deals not only with the fair itself but with its cultural effects. The most analytical studies include John G. Cawelti, "The World's Fairs of 1876, 1893, 1933," in Frederic Cople Jaher, ed., *The Age of Industrialism in America* (New York, 1968), 317–63; David F. Burg, *Chicago's White City of 1893* (Lexington, Ky., 1976), and Reid Badger, *The Great American Fair: The World's Columbian Exposition and American Culture* (Chicago, 1979). For a broader view of the effect of World's Fairs on culture, see Eugene S. Fergusen, "Expositions of Technology, 1851–1900," in Melvin Kranzberg and Carroll W. Pursell, eds., *Technology in Western Civilization* (2 vols.; New York, 1967), I, 706–26.

The City Beautiful Movement is treated in Blake McKelvey, *The Urbanization of America* (Rutgers, N.J., 1963), 122–26; Charles Nelson Glaab and A. Theodore Brown, *A History of Urban America* (New York,

1967); Jack Tager and Park Dixon Gorst, eds., *The Urban Vision* (Home-wood, Ill., 1970); and Mel Scott, *American City Planning Since 1890* (Berkeley, 1971), 31–109.

Charles Moore's *Daniel H. Burnham: Architect, Planner of Cities* (2 vols.; Boston, 1921) and *The Life and Times of Charles Follen McKim* (Boston, 1929) are basic sources as much as biographies. *McKim* is more analytical, *Burnham* more documentary; both are necessary starting points in connecting the world's fair of 1893, the City Beautiful Movement, and the rise of the new American cosmopolitanism. More recent and exhaustive is Thomas S. Hines, *Burnham of Chicago* (New York, 1974).

On the Roosevelt family's life in the White House, Sylvia Jukes Morris, *Edith Kermit Roosevelt: Portrait of a First Lady* (New York, 1980), is recent, readable, and complete. Hermann Hagedorn, *The Roosevelt Family of Sagamore Hill* (New York, 1951) is the best older social treatment of the Roosevelt family life.

Willard B. Gatewood, "Theodore Roosevelt: Champion of Governmental Aesthetics," *Georgia Review*, XXI (1967), 172–83, offers the best summary of Theodore Roosevelt's involvement with the aesthetics of his time, from the White House restoration to the establishment of the Fine Arts Commission, which was originated by TR and instituted under President Taft in 1910. See also Willard Gatewood, *Theodore Roosevelt and the Art of Controversy* (Baton Rouge, 1970), especially Ch. VII, "The Struggle for an Artistic Coinage," 213–35.

Glenn Brown, "Roosevelt and the Fine Arts," *American Architect*, CXVI (1919), 711–19, and "The Government and Art," *Outlook*, XCI (1909), 285–87, are genial contemporary appreciations of Roosevelt's role as promoter of the fine arts while president. See also Edwin C. Ranck, "What Roosevelt did for Art in America," *Art and Archeology*, VII (1919), 291–93.

Chapter Two

MANUSCRIPT SOURCES

Formal social life at the Roosevelt White House is exhaustively documented in the series of books, scrapbooks, and papers that comprise "Official Functions" with the "Official Diary of the President," 1902–1916,

24 vols., in Records of the Office of Public Buildings and Public Parks of the National Capital, RG 42, NA. The collection includes correspondence, formal menus and seating arrangments, guest lists, and even informal commentary, a marvelous potpourri of official life in Washington.

RG 42 is well supplemented by Series 15 in the Theodore Roosevelt Papers, LC. Series 15 includes the scrapbooks originally in the Roosevelt Memorial Association Collection, one of the first gifts that became a part of Harvard University's Theodore Roosevelt Collection. When the Library of Congress began microfilming the original Roosevelt Papers in 1968 jurisdiction over the scrapbooks was transferred from Harvard to the Library of Congress. Series 15 is now available as part of the 485 reels in the LC microfilm edition of the Theodore Roosevelt Papers. The scrapbooks are divided into four major categories: current events, personal, White House, and editorial comment. For social life in the White House, reels 461 and 462 (Series 15) are most useful, though there is considerable overlap between the categories. The White House reels include social columns of contemporary Washington newspapers and offer an exhaustive commentary on life at the White House with major events and social trivia given equal attention.

Some of the Roosevelt cabinet diaries are useful in showing how the administration carried out its duties, and for a discussion of some important issues of the time. The best is that of Oscar Straus who served as secretary of commerce and labor from December 17, 1906, to the end of Roosevelt's term. Straus, an influential businessman and the Roosevelt administration's official Jewish adviser (a standing joke between Straus and TR), was a regular visitor to the White House even before his cabinet appointment. Straus's meticulously typed diaries are in Box 22, Oscar Straus Papers, LC. The James Garfield Papers and the George von Lengerke Meyer Papers, both in LC, offer substantial cabinet diaries by Roosevelt's secretary of agriculture and postmaster general, but neither is of major significance for White House social life.

PUBLISHED SOURCES

By far the best of the memoirs written about TR is Owen Wister, *Roosevelt: The Story of a Friendship, 1880–1919* (New York, 1930). Wister was a close friend; he argued with the president, hunted with him, and visited the White House frequently. Wister is an essential source for information on the Roosevelt salon, political relations with the South, and life at the White House during Roosevelt's presidency. Wister is especially skillful in his treatment of literary and intellectual matters. Edward Wagenknecht, *The Seven Worlds of Theodore Roosevelt* (New York, 1958), an invaluable analysis of TR's nonpolitical life, concentrates on intellectual and literary matters and includes an extensive, useful bibliography.

Specialized studies of the Roosevelt intellect are rare. One of the best, Lewis Einstein, *Roosevelt: His Mind in Action* (Boston, 1930), was overshadowed almost immediately by Henry Pringle's more famous biography in 1931. The best full scale literary study is Aloysius Norton's *Theodore Roosevelt* (Boston, 1980) in Twayne's *United States Authors* series. See also the intellectual studies by David Burton, including *Theodore Roosevelt: Confident Imperialist* (Philadelphia, 1968) and *Theodore Roosevelt* (Boston, 1972). For Roosevelt's work in natural science, see Paul Cutright's excellent *Theodore Roosevelt the Naturalist* (New York, 1956) and John Burroughs, *Camping and Tramping with Roosevelt* (Boston, 1907), and *Life and Letters* (2 vols.; Boston, 1925).

The introductions to the collected editions of the *Works of Theodore Roosevelt* contain some useful early assessments and remembrances. See George Haven Putnam, "Roosevelt, Historian and Statesman," *Works, Mem. Ed.*, XI, *Nat. Ed.*, VIII; Brander Matthews, "Theodore Roosevelt as a Man of Letters," *Mem. Ed.*, XIV, *Nat. Ed.*, XII; and Hamlin Garland, "Roosevelt as Historian," *Mem. Ed.*, XII, *Nat. Ed.*, IX. Of interest is Charles W. Ferguson, "Roosevelt: Man of Letters," *Bookman*, LXIV (1927), 726–29; a centenary assessment is in Charles Fenton, "Theodore Roosevelt as a Man of Letters," *Western Humanities Review*, XIII (1959), 369–74. One of the most perceptive analyses of TR's influence is Don D. Walker, "Wister, Roosevelt, and James: A Note on the Western," *American Quarterly*, XII (1960), 358–66. Walker holds Henry James the novelist and Wister's friendship with the president as equally responsible for the trivialization of Wister's literary talent.

Kathleen Dalton argues in "Why Americans Loved Teddy Roosevelt/Or Charisma Is in the Eye of the Beholder," in Robert Brugger, ed., *Our Selves, Our Past: Psychological Approaches to American History* (Baltimore, 1981), 269–91, that Roosevelt's use of the symbolism of virility made his otherwise "sissy" literary and aesthetic interests acceptable in Victorian America. For Charles Freer's and TR's interest in Japanese culture see the bibliographic essay for Chapter Three herein.

Other personal accounts of TR of some interest include James Amos, *Theodore Roosevelt: Hero to His Valet* (New York, 1927); Lawrence F. Abbott, *Impressions of Theodore Roosevelt* (Garden City, 1919); and Archie Butt, *Letters*, edited by Lawrence Abbott (Garden City, 1925). Abbott was Roosevelt's editor at the *Outlook* and Butt his White House military aide. See also, Oscar Davis, *Released for Publication* (Boston, 1925), the memoirs of a Washington newsman; Joseph Leary, *Talks with TR* (Boston, 1920); Mike Donovan, *The Theodore Roosevelt I Knew* (New York, 1909); Arthur Dunn, *Gridiron Nights* (New York, 1915) and *From Harrison to Harding* (New York, 1922). Stefan Lorant's *The Life and Times of Theodore Roosevelt* (Garden City, 1959) contains a wealth of pictorial material and a useful commentary. Two family portraits are Alice Longworth, *Crowded Years* (New York, 1933), and Corrine R. Robinson, *My Brother Theodore Roosevelt* (New York, 1921). See also Frances E. Leupp, *The Man Roosevelt: A Political Sketch* (New York, 1904), the campaign biography for 1904, which catches the Roosevelt political image just before his biggest triumph; Frederick Iglehart, *Theodore Roosevelt as I Knew Him* (New York, 1919), and Frederick S. Wood, *Roosevelt as We Knew Him: Personal Recollections of 150 Friends* (Philadelphia, 1927). Nicholas Roosevelt, *TR: The Man as I Knew Him* (New York, 1967) offers youthful recollections and later considerations.

A useful popular history, Marie Smith's *Entertaining in the White House from Washington to Nixon* (Rev. ed.; New York, 1970) contains an excellent bibliography, many menus, and a fine collection of presidential anecdotes. Sylvia Jukes Morris' *Edith Kermit Roosevelt* (New York, 1980) is especially detailed on entertaining in the White House years and useful on the Roosevelt family life in general. For the salon as an international cultural phenomenon, see Peter Quennell, ed., *Affairs of the Mind: The Salon in Europe and America from the 18th to the 20th Century* (Washington, 1980).

Chapter Three

MANUSCRIPT SOURCES

The three best primary sources for information on Charles Lang Freer's and Theodore Roosevelt's struggle to establish the first national American art museum are in Washington, D.C. The richest collection is the Papers of Charles Freer located in the Library of the Freer Gallery of Art. The Freer Gallery's archive is substantial and includes letterbook copies of most of Freer's prolific correspondence, diaries, miscellaneous clippings, business accounts, and other correspondence.

Almost as important for the establishment of the Freer Gallery are the records in the Smithsonian Institution Archives. The Smithsonian archive contains most of the correspondence, budget reports, internal memoranda, minutes of board meetings, and details of the long liaison between Freer and the Smithsonian. All of the relevant material of the Freer-Smithsonian negotiations is in Record Unit 45, Office of the Secretary (Charles D. Walcott), 1907–1927, and mostly in Box 108. The bulk of the Smithsonian archive deals with matters that followed final acceptance of the gift in 1906. Surprisingly, there is relatively little duplication between the two collections. The Freer collection is most useful for Freer's own letters. The Smithsonian archive includes correspondence of the other principals, including Theodore Roosevelt.

The smallest of the three Freer collections is very important. In Box 20 of the Charles Moore Papers, LC, is a Freer Folder containing Moore's letters to his press confidants, annotated clippings, and miscellaneous notes that help to establish some otherwise inexplicable details in the complicated Smithsonian-Freer negotiations.

Roosevelt's cultural empathy with Japan and the Japanese culture is often overlooked, since most works dealing with Roosevelt and Japan are concerned with diplomatic affairs. For Roosevelt and Root's sympathy with the Japanese, their shock over California's discrimination against Japanese immigrants, and the diplomatic crisis that precipitated the cruise of the Great White Fleet in 1907–1908, see RG 59, Numerical File 1797, NA. This is a large and important source for American-Japanese relations and the Roosevelt administration's attempts to reassure the Japanese of American concern.

PUBLISHED SOURCES

The most complete study of Charles Freer is Helen Nebeker Tomlinson, "Charles Lang Freer: Pioneer Collector of American Art," (2 vols.; Ph.D dissertation, Case-Western Reserve University, 1979). Tomlinson's study encompasses Freer's life, his collecting activities, and his aesthetic friendships. The extensive bibliography is invaluable.

Much shorter but still essential is Aline B. Saarinen's "Charles Freer," in *The Proud Possessors* (New York, 1958), 118–43. The two best assessments of the Freer collection were contemporary: Ernest Fenellosa, "The Collections of Mr. Charles Lang Freer," *Pacific Era* (November, 1907), 57–66; and Lelia Mecklin, "The Freer Collection of Art," *Century*, LXIX (January, 1907), 65–83. One of the best recent assessments is Nicholas Clark, "Charles Lang Freer: An American Aesthete in the Gilded Era," *American Art Journal*, XI (October, 1979), 54–68. Still useful is the museum's own pamphlet, *The Freer Gallery of Art* (Washington, n.d.). The best source for the history of the Smithsonian is Geoffrey Hellman, *The Smithsonian: Octopus on the Mall* (Philadelphia, 1967), originally published as a series in the *New Yorker*.

For the changes taking place in American culture, Saarinen's *The Proud Possessors* is essential. The best contemporary accounts of the vast changes in American art and life are in Mark Sullivan's *Our Times* (6 vols.; New York, 1927–1935), especially Vol. I, *The Turn of the Century*, and Vol. II, *America Finding Herself*. For changes in world culture, especially Europe, see the monumental study by Jan Romein, *Watershed of Two Eras: Europe in 1900* (Middletown, Conn., 1978), and Edward Tannebaum's *1900: The Generation Before the Great War* (Garden City, 1976). Jackson Lears, *No Place of Grace: Antimodernism and the Transformation of American Culture, 1880–1920* (New York, 1981), is a synthesis that includes art, psychology, and religion in its sweeping reexamination of American society. Emily Rosenberg's *Spreading the American Dream: American Economic and Cultural Expansion, 1890–1945* (New York, 1982), and Alan Trachtenberg's *The Incorporation of America: Culture and Society in the Gilded Age* (New York, 1982) combine cultural and economic analysis.

Roosevelt's fascination with Japan can be found directly in the letters, especially to Cecil Spring Rice, March 19, 1904, MRL, IV, 759–61; to Baron Kentaro Kaneko, April 23, 1904, MRL, IV, 777–78; to George Trevelyan, May 13, 1905, MRL, IV, 1175; and Cecil Spring Rice, June 13, 1904, MRL, IV, 829–33. Roosevelt's long correspondence with his ambassador to Russia during the Russo-Japanese War, George von Lengerke Meyer, is candid and useful, *e.g.*, December 26, 1904, MRL, IV, 1078–80.

Virtually all the works on Roosevelt and Japan are primarily diplomatic. The most useful include: Raymond A. Esthus, *Theodore Roosevelt and Japan* (Seattle, 1966), which includes a good bibliography; Tyler Dennett, *Roosevelt and the Russo-Japanese War* (Garden City, 1925), *Americans in Eastern Asia* (New York, 1922), and "Could T.R. Have Stopped the War," *World's Work*, XLIX (1925), 392–99; Howard K. Beale, *Theodore Roosevelt and the Rise of America to World Power* (Baltimore, 1956); and Thomas A. Bailey, *Theodore Roosevelt and the Japanese American Crisis* (Palo Alto, 1934). See also Theodore Roosevelt, "The Japanese Question," *Outlook*, May 8, 1909, in *Works, Nat. Ed.*, XVI, 288–91; Sixth Annual Message to Congress, December 3, 1906, *ibid.*, XV, 385–87, and *Autobiography*, *ibid.*, XX, 368–74. Elihu Root's "The Real Question Under the Japanese Treaty and the San Francisco School Board Resolution," *American Journal of International Law*, I (1907), 273–86, is a useful summary.

For American-Japanese cultural relations, see Foster Rhea Dulles, *Yankees and Samurai: America's Role in the Emergence of Modern Japan* (New York, 1965). On European and Japanese cultural relations, see G. B. Sansom, *The Western World and Japan: A Study in the Interaction of European and Asiatic Culture* (New York, 1963). Although Charles H. Thornson and Walter H. C. Laves' *Cultural Relations of U.S. Foreign Policy* (Bloomington, Ind., 1963) deals with a later period, the book illustrates how culture, diplomacy, and politics are related and useful subjects for historical research. See also Morell Heald and Lawrence S. Kaplan, *Culture and Diplomacy* (Westport, Conn., 1977).

The relationship between culture and diplomacy is sensitively explored in Akira Iriye's works, *From Nationalism to Internationalism: U. S. Foreign Policy Before 1917* (London, 1977) and "Culture and Power:

International Relations as Intercultural Relations," *Diplomatic History*, III (1979), 115–28. Iriye's *Across the Pacific: An Inner History of American–East Asian Relations* (New York, 1967) is a comprehensive history of modern American-Asian relations from a unique international view; Ch. 4, "Imperialism—Japanese and American," 83–110, is especially useful.

Part Two

MANUSCRIPT SOURCES

Several record groups in the National Archives deal with naval history in the Roosevelt-Mahan era. The most general is RG 80, General Records of the Department of the Navy, which includes the letterbooks of the assistant secretary of the Navy. RG 45, the Naval Records Collection, includes area files classified by region, cipher files, confidential letters, personnel reports, and frequently useful miscellaneous information. RG 38 is Records of the Office of the Chief of Naval Operations, which include the important Office of Naval Intelligence files. RG 24, the Records of the Bureau of Naval Personnel, includes the Bureau of Navigation Records. RG 313 is the records of Naval Operating Forces.

The Operational Archives, which include the useful Navy General Board Records, are in a separate collection in the Naval Historical Center, Washington, D.C., Navy Yard. Records of the Joint Army and Navy Board, permanently established in 1903, are in RG 225.

State Department files are in RG 59, NA. The most useful categories include Despatches from American Ministers, Despatches from American Consuls, Instructions to American Ministers, and Notes from Foreign Legations to the State Department. All of these files were arranged by country until August 16, 1906, when the filing method changed to a numerical case file, in which all the categories were combined and related papers were assigned a numerical file number; in 1910 the decimal file system was instituted. Many important State Department papers are reprinted in *Papers Relating to the Foreign Relations of the United States*, dating from 1861 to the 1950s.

Bibliographical Essay

PUBLISHED SOURCES

For American diplomacy and naval policy, John A. S. Grenville and George Berkeley Young's *Politics, Strategy and American Diplomacy: Studies in Foreign Policy, 1873–1917* (New Haven, 1967) is an excellent starting point. Grenville and Young write about the interaction of politics, naval strategy, and diplomacy, and range widely through Europe, Asia, and the Americas. I am particularly indebted to their overall interpretation of the naval revolution, America's responses to Europe, and their knowledgeable treatment of the German threat under Wilhelm II. For Theodore Roosevelt specifically, Frederick Marks, III, *Velvet on Iron: The Diplomacy of Theodore Roosevelt* (Lincoln, Nebr., 1979) is an indispensable revision of the historiography of Roosevelt's foreign policy, correcting many of the old assumptions based upon personality and using new archival evidence from Great Britain and Germany. William R. Braisted, *The United States Navy in the Pacific, 1897–1909* (Austin, Tex., 1958), is authoritative and indispensable.

The most useful older book on Theodore Roosevelt's naval policies is Gordon Carpenter O'Gara, *Theodore Roosevelt and the Rise of the Modern Navy* (Princeton, 1943). The story of American naval planning cannot be told in a historical vacuum. The most useful studies are comparative. One of the best is Holger H. Herwig, *Politics of Frustration: The United States in German Naval Planning, 1889–1941* (Boston, 1976). See also Outten J. Clinard, *Japan's Influence on American Naval Power, 1897–1917* (Berkeley, 1947). Although both works concentrate on later eras, Vincent Davis's *The Admirals' Lobby* (Chapel Hill, 1967) and Richard D. Challener's *Admirals, Generals, and American Foreign Policy, 1898–1914* (Princeton, 1973) are valuable. For the American changes see especially Walter R. Herrick, *The American Naval Revolution* (Baton Rouge, 1966); Harold and Margaret Sprout, *The Rise of American Naval Power, 1776–1918* (Princeton, 1967); and Elting E. Morison, *Admiral Sims and the Modern American Navy* (Boston, 1942). See also Allen Westcott, ed., *American Sea Power Since 1775* (Philadelphia, 1947), and E. B. Potter, *The United States and World Sea Power* (New York, 1955).

For information on Alfred T. Mahan, W. D. Puleston's biography, *Mahan* (New Haven, 1939), is sympathetic and authoritative with a useful bibliography of Mahan's influential writing. Robert Seager, II, and Doris D. Maguire, *Letters and Papers of Alfred Thayer Mahan* (3 vols.; Annapolis, 1975), and Robert Seager, II, *Alfred Thayer Mahan: The Man and His Letters* (Annapolis, 1977), are essential. Mahan's most important books include *The Influence of Sea Power Upon History* (Boston, 1898), *The Interest of America in Sea Power Past and Present* (Boston, 1897), *The Lessons of Our War With Spain* (Boston, 1899), *The Problem of Asia and Its Effect Upon International Policies* (Boston, 1900), and *Naval Administration and Warfare: Some General Principles* (Boston, 1908).

Detailed general histories of European diplomacy include William Langer, *The Diplomacy of Imperialism, 1890–1902* (New York, 1951) and *European Alliances and Alignments* (New York, 1931); René Albrecht-Carrié, *The Concert of Europe* (New York, 1968) and *A Diplomatic History of Europe Since the Congress of Vienna* (New York, 1973).

The most useful general work on Great Britain is H. C. Allen, *Great Britain and the United States: A History of Anglo-American Relations, 1783–1852* (London, 1953). On Germany, Gordon A. Craig, *Germany, 1866–1945* (New York, 1978), is authoritative. See the bibliographic essay for later chapters for more specialized works on Germany and Great Britain.

General histories of American foreign policy include Thomas A. Bailey, *A Diplomatic History of the American People* (Englewood Cliffs, N.J., 1974); Samuel Flagg Bemis, *A Diplomatic History of the United States* (New York, 1936), *The Latin-American Policy of the United States* (New York, 1967), and Samuel Flagg Bemis, ed., *The American Secretaries of State and Their Diplomacy, 1776–1925* (18 vols.; New York, 1927–1929); Richard Leopold, *The Growth of American Foreign Policy* (New York, 1967); William Appleman Williams, *The Shaping of American Diplomacy* (2 vols.; Chicago, 1956) and *The Tragedy of American Foreign Policy* (Cleveland, 1959).

Good detailed diplomatic histories include Charles S. Campbell, *The Transformation of American Foreign Relations, 1865–1900* (New York, 1976); Foster Rhea Dulles, *America's Rise to World Power, 1898–1954* (New York, 1954); Norman Graebner, *An Uncertain Tradition: American Secretaries of State in the Twentieth Century* (New York, 1961), *Ideas and Diplomacy* (New York, 1964); and Robert Osgood, *Ideas and Self-Interest in America's Foreign Relations* (Chicago, 1965).

Essential to the study of Theodore Roosevelt are Frederick Marks, III, *Velvet on Iron: The Diplomacy of Theodore Roosevelt* (Lincoln, Nebr., 1980); Howard K. Beale, *Theodore Roosevelt and the Rise of America to World Power* (Baltimore, 1956); and A. L. P. Dennis, *Adventures in American Diplomacy* (New York, 1929).

For the Boer War, see Thomas Parkenham, *The Boer War* (New York, 1979); J. H. Ferguson, *American Diplomacy and the Boer War* (Philadelphia, 1939); and Thomas J. Noer, *Briton, Boer, and Yankee: The United States and South Africa* (Kent, Ohio, 1978). For the effect of the Spanish-American War on the Boer rebellion, see the fine essay by M. Boucher, "Imperialism, the Transvaal Press and the Spanish American War of 1898," *Kleio* (South Africa) V, (1973), 1–32.

The standard histories of the Monroe Doctrine are Dexter Perkins, *A History of the Monroe Doctrine* (Boston, 1955) and *The Monroe Doctrine, 1867–1907* (Baltimore, 1937). On the idea of the Monroe Doctrine, see Arthur B. Whittaker, *The Western Hemisphere Idea: Its Rise and Decline* (Ithaca, N.Y., 1954).

For American Populism, see Norman Pollack, *The Populist Response to Industrial America: Midwestern Populist Thought* (Cambridge, Mass., 1962); Walter Nugent, *The Tolerant Populists* (Chicago, 1967); Russel Nye, *Midwestern Progressive Politics* (East Lansing, Mich., 1951); and Lawrence Goodwyn, *The Populist Movement* (New York, 1978). George Rogers, ed., *The Turner Thesis* (Boston, 1956), in the *Problems in American Civilization* series, is an older sound introduction to the historiography of Frederick Jackson Turner's thesis.

The historiography of imperialism is already vast and still growing. The standard European works are: John Hobson, *Imperialism* (London, 1902; rpr. Ann Arbor, Mich., 1965); Parker Thomas Moon, *Imperialism and World Politics* (New York, 1926); Joseph A. Schumpeter, *Imperialism and Social Classes* (New York, 1951); William Langer, *Diplomacy of Imperialism* (New York, 1951); and V. I. Lenin, *Imperialism: The Highest Stage of Capitalism* (trans., New York, 1969).

The term *imperialism* has come under attack and for European historians it is no longer either sacrosanct or easily defined. Europe is the best starting point for making any convincing revision of imperialism. The most important part of the European revision is contained in the Robinson-Gallagher interpretations. Two Cambridge University historians, Ronald Robinson and John Gallagher, in a series of articles and books, have attacked the old economic basis of imperial expansion, and have argued that imperialism occurred more from accident than design; its main cause was the domestic politics of non-European colonial countries, and not the political ambitions of the occupying European nation. For their new strategic interpretation of imperialism, see Ronald Robinson and John Gallagher, *Africa and the Victorians: The Official Mind of Imperialism* (London, 1961); "The Partition of Africa," in *The New Cambridge Modern History: Material Progress and World Wide Problems, 1870–1898* (Cambridge, England, 1962) XI, 593–629; "The Imperialism of Free Trade," *Economic History Review*, 2nd Ser., VI (1953), 1–15; and Ronald Robinson, "Non-European Foundations of European Imperialism: Sketch for a Theory of Collaboration," in E. R. J. Owen and R. B. Sutcliffe, eds., *Studies in the Theory of Imperialism* (London, 1972), Ch. 5.

Useful compilations of the revisionist view and critiques of it can be found in William Roger Louis, ed., *Imperialism: The Robinson-Gallagher Controversy* (New York, 1976), and William B. Cohen, *European Empire Building* (St. Louis, 1980). See also William L. Langer, "A Critique of Imperialism," *Foreign Affairs* XIV (October, 1935), 102–15, an early attack on the economic assumptions of imperialism by one of the most influential of its historians, and John P. Halstead and Serafino Porcari, eds., *Modern European Imperialism: A Bibliography of Books and Articles* (2 vols.; Boston, 1974). On the history of how the use of the word itself developed, R. Koebner and H. D. Schmidt's *Imperialism: The Story and Significance of a Political Word, 1840–1860* (Cambridge, England, 1964) is essential. Wolfgang J. Mommsen, *Theories of Imperialism*, translated by P. S. Falla (Chicago, 1982), is a remarkably brief and clear historical synthesis.

On the idea of the balance of power, Moorhead Wright, ed., *Theory and Practice of the Balance of Power, 1486–1914* (Totowa, N.J., 1975) is a useful brief anthology. Also see E. W. Nelson, "The Origins of Modern Balance of Power Politics," *Medievalia et Humanistica*, I (1943), 124–42, and E. V. Gulick, *Europe's Classical Balance of Power* (Ithaca, N.Y., 1955).

On the Hague peace conferences, see Calvin de Armond Davis, *The United States and the First Hague Peace Conference* (Ithaca, N.Y., 1962) and *The United States and the Second Hague Peace Conference: American Diplomacy and International Organization, 1899–1914* (Durham, N.C., 1978). For Algeciras diplomacy, Eugene N. Anderson's *The First Moroccan Crisis, 1904–1906* (Chicago, 1930) is beneficial. James H. Hitchman, "The Platt Amendment Revisited: A Bibliographical Survey," *Americas*, 23 (1967), 343–69, discusses both American and Cuban views and examines the continuing disagreements.

Stephen Gwynn, ed., *The Letters and Friendships of Sir Cecil Spring Rice* (2 vols.; Boston, 1929), is a good compilation that includes much of the Roosevelt–Spring Rice correspondence.

The best biographies of John Hay are the early William Roscoe Thayer, *The Life and Letters of John Hay* (Boston, 1915), the more thorough Tyler Dennett, *John Hay: From Poetry to Politics* (New York, 1933), and the recent and more critical, Kenton J. Clymer, *John Hay: The Gentleman as Diplomat* (Ann Arbor, Mich., 1975). For Adee's enormous influence and expertise, see John A. De Novo, "The Enigmatic Alvey B. Adee and American Foreign Relations, 1870–1924," *Prologue*, VII (1975), 69–80.

Chapter Four

MANUSCRIPT SOURCES

Of particular value for naval planning and operations in the war of 1898 is RG 313, Records of Naval Operating Forces, NA, which includes William W. Kimball's war plan.

The Roosevelt letterbooks from when he was assistant Navy secretary are more illuminating than one might expect. Most of the letters are bureaucratic and routine; a few, however, are notable in shedding light upon the approaching war, the Long-Roosevelt relationship, and the actual war preparations. The letterbooks are in RG 80, Records of the Department of the Navy, NA.

Two major collections in the Massachusetts Historical Society, Boston, are important. The Papers of Henry Cabot Lodge is an enormous collection, still mostly unindexed and in the original file folders. This rich source contains, in addition to the voluminous correspondence of an active senator, Lodge's memorandum for his history of the war of 1898 and his correspondence with the Navy Department on Theodore Roosevelt's role in the war. Although some of John D. Long's journal from when he was secretary of the Navy has been published in John D. Long, *Journal*, edited by Margaret Long (Ridgie, N.H., 1946), there are gaps in the selection (mostly of peripheral material but not always). The printed edition tends to be partisan and defensive, especially when discussing the controversies concerning the differences between Secretary Long and Assistant Secretary Roosevelt. Using the original journals is preferable, though the printed version is convenient and in many cases adequate. The same preference applies to the *Papers of John Davis Long* published in the *Massachusetts Historical Society Collections*, LXXVIII (1931).

Other collections of some usefulness include the George Dewey Papers, LC, which contain the original Roosevelt order of February 25, 1898, the William McKinley Papers, LC, which are now in a microfilm edition with a full Presidential Papers index, the Alfred T. Mahan Papers, LC, the Stephen Luce Papers, LC, and the Moorfield Storey Papers, LC, which contain some material of value in the anti-imperialist movement.

PUBLISHED SOURCES

Until very recently Theodore Roosevelt has been considered by historians as primarily a disciple of Alfred Mahan and an amateur. That view has been effectively challenged by Peter Karsten, "The Nature of Influence, Roosevelt, Mahan, and the Concept of Sea Power," *American Quarterly*, XXIII (1971), 585–600. Karsten demonstrates that Roosevelt's naval scholarship was published and established before Mahan published his major works. Roosevelt's *The Naval War of 1812* (New

York, 1882), in *Works, Nat. Ed.*, VI, established Roosevelt's credentials as a naval intellectual and strategist before Mahan's influence began. Karsten argues that Roosevelt used Mahan's enormous prestige to further their mutual interest in naval expansion; Mahan used Roosevelt's political influence to further his own career. The two clearly understood that Roosevelt was the leader intellectually and politically. Although Roosevelt and Mahan frequently agreed on major naval issues, in several instances in the correspondence between the two men it was Roosevelt who corrected a tactical error by Mahan. Also see Peter Karsten, *The Naval Aristocracy: The Golden Age of Annapolis and the Emergence of Modern American Navalism* (New York, 1972), for a fuller discussion of the evolution of the new generation of naval intellectuals. Michael Corgan, "Mahan and Theodore Roosevelt: The Assessment of Influence," *Naval War College Review*, XXXIII (1980), 89–97, defends Mahan's primacy. For a full study of Roosevelt's naval role, see Gordon Carpenter O'Gara, *Theodore Roosevelt and the Rise of the Modern Navy* (Princeton, 1943); see also Elting E. Morison, *Admiral Sims and the Modern American Navy* (Boston, 1942). For a detailed examination of the pre-Mahan–Roosevelt period, Robert Seager, II, "Ten Years Before Mahan: The Unofficial Case of the New Navy, 1880–1890," MVHR, XL (1954), 491–512, is essential.

The older McKinley historiography often pictures him as a weak president easily influenced by the press or Congress. Lewis L. Gould's *The Presidency of William McKinley* (Lawrence, Kan., 1980) offers a reevaluation of McKinley's role in the Spanish-American War that takes into account the complexity of McKinley's diplomacy, the pressures of American domestic politics, and recognizes the president's keen sense of timing. See pages 59–90 especially. Also see Margaret Leech, *In the Days of McKinley* (New York, 1959), the most detailed account, and H. Wayne Morgan, *William McKinley and His America* (Syracuse, N.Y., 1963).

The fullest summary of John D. Long's secretaryship is Paolo E. Coletta, "John Davis Long, 6 March 1897–30 April, 1902," in *American Secretaries of the Navy* (2 vols.; Annapolis, 1980), 431–60. For Long's own assessment, see John D. Long, *The New American Navy* (2 vols.; New York, 1903). Jeffery M. Dorwart's *The Office of Naval Intelligence: The Birth of America's First Intelligence Agency, 1865–1918* (Annapolis, 1979) is a history of ONI that places Kimball and Roosevelt in proper historical perspective.

William Braisted was the first historian to cite William W. Kimball's war plan in the *United States Navy in the Pacific, 1897–1909* (Austin, 1958), 21–23. John A. S. Grenville and George Berkeley Young accord the Kimball plan its fullest treatment in *Politics, Strategy, and American Diplomacy: Studies in Foreign Policy, 1873–1917* (New Haven, 1967). For the view that Kimball's plan was not as decisive or as influential as Grenville and Young claim, see Ronald Spector, "Who Planned the Attack on Manila Bay?" *Mid-America*, LIII (1971), 94–102. For a detailed account of naval planning, before and after Kimball, see David F. Trask, *The War with Spain in 1898* (New York, 1981), 72–94. On the history of the United States Asiatic squadron, Dewey's temperament as commander, the history of the fleet's war preparations, and the sailing to Manila Bay, see the invaluable account in Robert Erwin Johnson, *Far China Station: The U.S. Navy in Asian Waters, 1800–1898* (Annapolis, 1979).

One of the most useful books on the debate between the imperialists and anti-imperialists is Robert Beisner: *Twelve Against Empire: The Anti-Imperialists, 1898–1900* (New York, 1968). Beisner illuminates the anti-imperialists' sense of frustration, their conservative opposition to any change, and their inability to work out political compromises or to stem the tide of modernization either in diplomacy or society. James A. Field's "American Imperialism: The Worst Chapter in Any Book," AHR, LXXXIII (1978), 644–83, is primarily an attack on the New Left emphasis on empire and economics. Field's dialectic (Walter LaFeber and Robert Beisner offer rejoinders in an AHR *Forum*) is a starting point to a more critical view of imperialism that is already present in recent European historiography.

Richard Koebner and H. D. Schmidt, *Imperialism: The Story and Significance of a Political Word, 1840–1960* (Cambridge, England, 1964) is an invaluable history of the changes in the meaning of the term. The modern use of the word *imperialism* began when J. A. Hobson (*Imperi-*

alism: A Study, 1902, rpr. Ann Arbor, Mich., 1965) used the Boer and Spanish-American Wars to establish the modern meaning of imperialism as part of the capitalistic expansion of which Hobson, an economist, was critical.

An especially perceptive essay, Robin W. Wink, "Imperialism," in C. Vann Woodward, ed., *The Comparative Approach to American History* (New York, 1968), 253–70, examines the similarities and differences of American and European expansion. M. Boucher's "Imperialism, the Transvaal Press and the Spanish American War of 1898," *Kleio*, V (1973), 1–32, offers an invaluable comparative view of the effect of the American war on the Boer War and on the idea of imperialism. See also David S. Landes, "Some Thoughts on the Nature of Economic Imperialism," *Journal of Economic History*, XXI (December, 1961). A good historiographical review is Hugh De Santes, "The Imperialist Impulse and American Innocence," in Gerald N. Haines and L. Samuel Walher, eds., *American Foreign Relations: A Historiographical Review* (Westport, Conn., 1981), 65–90.

American historiography has been determinedly anti-imperialistic beginning with the first historical accounts and continuing with the more sophisticated work of the New Left historians. E. Berkeley Tomkins, *Anti-Imperialism in the United States: The Great Debate, 1890– 1920* (Philadelphia, 1970), is a recent chronological compilation of the political and ideological issues raised by the anti-imperialist movement. One of the earliest anti-imperialist works was Walter Millis, *The Martial Spirit* (Cambridge, Mass., 1931), an antiwar, anti-imperialistic history of the war of 1898. One of the best of the older works, and still eminently useful, is Julius W. Pratt, *Expansionists of 1898: The Acquisition of Hawaii and the Spanish Islands* (Baltimore, 1936). One of the most influential essays is Richard Hofstadter, "Cuba, The Philippines, and Manifest Destiny," in *The Paranoid Style in American Politics and Other Essays* (New York, 1965), 145–87. Hofstadter combines intellectual, philosophical, and diplomatic history in castigating the new American expansionists as effectively as any writer ever has. He ingeniously uses the earlier movement of American manifest destiny to make his case for an indigenous American imperialism beginning in the early nineteenth century. Hofstadter takes the best of both worlds, however, and links

American expansion to both European imperialism and earlier American expansion. For the idea of manifest destiny, see Albert Weinberg, *Manifest Destiny* (Baltimore, 1935), and Frederick Merk, *Manifest Destiny and American Mission* (Cambridge, Mass., 1963).

William Appleman Williams' books about American empire are an essential part of the anti-expansionist school linking the old left antiwar scholars such as Walter Millis with the angry writers of the Vietnam generation. See especially *The Tragedy of American Diplomacy* (Cleveland, 1959); *Americans in a Changing World* (Harper, 1966); *Roots of the Modern American Empire* (New York, 1969); and *Empire as a Way of Life* (New York, 1980). David Healy's *U.S. Expansionism: The Imperialist Urge in the 1890's* (Madison, Wis., 1970) is a potpourri of people and ideas, juxtaposing economic imperialists, the ideas of an expanding society, and biographical support—Root and Roosevelt—in presenting a complex picture of American imperialism that is useful in its details, if only partly convincing in its overall interpretation. A much clearer and less ideological case for expansion is made in Walter LaFeber's brilliant *The New Empire: An Interpretation of American Expansion, 1860–1898* (Ithaca, N.Y., 1963), the least didactic of the New Left histories.

Some of the more thoughtful treatments include Richard Leopold's "The Emergence of America as a World Power: Some Second Thoughts," in John Braeman, Robert H. Bremer, and Everett Walters, eds., *Change and Continuity in Twentieth Century America* (New York, 1966); Ernest May, *Imperial Democracy: The Emergence of America as a Great Power* (New York, 1961) and *American Imperialism: A Speculative Essay* (New York, 1968).

See also Thomas A. Bailey, "America's Emergence as a World Power: The Myth and the Verity," PHR, XXX (1961), 1–16; Barton J. Bernstein and Franklin A. Lieb, "Progressive Republican Senators and American Imperialism, 1898–1916: A Reappraisal," *Mid-America*, L (1968), 163–205; Willard Gatewood, Jr., "Black Americans and the Quest for Empire, 1893–1903," JSH, XXXVIII (1972), 545–66; and William E. Leuchtenburg, "Progressivism and Imperialism: The Progressive Movement and American Foreign Policy, 1898–1916," MVHR, XXXIX (1952), 483–504. An economic historian's assessment can be found in Robert Zevin, "An Interpretation of American Imperialism," *Journal of Economic History*, XXXII (1972), 496–512.

Older interpretations, still useful, include Fred Harvey Harrington, "Literary Aspects of American Anti-Imperialism, 1898–1902," *New England Quarterly*, X (1937), 650–67; "The Anti-Imperialist Movement in the United States, 1898–1900," MVHR, XXXII (1935), 211–30; James A. Zimmerman, "Who Were the Anti-Imperialists and the Expansionists of 1898 and 1899? A Chicago Perspective," PHR, XLVI (1977), 589–602; Thomas A. Bailey, "Was the Presidential Election of 1900 a Mandate on Imperialism?" MVHR, XXIV (1937), 43–52; E. Berkeley Thompkins, "Scylla and Charybdis: The Anti-Imperialist Dilemma in the Election of 1900," PHR, XXXVI (1967), 143–61; Richard E. Welch, Jr., "Motives and Policy Objectives of Anti-Imperialists, 1898," *Mid-America*, LI (1969), 119–29; and Christopher Lasch, "The Anti-Imperialists, the Philippines, and the Inequality of Man," JSH, XXIV (1958), 319–31.

Rubin Francis Weston, *Racism in U.S. Imperialism: The Influence of Racial Assumptions on American Foreign Policy, 1893–1946* (Columbia, S.C., 1972), is a study of the racial complications in American expansion. Richard E. Welch, Jr., *Response to Imperialism: The United States and the Philippine-American War, 1885–1902* (Chapel Hill, 1979), in spite of its title, is a well-balanced study of the American-Philippine war that is not sidetracked by the question of imperialism. Some useful compilations in college texts include Thomas G. Patterson, ed., *American Imperialism and Anti-Imperialism* (New York, 1973); Marilyn Blatt Young, *American Expansion: The Critical Issues* (Boston, 1973); A. E. Campbell, *Expansion and Imperialism* (New York, 1970), and Thomas P. Greene, *American Imperialism in 1898* (Boston, 1955). H. Wayne Morgan's *America's Road to Empire* (New York, 1967) is a brief history by the biographer of President McKinley.

Albert Beveridge and Theodore Roosevelt are often cited as stereotype American imperialists and jingos. For an examination of the sharp differences between the extreme nationalism of Beveridge and the foreign policy of Roosevelt's presidency, see John Braeman, *Albert J. Beveridge: American Nationalist* (Chicago, 1971), especially Ch. 5, "The Ebbing of Imperialism," 56–67.

Chapter Five

MANUSCRIPT SOURCES

On the Philippine-American War, the Papers of William Howard Taft, LC, are a necessary adjunct to the Roosevelt Papers. Taft was the first American governor of the Philippines and head of the Second Philippine Commission. The Elihu Root Papers, LC, are largely the official records of his bureaucracy and less personal than either Taft's or Roosevelt's papers. Much of the important Root material will be found in either the Taft or Roosevelt collections. The Root Papers, nonetheless, are still essential for historians of the period. For the Philippine war, the Philippine Insurgent Records, RG 126, NA, compiled by Captain John R. M. Taylor, are an important collection. Captain Taylor's own unpublished history, "A History of the Philippine Insurrection Against the United States, 1899–1903" (1906), in galley proofs with an administrative history of the War Department's project to publish it, is in RG 350, NA. Taylor's history is a narrative account of the Filipino independence movement that is broader than its title suggests. Both the history and the accompanying documents, called exhibits, are still useful. For the corrected galley proofs of Taylor's work, see Microcopy 719, Roll 9, in RG 350.

PUBLISHED SOURCES

The most complete account of Theodore Roosevelt's involvement in the Philippines is Oscar M. Alfonso, *Theodore Roosevelt and the Philippines, 1897–1909* (Quezon City, Philippines, 1970). Although Alfonso's work began as a dissertation (University of Chicago, 1966) his book goes well beyond an academic exercise. Alfonso carefully weighs the sympathetic claims for Filipino independence against the efforts of the Roosevelt administration. Much more sympathetic to William Howard Taft than to Roosevelt, whom he regards as the stereotyped social Darwin imperialist of his time, Alfonso concludes that Roosevelt's administration may have been the Philippines' Achilles heel. Alfonso's book is invaluable; he has done extensive work in the Taft and Roosevelt papers, reviews the military and political matters on both sides, and in spite of his personal sympathies has written a spirited and balanced historical account of a difficult subject. The fullest historiographical summary is Peter W. Stanley, "The Forgotten Philippines," in Ernest R. May and James C. Thomson, Jr., eds., *American – East Asian Relations: A Survey* (Cambridge, Mass., 1972), 291–316.

The Philippine-American War is attracting younger scholars who are using cultural materials in their more sophisticated analyses. An excellent example of the more complex treatment is Peter W. Stanley, *A Nation in the Making: The Philippines and the United States, 1899–1921* (Cambridge, Mass., 1974). Stanley uses culture and class as well as diplomacy in examining the many-sided conflicts between Filipino and American nationalisms. Morrell Heald and Lawrence S. Kaplan, "Conscience and Consciousness in the Philippines: The Imperial Impulse, 1898–1903," in *Culture and Diplomacy* (Westport, Conn., 1977), 124–58, follow the same careful approach. They examine McKinley's ambivalence in cultural as well as political terms and make good use of American underestimation of Philippine nationalism. Stanley, Heald, and Kaplan have written sensitive, balanced accounts in which American good faith as well as American mistakes are illuminated.

Richard E. Welch, Jr., has written many articles on the Philippine war; his best work is his recent book, *Response to Imperialism: The United States and the Philippine-American War, 1899–1902* (Chapel Hill, N.C., 1979). In spite of its title, Welch's book is not a diatribe against imperialism but a careful scholarly account that concentrates equally on the actual war, American domestic politics, and the ideological arguments of the anti-imperialists.

John Morgan Gates, *Schoolbooks and Krags: The United States Army in the Philippines, 1898–1902* (Westport, Conn., 1973), is a valuable military history that illuminates the American idealism and the social advances brought about by the untimely war. Glenn Anthony May, *Social Engineering in the Philippines: The Aims, Execution and Impact of American Colonial Policy, 1900–1913* (Westport, Conn., 1980), analyzes rather than moralizes, and argues that the main reforms of American progressivism may have had their first dress rehearsal in the Philippines.

A detailed and critical account of the military conduct of the war is Stuart Creighton Miller, *Benevolent Assimilation: The American Conquest of the Philippines, 1899–1903* (New Haven, 1982). The view from the Filipino side is well represented in Philippine historian Teodoro A.

Agoncillo's works, especially *Malolos: The Crisis of the Republic* (Quezon City, Philippines, 1960). One of the most important treatments of the Philippines in context is William Braisted, *The United States Navy in the Pacific, 1897–1909* (Austin, 1958), a necessary adjunct to any political or diplomatic interpretation of the Philippine war.

Ralph Eldin Minger's *William Howard Taft and the United States Foreign Policy: The Apprenticeship Years, 1900–1908* (Urbana, Ill., 1975) is a judicious account of Taft's work as administrator and peacemaker. Representing the shrill arguments of historical presentism by equating protest over Vietnam with the anti-imperialist objections to the Philippines is Daniel B. Schirmer, *Republic or Empire: American Resistance to the Philippine War* (Cambridge, Mass, 1972), more a modern anti-imperialist tract than a balanced history.

For American Philippine policy statements, see Elihu Root, *The Military and Colonial Policy of the United States* (Cambridge, Mass., 1916); an anti-imperialist history is given in Moorfield Storey and Marcial P. Lichiano, *The Conquest of the Philippines by the United States* (New York, 1926). An older account is Garel A. Grunder and William E. Livezey, *The Philippines and the United States* (Norman, Okla., 1951).

Jacob Gould Schurman's *Philippine Affairs: A Retrospect and Outlook* (New York, 1902) is a firsthand account by the head of the Philippine Commission and president of Cornell University. Henry Cabot Lodge's *The War With Spain* (New York, 1900) is one of the oldest naval histories; David Trask's *The War with Spain in 1898* (New York, 1981) is the newest. For McKinley's role, see Lewis L. Gould, *The Presidency of William McKinley* (Lawrence, Kan., 1980). A good review of the war's political historiography is in Joseph A. Fry, "William McKinley and the Coming of the Spanish American War: A Study of the Besmirching and Redemption of a Historical Image," *Diplomatic History*, III (1979), 77–98.

Useful articles include James K. Eyre, "Russia and the American Occupation of the Philippines," MVHR, XXVIII (1942), 539–652, which argues that occupation by the U.S. was necessary to world peace, and Paolo E. Coletta, "McKinley, the Peace Negotiations, and the Acquisition of the Philippines," PHR, XXX (1961), 341–50. Also see William R. Braisted, "The Philippine Naval Base Problem, 1898–

1909," MVHR, XLI (1954), 21–40, and "The United States Navy's Dilemma in the Pacific," PHR, XXVI (1957), 235–44; Kenneth E. Hendrickson, "Reluctant Expansionist—Jacob Gould Schurman and the Philippine Question," PHR, XXXVI (1967), 405–21; Geoffrey Seed, "British Views of American Policy in the Philippines Reflected in Journals of Opinion, 1898–1907," *Journal of American Studies*, II (April, 1968), 49–64; and Gary C. Ness, "Proving Ground for a President: William Howard Taft and the Philippines, 1900–1905," *Cincinnati Historical Society Bulletin*, XXXIV (1976), 204–23. Other articles include E. Ranson, "British Military and Naval Observers in the Spanish-American War," *Journal of American Studies*, III (1969), 33–56; Julius Pratt, "The Large Policy of 1898," MVHR, XIX (1932), 219–42; George Auxier, "Middle Western Papers and The Spanish American War," MVHR, XXVI (1940), 523–34; Thomas A. Bailey, "Dewey and the Germans at Manila Bay," AHR, XLV (1939), 59–81; L. B. Shippee, "Germany and the Spanish American War," AHR, XXX (1927), 754–77; Seward Livermore, "The American Naval Base Policy in the Far East, 1850–1914," PHR, XII (1943), 33–52; "American Strategy, Diplomacy in the South Pacific, 1890–1914," PHR, XIII (1944), 113–35; and J. Fred Rippy, "The European Powers and the Spanish American War, *James Sprunt Historical Studies,* XIX (1927), 22–52.

Especially interesting is a contemporary article by Admiral Stephen Luce, "The Benefits of War," *North American Review*, CLIII (1891), 672–83. In the same general vein is John P. Mallan, "Roosevelt, Brooks Adams, and Lea: The Warrior Critique of the Business Civilization," *American Quarterly*, VII (1956), 216–30.

Chapter Six

MANUSCRIPT SOURCES

The Richard Olney Papers and the Grover Cleveland Papers, LC, are extensive collections dealing with pre-Rooseveltian diplomacy with Great Britain. The Cecil Spring Rice Papers at Churchill College, Cambridge, England, the James Bryce Papers in the Bodelian Library, Oxford University, Oxford, England, and Arthur Lee's correspondence at the Courtauld Institute, London, are three major collections of English writers with whom Theodore Roosevelt corresponded regularly. The John Hay Papers, LC, are extensive and essential.

PUBLISHED SOURCES

Stephen Gwynn, ed., *The Letters and Friendships of Sir Cecil Spring Rice* (2 vols.; Boston, 1929), and Arthur Lee, *A Good Innings* (3 vols.; n.p., 1940; selected edition, London, 1974), supplement the full representation in both MRL and the Theodore Roosevelt Papers, LC.

The best histories of Anglo-American diplomacy are H. C. Allen, *Great Britain and the United States: A History of Anglo-American Relations, 1783–1952* (New York, 1953); Lionel Gelber, *The Rise of Anglo-American Friendship: A Study in World Politics, 1898–1906* (New York, 1938); R. G. Neale, *Great Britain and United States Expansion, 1898–1900* (East Lansing, Mich., 1966); Charles S. Campbell, Jr., *Anglo-American Understanding, 1898–1903* (Baltimore, 1957); Charles S. Campbell, Jr., *From Revolution to Rapprochement: The United States and Great Britain, 1783–1900* (New York, 1974); and Richard Heathcote Heindel, *The American Impact on Great Britain, 1898–1914* (Philadelphia, 1940). For the Fenian invasion, see Leon O'Broin, *Fenian Fever: An Anglo-American Dilemma* (New York, 1971).

David Burton's works bear heavily on Theodore Roosevelt's relations with the British. For the fullest treatment, see David Burton, *Theodore Roosevelt: Confident Imperialist* (Philadelphia, 1968). More specific is Burton's "Theodore Roosevelt and his English Correspondents: The Intellectual Roots of the Anglo-American Alliance," *Mid-America*, LIII, (1971), 12–34; and "Theodore Roosevelt and the Special Relationship with Great Britain," *History Today* (August, 1973), 527–35. For an excellent summary of Anglo-American relations, see Lyle A. McGeoch, "Lord Lansdowne and the American Impact on British Diplomacy, 1900–1905," *Theodore Roosevelt Association Journal* (Fall, 1981), 13–18.

For Cleveland's and Olney's diplomacy, see John A. S. Grenville and George Berkeley Young, *Politics, Strategy and American Diplomacy: Studies in Foreign Policy, 1873–1917* (New Haven, 1967). Allen Nevins' *Grover Cleveland: A Study in Courage* (New York, 1932) is the most complete work on Cleveland. See also, Horace Samuel Merrill, *Grover Cleveland: Bourbon Leader* (Boston, 1957).

On the effect of the Boer War upon American-British relations, see James H. Ferguson, *American Diplomacy and the Boer War* (Philadephia, 1939), and Byron Farwell, "Taking Sides in the Boer War," *American Heritage*, XXVIII (April, 1976), 20–25, 92–97.

For studies on John Hay, see William Thayer, *The Life and Letters of John Hay* (Boston, 1915), the earliest Hay biography. Tyler Dennett, *John Hay, From Poetry to Politics* (New York, 1933), and Kenton J. Clymer, *John Hay: The Gentleman as Diplomat* (Ann Arbor, Mich., 1975), are two of the best.

Chapter Seven

MANUSCRIPT SOURCES

The Papers of Henry White, LC, are a necessary adjunct to the John Hay and Theodore Roosevelt Papers, LC. Elihu Root's Papers are informative, particularly the oversize atlases specially made for the Alaskan boundary commissioners, containers 222–226, LC. The Henry Cabot Lodge Papers, Massachusetts Historical Society, are useful.

PUBLISHED SOURCES

The most complete treatment of the Alaskan boundary dispute and Canadian-American diplomacy is in Charles Callan Tansill, *Canadian-American Relations, 1875–1911* (New Haven, 1943). See also Thomas A. Bailey, "Theodore Roosevelt and the Alaska Boundary Settlement," *Canadian Historical Review*, XVIII (1937), 123–30. British Columbia geologist Lewis Green's *The Boundary Hunters: Surveying the 141st Meridian and the Alaskan Panhandle* (Vancouver, 1982), an extensive geographical and historical study, is critical of TR.

For information on the American diplomats who served on the Alaskan boundary commission, John Garraty, *Henry Cabot Lodge* (New York, 1953), Philip Jessup, *Elihu Root* (2 vols.; New York, 1938), and Allan Nevins, *Henry White: Thirty Years of American Diplomacy* (New York, 1930), are invaluable.

The British diplomats are represented by John A. S. Grenville, *Lord*

Salisbury and Foreign Policy: The Close of the Nineteenth Century (London, 1964); J. L. Garvin, *The Life of Joseph Chamberlain* (2 vols.; London, 1933); and E. C. Dugsdale, *Arthur James Balfour, 1848–1906* (New York, 1937). For Canada's diplomacy, see R. Craig Brown, *Canada's National Policy, 1883–1900* (Princeton, 1964).

Epilogue

PUBLISHED SOURCES

Henry James's life is told in Leon Edel, *Henry James* (5 vols.; Philadelphia, 1962–72). The account of James's late American visit is in Henry James, *The American Scene* (New York, 1907), Ch. 9.

The best revisions on TR and Panama are Frederick Marks, III, *Velvet on Iron: The Diplomacy of Theodore Roosevelt* (Lincoln, Nebr., 1979), and Robert A. Friedlander, "A Reassessment of Roosevelt's Role in the Panamanian Revolution of 1903," *Western Political Quarterly*, XIV (1961), 535–43. For an overview of Roosevelt's later diplomacy in Latin America, see Marks, *Velvet on Iron*; David A. Lockmiller, *Magoon in Cuba: A History of the Second Intervention, 1906–1909* (Durham, N.C., 1938); Russell H. Fitzgibbon, *Cuba and the United States, 1900–1935* (Menasha, Wis., 1935); and Howard C. Hill, *Roosevelt and the Caribbean* (Chicago, 1927). Thomas A. Bailey's *Theodore Roosevelt and the Japanese American Crisis* (Palo Alto, Calif., 1934) and Raymond Esthus' *Theodore Roosevelt and Japan* (Seattle, 1967) are good starting points for research in Roosevelt's Asian diplomacy. For the Hague peace conference, see Calvin de Armond Davis, *The United States and the Second Hague Peace Conference: American Diplomacy and International Organization, 1899–1914* (Durham, N.C., 1976). On Morocco and Algeciras, see Eugene N. Anderson, *The First Moroccan Crisis, 1904–1906* (Chicago, 1930).

Oliver W. Larkin's standard art history, *Art and Life in America* (New York, 1949), is a synthesis of culture, politics, and social life. For nineteenth-century American art history, see James Flexner, *That Wilder Image* (Boston, 1962), and Barbara Nowak, *American Painting of the Nineteenth Century* (New York, 1969).

Arthur Frank Wertheim's *The New York Little Renaissance: Iconoclasm,*

Modernism, and Nationalism in American Culture, 1908–1917 (New York, 1976), is extremely useful with excellent chapters on the modernist fight with genteel culture, and on the Ash Can school of urban realists led by Robert Henri. Wertheim is equally adept with the art and politics of the period. See Ch. 11, "The Cultural Nationalists," 167–85. Especially notable is his portrait of Herbert Croly. Croly's *The Promise of American Life* (New York, 1909) is both a history of Roosevelt's presidency and a blueprint for Roosevelt's political future. Croly's term *New Nationalism* became the slogan of Theodore Roosevelt's new movement that culminated in the Bull Moose third party. Wertheim deals with the period before Croly began his new political writing career, when he was editor of the *Architectural Record* and preached an idealistic cultural nationalism.

For Gertrude Stein's influence, see the Museum of Modern Art's *Four Americans in Paris: The Collections of Gertrude Stein and Her Family* (New York, 1970), the detailed catalog of the monumental Stein family show in New York. William Innes Homer's *Robert Henri and His Circle* (Ithaca, N.Y., 1969) is the fullest of the artistic biographies for the period.

Influential American expatriates are treated in George Wickes, *Americans in Paris, 1903–1939* (Garden City, 1969). See also Ishbel Ross, *The Expatriates* (New York, 1970). Mark Sullivan's *Our Times* (6 vols.; New York, 1927–35) offers the fullest social history of the new century. Dale Kramer, *Chicago Renaissance* (New York, 1966), supplements Henry May's *End of American Innocence* (New York, 1959) in telling of Chicago's aesthetic leadership. Irving Howe, *World of Our Fathers: The Journey of the East European Jews to America and the Life They Found and Made* (New York, 1976), Moses Rischin, *The Promised Land: New York's Jews, 1870–1914* (Cambridge, Mass., 1962), and Ronald Sanders, *The Downtown Jews* (New York, 1969), are detailed histories of the new Yiddish-American culture and the East-Side renaissance.

For the movement of European art to America, see especially Aline B. Saarinen, *The Proud Possessors* (New York, 1958). For the Armory Show, see Milton W. Brown, *The Story of the Armory Show* (New York, 1963), and J. Meridith Neil, "The Impact of the Armory Show," *South Atlantic Quarterly*, LXXIX (1980), 375–85.

Changes in American urban culture are well summarized in Gunther Barth, *City People: The Rise of Modern City Culture in Nineteenth Century America* (New York, 1980). A highly sophisticated analysis of change in American culture, T. J. Jackson Lears, *No Place of Grace: Antimodernism and American Culture, 1880–1920* (New York, 1981), uses cultural and intellectual sources.

The most widely accepted historical synthesis of the Theodore Roosevelt era is found in the works of historians Samuel P. Hays and Robert Wiebe, who emphasize the idea of institutional order as the main heritage of the progressive reform movement. See Wiebe, *The Search for Order* (New York, 1967), "Business Disunity and the Progressive Movement, 1901–1914," MVHR, XLIV (1958), 664–85, and *Businessmen and Reform* (Cambridge, Mass., 1962). Hays's earliest and most influential books include *Conservation and the Gospel of Efficiency* (Cambridge, Mass., 1958) and *The Response to Industrialism, 1885–1914* (Chicago, 1957). Of particular interest is his *American Political History as Social Analysis* (Knoxville, Tenn., 1980), a collection of Hays's historical essays and a memoir that traces the development of his historical ideas. See especially Introduction, 1–46, and "The New Organizational Society," 244–63.

See also Alfred D. Chandler, Jr., "The Origins of Progressive Leadership," in MRL, VIII, 1462–65; John Morton Blum, *The Republican Roosevelt* (Cambridge, Mass., 1954); and John Braeman, "Seven Progressives," *Business History Review*, XXXV (1961), 531–92. Still useful is Herbert Croly's original contemporary account of Roosevelt's presidency, *The Promise of American Life* (New York, 1909). Perhaps the final word on the Progressive movement and a persuasive critique of the structuralist thesis is Peter G. Filene, "An Obituary for the Progressive Movement," *American Quarterly*, XVII (1970), 20–34.

Index

237

Scott, Sir Walter, 11, 62
Scripps, James E., 31, 66
Seward, William, 155
Shakespeare, William, 49
Shantung Province, China, 127, 139
Siam, 162
Sicard, Rear Admiral Montgomery, 113, 114
Sino-Japanese War, 5, 98
Skyscrapers, 195
Sloan, John, 194
Smalley, George, 179
Smithsonian Institution, 67, 72–90
Social engineering, 151
Sorrento, Italy, 50
Sousa, John P., 60
South Africa, 23, 98
South Atlantic Squadron, 110
Spain, 68, 99, 102, 104, 111, 157
Spanish-American War, 68, 98, 100, 102, 104–34, 135, 157, 163, 166, 190. *See also* Manila Bay, Battle of; Philippines; San Juan Hill, Battle of; Roosevelt, Theodore—and foreign affairs: Dewey cable legend
Spanish Armada, 95
Spring Rice, Cecil Arthur, 102
State Department (U.S.), 102
Staunton, Va., 193
Steiglitz, Alfred, 197
Stein, Gertrude, 68, 194
Stein, Leo, 68, 194
Sternberg, Herman Speck von, 102
Story of Panama, 9
Strategic necessity, 3, 115, 144, 153, 186
Straus, Oscar, 61
Strether, Lewis Lambert, 190–91, 193, 198
Submarines, 111
Suez Canal, 10, 196
Sugar, 115
Sullivan, Louis, 28, 195
Sundry Civil Act (1902), 39
Supreme Court, 60
Surrealism, 13
Symons, Colonel Thomas W., 60
Symphony orchestras, 196

Taft, William H., 9, 143, 146, 147, 151
Tahawis, 18
Tahiti, 74
Tariffs: of 1890, p. 156; lumber, 174;

sugar, 109; Wilson-Gorman, 109, 110
Taylor, Henry C., 113
Tennis Cabinet, 63
Texas, 154
Thames and Severn tunnels, 62
Thayer, Abbott H., 70, 75
"Theodore Rex" (James), 191
Third World, 24, 109, 153
Thomas Hart Benton (Roosevelt), 49
Tiffany, Louis, 26, 27, 44
Tobacco, 115
Tolstoy, Leo, 49
Torpedos and torpedo boats, 111
Transcontinental railroads (U.S.), 194
Transvaal, 97, 177
Trevelyan, George Otto, 48
Tuckerman, Emily, 62
Turkey, 48, 148
Turner, Frederick Jackson: frontier thesis, 6, 28, 30, 99, 107
Turner, J. M., 51
Twain, Mark, 62
291 Gallery, 197
Two Nudes (Rouault), 196
Tyron, Dwight W., 70, 75

Union party, 76
Union Station (Washington, D.C.), 33
Union Trust Company (Detroit), 77
United States: and Algeciras Conference, 102; anticolonialism, 137; and Asian nationalism, 137; in athletic competition, 108; avoidance of European imperialism, 107; belief in messianic democracy, 136; sees Britain as part of Europe, 167; California school segregation crisis, 189; colonial dilemmas, 137; diplomatic reorganization (1893), 156; economic growth, 11, 64, 65; geographical isolation, 161; and German threats, 139; growth and influence, 186; immigration, 196; internationalism, 198; Great White Fleet, 103, 189; and Morocco, 102; as naval power, 99, 175; provincialism vs. nationalism in, 67; and technological changes, 106; world trade ambitions, 99. *See also* Cleveland, Grover; Cosmopolitanism; Cultural change; Germany; Great Britain; Monroe Doctrine; Philippines; Roosevelt, Theodore;